The Politics of Revelation
in the English Renaissance

The Politics
of Revelation in the
English Renaissance

Esther Gilman Richey

University of Missouri Press
Columbia and London

Copyright © 1998 by
The Curators of the University of Missouri
University of Missouri Press, Columbia, Missouri 65201
Printed and bound in the United States of America
5 4 3 2 1   02 01 00 99 98

Library of Congress Cataloging-in-Publication Data
Richey, Esther Gilman, 1954–
    The politics of Revelation in the English Renaissance / Esther
Gilman Richey.
        p.   cm.
    Includes bibliographical references and index.
    ISBN 0-8262-1166-6 (alk. paper)
    1. English literature—Early modern, 1500-1700—History and
criticism.   2. Bible. N.T. Revelation—Criticism, interpretation,
etc.—England—History—17th century.   3. Politics and literature—
Great Britain—History—17th century.   4. Christianity and
literature—England—History—17th century.   5. Christian
literature, English—History and criticism.   6. Apocalyptic
literature—History and criticism.   7. England—Church
history—18th century.   8. Prophecies in literature.   9. Prophecy—
Christianity.   10. Renaissance—England.   I. Title.
PR438.R45R53   1998
820.9'3823—dc21   98-3089
                                                            CIP

⊗™ This paper meets the requirements of the
American National Standard for Permanence of Paper
for Printed Library Materials, Z39.48, 1984.

Designer: Mindy Shouse
Typesetter: Bookcomp, Inc.
Printer and Binder: Thomson-Shore, Inc.
Typefaces: Minion

For Bill

Contents

ACKNOWLEDGMENTS ix
INTRODUCTION 1

1 Historic Recoveries
Spenserian Apocalyptic and the True Church 16

2 War and Peace
Prophecy in Thomas Brightman and Lancelot Andrewes 36

3 Subverting Paul
The True Church and the Querelle des Femmes *in Aemilia Lanyer* 60

4 Admitting Adultery
Donne's Versions of the True Church 84

5 Body Language
The Political Design of Herbert's Temple 106

6 Contestatory Measures in "On the Morning," *Comus,* and *Paradise Lost* 130

7 Feminist Authority in Eleanor Davies's Prophecies 173

8 Re-Covering Paul
The True Church and the Prophecies of Mary Cary, Anna Trapnel, and Margaret Fell 196

9 Henry Vaughan's Concealed Temple 219

BIBLIOGRAPHY 231
INDEX 247

Acknowledgments

Like those I consider here, my own "habit of words" has been shaped and transformed by my family, teachers, colleagues, and students. I am deeply grateful to my parents, Bill and Shirley Gilman, not only because they taught me language, but also because they taught me the language of the Bible. Elizabeth McCutcheon introduced me to the extraordinary playfulness of Renaissance texts and gave me the courage to continue in a field that is often fraught with peril. Christopher Grose dazzled me with the intricate twists and subtleties of Miltonic narrative, and I remain dazzled still. His words and ideas continue to inform my thinking and teaching. Jonathan Post's political and historical awareness—along with his encouragement—helped me to become a scholar. Friends near UCLA or within the program made life, even as a student, unbelievably happy, especially Lynn Huizenga, David Case, Tom and Lisa Burkdall, and Kevin and Robyn Dettmar. My colleagues at Virginia Tech furthered my education through daily conversation: Tom Gardner by making me aware of the tensions and limits of language, Ernest Sullivan by turning textual editing into a detective mystery, and Sara Thorne-Thomsen by leading me to a number of delightful women writers in the Renaissance. Virginia Tech provided me with several grants to carry out research at the British Library and the Huntington Library, archives tremendously important in facilitating my completion of this project. The VPI English Department also gave me, in the final stages of the book, a splendid research assistant, John Wright. His thoroughness and diligence were invaluable. David Radcliffe, Margaret Shaw, Karen Swenson, Linda Anderson, and Judy Hood offered continual emotional and intellectual support during my time at VPI, as did another intellectual community in South Carolina: Stan and Melissa Dubinsky, Nina and Arnie Levine, and Amittai Aviram. Sensitive and perceptive readers helped me revise portions of the book, especially those at *SEL* and the

University of Missouri Press. I am especially grateful to Annette Wenda, who made the copyediting a joy. *SEL* and *ELR* have graciously allowed me to reprint portions of articles appearing first in their journals. Most important of all, my husband, Bill, has provided a conceptual framework to my life and work, filling our times together with intellectual awareness, witty commentary, music, and laughter. He has also rescued me repeatedly from major tragedies at the computer, and that this book is printed at all is due very much to him. Finally, the English Department at the University of North Carolina at Charlotte has done me the greatest favor of all by giving me a place with them and thereby bringing all my loves together.

The Politics of Revelation
in the English Renaissance

Introduction

If the Spirit by such revelation have discovered unto them the secrets of that discipline out of Scripture, they must profess themselves to be all (even men, women, and children) Prophets.
>—Richard Hooker, *Of the Laws of Ecclesiastical Polity*

RICHARD HOOKER's words indicate that the status of the prophet during the Renaissance was frighteningly open-ended, enabling people to "profess" this ability regardless of their age, gender, or limited educations. In this rather singular instance, the political, social, and spiritual restrictions so basic to the culture no longer applied. The role of the prophet was similarly limitless, since, as William Kerrigan has informed us, the term could refer to "a teacher, preacher, poet, or inspired interpreter of the Bible." Indeed, Bishop Griffith Williams offers so extensive a range of possibilities in *The True Church* of 1629 that the role appears almost as infinite as the "Spirit" who inspires it. Beginning each citation with the qualifying word *sometimes,* Williams includes 1) those "that are deare and beloved of God," 2) those "that doe interpret the words and mind of God," 3) those "which have immediately heard the words of God, from his owne mouth, either by dreams or visions," 4) those "that by the Inspiration of Gods Spirit doe interpret the Scriptures, and especially the obscurest and hardest of places," 5) those "that were set apart, after a speciall manner, to do the service of God," 6) those "that are moved by the Spirit, good or bad, as it were by enthusiasme, to speak strange and unwonted things," 7) those "which do foretell things to come, and those things doe come to pass," and finally, 8) those "that doe reveal things past, so they be such as are unknowne, obscure, and secret."[1]

---

1. Kerrigan, *The Prophetic Milton,* 13; Williams, *The True Church Shewed to all men that desire to be members of the Same,* 504–5.

1

By Williams's account, the prophet spanned the gap between private and public spirituality, revealing on the one hand the intimacy of a relationship with God, and on the other, a calling to social and political service. Gifted in interpretation, he found meaning in the margins of the written and unwritten Word, revealing what was hitherto indecipherable and expressing what was hitherto unimagined. He observed the secrets encoded in time, unearthing the mysteries hidden in history and forecasting the events to come. In short, he glimpsed the matters of this world through the optical lenses of the next.

Despite Williams's rather comprehensive list, he was, by 1629, aware of the spiritual ramifications of the prophet's role and not at all sanguine about the politically charged and subversive opportunities that such a role opened up. Immediately following his definition, he attempted to delimit these problematic areas by asserting that the "most principall Prophet" was Christ, while all others were "lesse principall." Then, he noted, the "lesser" prophets had "a two-fold office. First to declare the will of God from one language into another, because all men had not the Scriptures in those days in their own vulgar speech. Secondly, to shew the will of God that was most especially revealed to them by God himselfe."[2] With one deft move, Williams had abandoned the slippery territory involving "revelations" and had set the prophet on firmer ground: he was now a translator, an illuminator of Scripture for the "vulgar" and unlearned. Clearly, a man skilled in languages and hermeneutics, the prophet was, not surprisingly, very much like Williams himself. But Williams did not stop there. The predictive dimension of prophecy, he now asserted, had vanished by the time of the New Testament. Consequently, later prophets "did not excell in the gift of fore-shewing things to come" but were instead "worthy interpreters of holy scriptures" and "could wisely apply the same according to the present use, for the edification of God's Church."[3] The role of the prophet, then, was not only safe but also orthodox: it was more interpretive than predictive, more interested in edification and application than uncovering divine secrets, more concerned with life in the present moment than with past or future events.

In seeking to close the door on contemporary predictions and revelations, Williams inadvertently left one small window wide open. The "obscurest and hardest" parts of Scripture, the books of Daniel and Revelation, still lay within the contemporary prophet's purview, and these allowed radical

2. Williams, *True Church Shewed*, 504.
3. Ibid., 507.

puritans such as Thomas Brightman ample opportunity to carry out politically charged readings. "It is a matter with one consent acknowledged," Brightman wrote,

> that the Revelation doth still require necessarily a Revelation, and this voice of the Lord is sounding continually in thine eares: The Lord hath spoken who can but Prophecy, Amos 3.5. For the Lord hath not onely spoken by dreames and visions of old, but he speaketh also every day, even as often as he inlighteneth the mindes of his servantes, that they may be able to search out the hidden truth of his word, and to bringe it forth into the champion world.[4]

Brightman's assessment of the prophet's role not only fit within Williams's carefully chiseled definition, but also made "prophesying" (through the revelation of Revelation's "visions and dreams"), an ongoing, contemporary act. In attempting to contain the politically subversive dimension of prophecy, it seems, Williams had refused to take the final step: he had refused to limit either sermons on Revelation or the introduction into print of various commentaries on this most cryptic and symbolic of texts.

Consequently, the "obscurest and hardest" parts of Daniel and Revelation quickly became a veritable minefield of charges and countercharges in the ecclesiastical and spiritual debates of the early seventeenth century. Numerous commentaries on Revelation by Brightman, Napier, Forbes, and others entered the public domain, often attaining political and spiritual significance that extended far beyond the implications of the original text.

This lesson King James himself unhappily learned in 1618 at the outbreak of the Thirty Years' War when George Abbot, archbishop of the English Church, directed the king back to his own *A Paraphrase upon the Revelation.* James had there outlined the necessary militancy of Protestant kings: "The time shall come before the consummation, that they shall hate the whore, who abused them so strongly and long, and shall make her to be alone, for they shall withdraw from her their subjects the nations that were her strength, and shall make her naked, for they shall discover the mysterie of her abominations, and shall eat her flesh, and burne her with fire." Slyly cramming James's own words down his throat, Abbot suggested that James carry out the role he had once assigned himself, a wish he expressed in even more graphic and violent terms: "That by piece and piece, the Kings of the Earth that gave their power unto the Beast (all the work of God

---

4. Brightman, *A Revelation of the Revelation that is . . . the Revelation of St. John,* opening letter "To the Holy Reformed Churches of Britany, Germany and France."

must be fulfilled) shall now tear the whore, and make her desolate, as St. John in his revelation hath foretold."[5] For Abbot, the moment James had identified as the "time" that "shall come" was here. James need only fulfill his divinely appointed destiny by taking action against the Roman "whore"— action requiring that he immediately "tear" her to pieces. In practical terms, this meant that James would now declare war on the "Anti-Christian" forces of Spain and march to the aid of his Protestant son-in-law, Frederik of Bohemia.[6]

But Abbot's militant desires were far from what James himself had in mind. At this very moment he was negotiating with Spain to bring about a marriage between his son Charles and the infanta, Maria—a marriage, he believed, that would unite opposing nations and effectively silence the rumblings of war. Linked on the one hand to Protestant Germany through his daughter, Elizabeth, and on the other to Catholic Spain through his son Charles, James prepared to usher in a golden age of Christian peace and unity. Like the peacemaking emperors Augustus Caesar and Constantine, James would achieve in his family as well as his kingdom the *via media*.[7]

Ironically, in opting for peace rather than war, James chose to dismiss a crucial aspect of the "Constantinian" character encoded in contemporary interpretations of the Apocalypse. Putting aside the notion of imperial conquest written into Foxe's *Acts and Monuments* and nearly all commentaries on Revelation, James began to advocate an alternative, pacifistic understanding of prophecy. Other versions, in particular those with militant overtones, now came to be seen as so many attempts to circumscribe his

5. King James I, *The Workes of the Most High and Mightie Prince, James,* 56. James I, in *Paraphrase upon the Revelation* (reprinted in *Workes*), takes the same position as Bale, Foxe, and Brightman: "The Pope's empire is the outward part of the Temple; the true church is in *Sancto Sanctorum,* but under the persecution of these hypocrites for a certain space" (32). Abbot is quoted in Kenneth Fincham and Peter Lake, "The Ecclesiastical Policy of King James I," 198.

6. For further discussion of James's foreign policy, see W. B. Patterson, "King James I and the Protestant Cause in the Crisis of 1618–1622."

7. Thomas Cogswell analyzes the English reaction to James's plans in "England and the Spanish Match." He also argues that this "furore over the Infanta established a certain political pattern which was to recur in subsequent years" (128). Since it was "a Catholic scare with an important difference," one that involved the monarch directly, it "became much harder to dismiss" the possibility that the sovereign was "plotting to subvert the Reformed religion" (129). See also Julian Davies, *The Caroline Captivity of the Church: Charles I and the Remoulding of Anglicanism, 1625–1641;* Peter Lake, "The Significance of the Elizabethan Identification of the Pope as Antichrist"; Peter Lake, "Anti-popery: the Structure of a Prejudice"; and Peter Lake, "Constitutional Consensus and Puritan Opposition in the 1620s: Thomas Scott and the Spanish Match."

behavior, limiting his course of action and imperiling his freedom. With King James's death and King Charles's marriage in 1625 to the French Catholic princess Henrietta Maria, apocalyptic designs involving the destruction of the "Romish" whore proved altogether at odds with royal interests. The king and court would henceforth view commentaries on Revelation with suspicion and, by the 1630s, would begin to suppress them.[8]

In the interim, we find the political tension and controversy surrounding Revelation steadily increasing, reaching something of a boiling point in one of Robert Sanderson's sermons of 1628. Sanderson then identifies the prophetic terms in which the Church of England is being challenged from within and without as the voices lobbying for reform become more and more threatening:

> They judge our Church as halfe popish, and Anti Christian, for retaining some ceremonies used in poperie, though wee have purged them from their superstitions, and restored them to their Primitive use. Their great admired opinion of the Revelation, *maketh our Church in the Linsey-Welsey* Laodicean Church; neither hot nor cold. And some of them have slovenly compared our late gracious Sovereign Queen Elizabeth of most blessed memorie to a sluttish husewife; that having swepe the house, yet left the dust and dirt behinde the doores.[9]

Behind Sanderson's voice are a series of other voices—those calling names, making "slovenly" comparisons, criticizing the presence of ceremonies, all, Sanderson asserts, because of a "great admired opinion of the *Revelation.*" Such criticism is misinformed, he carefully points out, since the church is not "popish," but "primitive"; not corrupt, but true to its foundation in antiquity. The church is indeed "reformed," he argues, both purged of its "superstitions" and restored to an originary purity.

---

8. Christopher Hill, Anthony Milton, and David Norbrook all discuss the suppression of apocalyptic commentary during the 1630s (Hill, *Antichrist in Seventeenth-Century England*, 38–39; A. Milton, *Catholic and Reformed: The Roman and Protestant Churches in English Protestant Thought, 1600–1640*, 119; Norbrook, *Poetry and Politics in the English Renaissance*, 244–45). Shiela Lambert, in contrast, suggests that such suppression was highly dramatized and politicized, but not actually occurring ("Richard Montagu, Arminianism, and Censorship"). Regardless of whether Revelation was or was not suppressed, apocalyptic commentary was indeed the subject of political, ecclesiastical, and social debate. For further discussions of seventeenth-century prophecy, see Le Roy Edwin Froom's seminal study, *The Prophetic Faith of Our Fathers*, especially volumes 1 and 2, as well as Paul Christianson, *Reformers and Babylon*; Katherine Firth, *The Apocalyptic Tradition in Reformation Britain, 1530–1645*; and C. A. Patrides and Joseph Wittreich, eds., *The Apocalypse in English Renaissance Thought and Literature*.

9. Sanderson, *Ten Sermons*, 43.

What rings in our ears, however, is not so much Sanderson's defense as his reference to "some" who have labeled Elizabeth a "sluttish husewife." By conflating the recent queen with an impure church and thus with adultery, such commentators had hinted at their desire to see the "woman" of the Apocalypse restored to purity, now represented in domestic terms as a woman willing to carry out a thorough "housecleaning" of the house of God. It is hardly surprising, then, that during the Parliaments of 1621 and 1624, both houses became zealous about maintaining the purity of the church, often angrily contesting what they saw as the increasing Romishness of the bishops.

One of the bishops who quickly came under parliamentary attack was Joseph Hall, his publication of *The Old Religion* appearing unnecessarily sympathetic to Rome. Hall's response was characteristic: "Censure not," he appealed, "where there is the same truth clad in a different, but more easy habit of words."[10] In highlighting the "habit of words" that allows the truth to appear in different fashions, Hall calls attention to the way "truth" takes a variety of continually altering forms. Certainly, the awareness that truth can be "covered" and "re-covered" in oppositional ways is the "darke conceit" at the center of the first book of *The Faerie Queene* where Una remains veiled, shining forth only in brief and illuminating flashes. And this same "habit of words" figures prominently in the writings of poets, preachers, and prophets of the seventeenth century who, like Spenser, return to Revelation to re-cover the truth.

My emphasis on Revelation is not new to seventeenth-century studies since apocalyptic interpretation has been treated extensively in surveys of Renaissance apocalyptic commentary and in historical accounts of the English civil war—in Christopher Hill's work particularly. This study diverges from those, however, in that I do not pursue an exclusively "radical," millenarian, or Miltonic focus. Instead, I evaluate a series of figures, both men and women, engaged in apocalyptic debate from a range of ecclesiastical and political perspectives. By analyzing their texts within the context of history and ecclesiastical politics, I am able to show how some writers previously considered "literary" actually participate in the hottest controversies of the seventeenth century.

---

10. Hall, *The Old Religion*, 734. Joseph Hall was attacked on two fronts: the more zealous reformers were angered at the Romish stance of *The Old Religion*, while, on the opposite side, Laud forced him to revise his commentary on Revelation to soften its militancy against Rome.

Introduction

I begin with a brief overview of a text long recognized as both literary and apocalyptic: Spenser's "Legende of the Knight of the Redcrosse,
or Holinesse." Spenser's work provides an important point of origin for
this study since his transcendent and militant model of the church holds
together so brilliantly at the end of the Elizabethan era but quickly unravels
under the pressures of Stuart religion and politics. Over the course of the
seventeenth century, Spenser's apocalyptic paradigm undergoes a series of
transformations into a variety of new forms as Protestant militancy against
Rome becomes increasingly less acceptable at Court.

While Spenser and Milton's apocalyptic narratives are crucial to this book,
I do not focus exclusively upon them, treating them simply as nodal points in
an ongoing apocalyptic debate rather than as the most significant prophetic
writers of the age. By situating Milton within the ecclesiastical controversies
of his own particular moment, I am able to demonstrate how his early work,
"On the Morning" and *Comus,* undercuts the "royalist" and "conformist"
responses of writers such as Donne and Herbert published around the same
time. Such contextualizing accomplishes two purposes. It makes Milton a far
stronger prophetic voice at a time when he is generally considered "courtly"
and "metaphysical." And it grounds the metaphysical poets far more firmly in
the political, ecclesiastical, and social controversies confronting the English
Church. Their poetics emerge as neither "apolitical" nor entirely devotional,
but deeply concerned with the questions and crosscurrents of the time. I am
thus able to fill significant gaps in the prophetic continuum, to demonstrate
that conformist writers such as Andrewes, Donne, Herbert, and Vaughan
use apocalyptic imagery to address such questions as whether the pope was
Antichrist, the bride of Christ was "pure," or the structure of the temple was
a model of ecclesiastical reform.

Another major focus of this study is how women writers of the time
rework apocalyptic material to suit their own social and spiritual agendas.
Rather than accepting the Pauline passage mandating female silence, they
authorize their prophetic writings and gender by identifying themselves both
with Joel's prophetic handmaids and with Saint John's "woman clothed with
the sun." Because we have not been very attentive to these alternative strands
of prophecy—on the one hand political and conformist, on the other radical
and feminist—what was in the seventeenth century an extremely volatile
debate over apocalyptic interpretation has become a one-sided discussion.
I seek to recover the dynamism of this initial dialogue by drawing on a
number of writers from each gender as well as from radical and conformist

groups as I trace the shifting representations of the apocalyptic bride and temple over time.

The fact that some of these writers recover apocalyptic truth with pacifistic rather than militant intention goes far toward resolving one of the literary mysteries of the seventeenth century. We have, for some time, accepted without question Barbara Lewalski's interpretation of a generic split between the religious poets of this period: that Spenser and Milton, for example, differ from Herbert and Donne in their choice of biblical models, genres, and audiences. The prophetic poem, in Lewalski's view, emerges as public, symbolic, and apocalyptic, drawn from the coded language of Revelation, while the meditative lyric is private, expressive, and reflective, drawn from the meditative verse of the Psalms.[11] This book will demonstrate that, contrary to Lewalski's viewpoint, the designs operating within the metaphysical lyric often derive from the same apocalyptic material chosen by Spenser and Milton: the bride and the temple of Saint John the Divine. What sets these poets apart from one another is neither their biblical model nor a difference in audience, but the ecclesiastical and spiritual politics that inform and transform their apocalyptic representations.

To understand how these representations highlight the ecclesiastical, spiritual, and political commitments of each writer, I draw on the work of Stuart historians Peter Lake, Anthony Milton, Kenneth Fincham, and others. These men have attempted, as Kenneth Fincham puts it, "to nudge the current historigraphical debate away from an obsessive preoccupation with one doctrine—predestination—and towards an appreciation of a range of contentious issues: conformity, order, worship, clerical authority and wealth, even attitudes toward the Church's own past."[12] Abandoning the dichotomy between "Anglicans and Puritans" as inappropriately reductive, Fincham locates at least four different groups engaged in ecclesiastical debate: moderate puritans, radical puritans, conformist Calvinists, and anti-Calvinists. Of the four, the group he holds most accountable for the political and ecclesiastical turmoil culminating in the English civil war is the "anti-Calvinists," the English Churchmen close to James I and Charles I during the early decades of the seventeenth century. These churchmen, he argues, went well beyond attacking the Calvinist doctrine of the English Church. They also implemented a series of substitutions, replacing the Calvinist emphasis on internal piety with an elaborate public worship service based on the prayer

11. Lewalski, *Protestant Poetics and the Seventeenth-Century Religious Lyric*, 4.
12. Fincham, ed., *The Early Stuart Church, 1603–1642*, 1–2.

book and canons, the Calvinist belief in "saving grace" with a "sacramental" grace received in the Eucharist, and the Calvinist obsession with destroying the Roman "whore" with a "bride" interested neither in purifying separation nor in militancy against Rome. Rather, this "bride" wished to draw into her "body" a community of believers committed both to pacifism and to episcopal lines of authority. Because these innovations in doctrine and ceremony were intended to decenter and even remove the Calvinist beliefs at the core of the later Elizabethan church, historian Peter Lake has labeled this group "avant-garde conformists."[13]

Such clarifications by Peter Lake, Kenneth Fincham, and others have enabled me to consider poets and prose writers of the seventeenth century within the context of Stuart debates over worship, ceremony, and apocalyptic history, where seemingly minor observances such as kneeling, bowing, preaching, and praying encode political as well as spiritual positions. In carrying out my analysis, I focus less on reformation theology than on ecclesiastical politics, partly because many theological treatments of literary figures have already been taken up (Georgia Christopher's brilliant analysis of Milton's attention to Luther in *Milton and the Science of the Saints;* Christopher Hodgkins's, Richard Strier's, and Gene Edward Veith Jr.'s sensitive studies of the interplay of Luther and Calvin on George Herbert's work; David Norbrook and John King's reformation readings of Spenser; and Stephen Honeygoskey's powerful analysis of Milton's ecclesial theology, for example).[14] Partly too, I have wished to maintain a political rather than a theological focus, one I find particularly conducive to interpretations of the book of Revelation. Because this text quite literally uncovers each writer's ecclesiastical and social commitments as he or she unveils its mysteries, it enables us to see how diverging histories of the church, attitudes toward church structure, and assessments of ceremonies enter into contestatory dialogue with one another. Each writer's "habit of words" is, in this sense, both theologically and politically motivated.

If historians have enabled me to identify significant political and ecclesiastical issues under contention in the Stuart church, literary historians have

13. See Lake, "Lancelot Andrewes, John Buckeridge, and Avant-Garde Conformity at the Court of James I."

14. See Christopher, *Milton and the Science of the Saints;* Hodgkins, *Authority, Church, and Society in George Herbert: Return to the Middle Way;* Strier, *Love Known: Theology and Experience in George Herbert's Poetry;* Veith, *Reformation Spirituality: The Religion of George Herbert;* Norbrook, *Poetry and Politics;* King, *Spenser's Poetry and the Reformation Tradition;* and Honeygosky, *Milton's House of God: The Invisible and Visible Church.*

made me aware of the extent to which these variables inform the poets and prose writers of the seventeenth century. Sidney Gottlieb, Achsah Guibbory, and Michael Schoenfeldt have emphasized the social, economic, and political discourses operating within the "private" form, while Ted-Larry Pebworth, Claude J. Summers, and John N. Wall have turned the expressive function of the lyric on end by arguing that it is often didactic and liturgical, aimed at both building up the spiritual community and containing ecclesiastical controversy.

Once I became aware of the politics encoded in the lyric and prose writers of the period, economic issues, particularly those articulated by New Historicist critics, also came into view. Louis Montrose, Stephen Greenblatt, Jonathan Goldberg, Jonathan Dollimore, and David Norbrook have called attention to the subtle political and economic transactions evident in the rhetorical maneuvers of Renaissance writers. I diverge from these critics in my attempt to show the other, transcendent side of materialist discourse, a dual "habit of words" perfectly encoded in the pun on "profit/prophet" itself. The prophet's words, I suggest, often indict the profit and power of the Stuart court, words that invoke a God deeply committed to the marginalized and powerless. Nearly all of the writers I consider here, whether avant-garde conformists, conformists, Presbyterians, or Fifth Monarchists, condemn those economic exchanges in which spirituality becomes simply one more counter in the politics of Stuart culture. Thus, Andrewes claims as his ultimate value a transcendent "profit" determined only in heaven, Donne calls for inward transformation in an attempt to reform the mercenary members of the present church, Milton skewers those living in "lewdly pampered luxury," and Lanyer, Davies, Cary, and Fell request a complete reworking of social and political inequities, not just for the female gender but for the entire "common wealth." By surveying these writers, I demonstrate how apocalyptic discourse seeks to expose corrupt economies to a readership, either to bring about their purification or to overturn the very structures of power that have brought them into being.

Once English Churchmen and Presbyterians, poets and prophets, and men and women are heard participating in the same apocalyptic debate, the political dynamics of that dialogue emerges, one in which persons discussing the "same truth" quickly part company over the "clothing" that the truth must assume in the seventeenth-century church. We therefore find them disagreeing about the "invisibility" or "visibility" of the church in history, its Presbyterian "discipline" or episcopal design, its unceremonial or ceremonial worship, and, of course, the lay or episcopal status of its prophets.[15] These issues, derived from careful readings of apocalyptic texts, concern radical prophets such as Thomas Brightman, John Milton, and Eleanor Davies as well as conformist churchmen such as Lancelot Andrewes, George Herbert, and John Donne. In grounding this apocalyptic debate historically, I arrange the chapters of the book in chronological order.

The first chapter, "Historic Recoveries: Spenserian Apocalyptic and the True Church," focuses on Spenser's "Legende of the Knight of the Red-crosse, or Holinesse" where the ecclesiastical history of the true church is woven together through the visible and invisible narrative strands of Redcrosse and Una, while it is threaded against and partially unraveled by the corrupt histories of "Una" and Duessa. In attempting to seduce Redcrosse to alternative versions of history, these women reveal their visible Presbyterian and Romish origins, origins that Redcrosse fails to recognize. Through just such "historicall fictions" framing Book 1, Spenser constructs an apocalyptic narrative for his own time, one that attunes his readership to the presence of the oppositional histories being presented in the ecclesiastical debates of the 1580s as well as to the multifaceted and creative character of prophecy.

Chapter 2, "War and Peace: Prophecy in Thomas Brightman and Lancelot Andrewes," analyzes the commentary of the radical puritan Thomas Bright-man. His *Revelation of the Revelation* equated the Church of England with the corrupt Laodicean church and called for an immediate rejection of episcopacy as well as an open embrace of Presbyterianism. In interpreting the woman of the Apocalypse, Brightman associates the pain of her "labor" with the persecution that the primitive church undergoes. Ironically, the child she produces, Constantine the Great, brings a peace that immediately corrupts the church, driving the woman into the invisible inner portion of the temple. Only by rejecting peace and declaring war on the Romishness of the episcopal hierarchy, Brightman asserts, will the church emerge in all her purity. In taking this stand, Brightman departs in his apocalyptic rhetoric both from moderate conformists in the English Church such as Spenser and from the avant-garde conformists gaining power in the Stuart court. I assess this latter group through the Whitsunday sermons of Lancelot

---

15. Especially valuable have been essays in Peter Lake and Maria Dowling, eds., *Protestantism and the National Church in Sixteenth-Century England;* Fincham, *Early Stuart Church;* and A. Milton's comprehensive study, *Catholic and Reformed.*

Andrewes, who, in redefining prophecy for King James, spearheads a shift in court preaching and writing. Arguing that the true church has always been material and visible, Andrewes equates the male and female prophets of the age with the curse of Babel. Only God's true prophets, he indicates, can turn cacophony into unity, making a harmony of divine and human languages by rejecting any discourse that sponsors social or political division.

One of the many voices that Andrewes attempts to silence in his reconsideration of prophecy is that of women, efficiently achieved by quoting Paul's, "I suffer not a woman to teach, nor to usurp authority over the man, but to be in silence" (1 Tim. 2:12). In my third chapter, "Subverting Paul: The True Church and the *Querelle des Femmes* in Aemilia Lanyer," I show how Aemilia Lanyer responds to interpretations like Andrewes's by appropriating an alternative hermeneutic method from a prophetic tradition available in the *Querelle des Femmes*. Following the lead of Cornelius Agrippa, she reinterprets Paul's analysis of the Fall to recover a Gospel narrative produced by women and authorized by Christ.

As I have suggested here, the prophetic debate became hotter during the late 1620s and early 1630s as apocalyptic formulations took on subversive, politically dangerous connotations for King James and King Charles. Chapter 4, "Admitting Adultery: Donne's Versions of the True Church," demonstrates how Donne responds to this dilemma by underscoring the difficulty and danger of interpreting the Apocalypse of Saint John as a political document about the way national or ecclesiastical affairs should be conducted. Consequently, whenever Donne takes up the issue of the Antichrist and popery in his sermons, he dramatizes the proliferating ambiguities that result from a reading of the "letter" itself. Here, as in Holy Sonnet 18, Donne reaches ecclesiastical consensus regarding the true church by obscuring altogether the Spenserian opposition between Una and Duessa. The true church, he hints, is both bride and whore.

The fifth chapter, "Body Language: The Political Design of Herbert's *Temple*," considers how George Herbert enters into this debate over prophecy and the origins of the true church. Similar to Spenser, Andrewes, and Donne, he seeks to interpret the apocalyptic letter, but he chooses not to destabilize either John's epistle or the method of interpreting it. Rather, he traces the "Temple" within the text of the Apocalypse to the first Christian temple of Constantine's reign. By reconstructing and modifying this primitive structure according to the controversies of his time, he contests both Laudian and Puritan positions and establishes betweenness itself as the highest art.

Chapter 6, "Contestatory Measures in 'On the Morning,' *Comus,* and *Paradise Lost*" shows how John Milton's "On the Morning of Christ's Nativity" counters the pacifistic version of prophecy promoted by Andrewes, Donne, and Herbert. While Milton begins his poem by entertaining the Virgilian "harmonies" of the Caroline court, he rejects such utterance before the poem is half over. Milton thus acknowledges "mythic" prophecy in order to silence it, revealing in the process its delusional attempt to avoid a linear and redemptive understanding of history. His next work, *Comus,* responds still more powerfully to ecclesiastical controversy. In his rewriting of the Apocalypse, the lady—again representative of the true church—finds that journeying into the wilderness does not enable her to escape corruption, but brings her face-to-face with its embodiment, the licentious and fleshly Comus. Through their ensuing debate, Milton exposes the profit motives behind the avant-garde wing of the English Church, attacking along the way the Laudian emphasis on the Episcopalian priesthood, vestments, sacraments, and canon law. Milton's antiprelatical tracts and *Paradise Lost* move the debate into still wider territory as the conflict assumes universal proportions. The debate now hinges on the difference between free inspiration and the constraints of tradition. Because the latter inevitably rigidifies into a variety of self-authorizing political, ecclesiastical, and social forms—whether avant-garde conformism, feminism, or Presbyterianism—Milton seeks to create a discerning readership, one capable of sorting out coercive interpretations that seduce and thereby control the interpreting subject.

During the Interregnum, the prophet Eleanor Davies assumes an even more forceful apocalyptic role than does John Milton as she calls down judgment on King Charles and his wife, "the Whore of Babylon," Henrietta Maria. In the seventh chapter, "Feminist Authority in Eleanor Davies's Prophecies," I examine how Davies's feminist, apocalyptic focus places her in repeated conflict not only with the Stuart court, but also, in the long run, with Parliament. Consequently, Davies's prophecies predicting the fall of Charles are revised by the Presbyterians before they go into print; in these later, altered versions, Davies's feminist "handwriting" no longer appears.

Chapter 8, "Re-Covering Paul: The True Church and the Prophecies of Mary Cary, Anna Trapnel, and Margaret Fell," traces the shifting apocalyptic formulations of "temple" and "bride" through the prophecies of three women who adopt very different prophetic styles. Each, like Aemilia Lanyer, finds it necessary to contest the standard Renaissance interpretation of Paul. Mary Cary does so by appropriating his communal vision, Anna Trapnel, by feminizing his paradoxical life, and Margaret Fell, by contextualizing his words. In this way, each of these women argues for greater freedom for women within the church and, at the same time, for further social and political reform.

In the last chapter of this study, "Henry Vaughan's Concealed Temple," I come full circle by examining how the politically exiled English Churchman Henry Vaughan returns to Spenser's apocalyptic paradigm to align his own prophetic discourse with the destroyed temple and the marginalized "woman in the wilderness." Now Herbert's *Temple*—ventriloquized through Vaughan—is radically destabilized. Building out of fragmentary bits and pieces of Herbertian poetics, Vaughan attempts to refashion an ecclesiastical home in the midst of political chaos and against overwhelming loss. Gone is the Herbertian restraint, the highly conscious attempt to include. In its place, we hear an angry apocalyptic voice, proclaiming the truth in the wilderness and foreseeing, in his brightest, most visionary moments, the return of the true church.

All of these seventeenth-century rewritings of the Apocalypse uncover, through the multifaceted interpretations of the hidden temple and the woman clothed with the sun, the political and ecclesiastical commitments of the writers themselves. But because these writers invoke a poetics of transcendence through the social, economic, and spiritual profit of their words, they register that mysterious change in signature that occurs when the wholly Other becomes articulated through the human.[16] Indeed, the power behind the sermons, lyrics, and pamphlets of the age resides in the writer's ability to refer beyond his or her own material articulations to that transcendent, immaterial voice that can never be wholly contained, a voice that opens human discourse up both to representational innovation and to divine Presence.[17]

---

16. I am indebted here to the work of my colleague Tom Gardner, who has analyzed how Heidegger and Wittgenstein provide a theoretical and philosophical model for understanding the way American poets come to terms with the limits of language.

17. Thomas Cooper, in *An answer in defense of the truth against the Apology of private mass*, analyzes the way figurative language contains divine mysteries, especially evident in Christ's "This is my Body": "What can be more plainly spoken against that interpretation that you make upon these words of Christ; wherebye you do bind us to a servile and literal sense of this word, 'Is,' and in such sort take the signs of this sacrament for the things signified" (210). Calling the Romish interpretation of Christ's words "sluttish eloquence," Cooper suggests that Rome has been ravished to such usage by a "mocking spirit" (215). The English Churchmen would increasingly claim the tendency of both Roman Catholics and Presbyterians to misread the Word by literalizing it. In doing so, both groups missed a Mystery that resided neither in the "naked Word" highlighted by the Puritans nor the "Body" highlighted by Rome, but in the mysterious realm between—a tension that metaphor sets in motion. Joseph Hall would return

Introduction

This book accordingly highlights the matrices of religious, historical, and political variables that bring numerous works together under the term *prophecy*, while accounting for the ideological distinctions that separate them. It diverges from Debora K. Shuger's *Habits of Thought in the English Renaissance* by focusing only on the "more easy habit of words" employed in the apocalyptic revisions of the time, words that clothe "the same truth" in order to recover a more acceptable prophetic form. Paradoxically, such discourse also uncovers a number of material and surprisingly transcendent differences.

---

to the words "This is my body" to highlight the "somewhat more" within human memory and reflection that turns absence into Presence: "He adds, *Do this in remembrance of me:* remembrance implies an absence; neither can we more be said to remember that which is in our present sense, than to see that which is absent" (*The Old Religion*, 665).

1

Historic Recoveries

Spenserian Apocalyptic and the True Church

[Revelation] contayneth the universall troubles, persecucions and crosses, that the churche suffred in the primative spryng, what it suffreth now, and what it shall suffre in the latter tymes by the subtyle satellites of antichrist.
—John Bale, *The Image of Bothe Churches*

T HE RATHER lengthy title of John Bale's *The Image of Bothe Churches* not only promises "a very frutefull exposicion" of the "heavenly Revelacion" of Saint John but also offers a text read in the context of "the most auctorised historyes." As the ultimate "holye oracle" and a "light to the cronicles," Revelation, he asserts, will unravel the mysteries of every past and future event, providing powerful parallels for the present church. As time and space converge in Bale's commentary, his own exile from England with other "beleving brethren" reenacts the three-and-a-half-year exile of the prophets Elias, Daniel, and Saint John and designates the true church's repeated flight from political corruption. From this divinely appointed "resting place," Bale commits his text to paper under the very conditions that brought Revelation into existence—a time of persecution—offering a spiritual and political "rebuke" to the country he has left behind. "Contempt of the gospel," he warns, "now reyneth [in England] above all in the clergye."[1]

John Foxe, like Bale before him, foregrounds the intersection of ancient chronicle, divine Revelation, and contemporary history, but he provides a far more conciliatory moment for the writing of his text. Identifying his *Actes and Monuments of these latter perillous dayes* as a sequel to the work of the patristic historian Eusebius, Foxe traces his political and spiritual lines back to Eusebius's imperialist theology. He accordingly rejects the sharp

---

1. Bale, *Image of Bothe Churches after the moste wonderfull and heavenly Revelacion of Sainct John the Evangelist, Contaynyng a very frutefull exposicion or Paraphrase upon the same. Wherin it is conferred with other scripturs, and most auctorised historyes*, A5v–A6r.

division between secular and spiritual authority established by Bale, finding in Eusebius's celebratory union of state and church under Constantine a model for the political and spiritual realities of Elizabeth's rule. Just as Constantine patronized Eusebius's chronicles, then, Foxe requests Queen Elizabeth to provide him with the same "favour and furtheraunce" for the work he has in hand.[2]

In authorizing his text on the basis of this ancient model, Foxe seeks to sanction the emergence of the English Church as a political and spiritual body by tracing its decline from Constantinian rule and its eventual return to this ideal. During the time of decline, the lines of the true church can be glimpsed in the marginalized and martyred believers who resist spiritual corruption and later are identified in *Actes and Monuments* as those enduring Romish persecution.[3] Designating Rome's spiritual authority as the instrument of oppression, Foxe contrasts this corrupt claim with England's appropriate rule: the latter follows the Constantinian ideal in which the church remains subordinate to the state. Foxe thus aligns the English Church with the primitive church of the past and with an originary purity that is both episcopal in structure and orthodox in doctrine.

Drawn to but not defined by these historical and ecclesiastical narratives, Spenser offers a significantly more subtle version of the true church in his "Legende of the Knight of the Redcrosse, or Holinesse." Like Bale and Foxe before him, Spenser traces the history of the true church in time, but he negotiates far more circumspectly between the division of church and state highlighted by Bale or the imperialistic union celebrated by Foxe. As Ake Bergvall has shown, Spenser achieves this synthesis by grafting the theological stock of Augustine, Luther, and Bale onto that of Eusebius and Foxe, thereby deepening the distinction between the secular and the spiritual realms, even as he celebrates the divinely sanctioned reign of the queen in bringing them together.[4]

But Spenser necessarily goes further than this in creating a nuanced synthesis of political and spiritual positions—and for reasons located not only in the final word of his title but also in contemporary debates over holiness taking place at the time. By the 1580s and 1590s, the English Church was under attack on two fronts: the Presbyterians were arguing that the

2. Foxe, "Dedication to Queen Elizabeth," in *Actes and Monuments of these latter perillous dayes,* n.p.

3. See Jane Facey, "John Foxe and the Defence of the English Church."

4. Bergvall, "Between Eusebius and Ausgustine: Una and the Cult of Elizabeth."

English Church needed to be purified of its Romish episcopal structure and restored to a visible "Presbyterian" model—the structure, they claimed, of the church in antiquity.[5] The Roman Catholics argued, on the other hand, that the English Church had abandoned its visible foundation in antiquity and was accordingly guilty of heresy.

Spenser's response to these debates is not only aesthetically illuminating but also historically, politically, and spiritually astute. Through the dual narratives of Una and Redcrosse, he dramatizes the mysterious tension joining the invisible, spiritual dimension of the church (represented by Una), to its visible, institutional structure (represented by Redcrosse)—a "double" government articulated by the archbishop of the church, John Whitgift:[6]

> There is a double government of the Church, the one spiritual, the other external. Christ only, and none other, by the operation of his Spirit and direction of his word, spiritually governeth his church, and reigning in the consciences of the faithful guideth their minds in all matters of devotion, faith, and holiness; and this is the spiritual kingdom of Christ, so much spoken of in the scriptures, and specially in the prophets . . . The external government hath both a substance and a matter about which it is occupied, and also a form to attain the same, consisting in certain offices and functions, and in the names and titles of them. The substance and matter of government must indeed be taken out of the word of God, and consisteth in these points, that the word be truly taught, the sacraments rightly administered, virtue furthered, vice repressed, and the church kept in quietness and order.[7]

Following Whitgift, Spenser makes the distinction between Una and Redcrosse central to his poetry while reinforcing their necessary interdependence and union. In this way he models for his readership what Peter Lake calls the "abhorrence with which hard line conformist divines viewed any hint of slippage between the spiritual or political spheres—or stated differently, between the visible and invisible church."[8]

The reason Spenser takes such a strategy is clear: the Roman Catholics and Presbyterians each pointed back to a visible church founded directly by

---

5. See *The Reformation of Our Church* for the Presbyterian position and Matthew Sutcliffe, *Ecclesiastical Discipline,* for the conformist position.

6. See Peter Lake, *Anglicans and Puritans? Presbyterianism and English Conformist Thought from Whitgift to Hooker,* chapter 1, for an analysis of this controversy.

7. John Whitgift, *The Defence of the Answer to the Admonition,* 48:6.

8. Lake, *Anglicans and Puritans?* 127.

Christ, one continuing for the Roman Catholics through the authority of the pope and one for the Presbyterians through the "discipline" or "platform" of the godly. To create a space for the English Church that placed it beyond the claims of such visible models, Spenser and other conformists constructed a version of the true church in which its transcendent dimension necessarily remained distinct from its visible, ecclesiastical institution. And Spenser makes this distinction even sharper. Representing the relationship between Una and Redcrosse as a protracted engagement, he refuses to "marry" them within the poem. Instead, through a psychological and sexual tension that extends across historical time, he depicts the transcendent hope of Una, who, while she guides and directs the external government of the church, never becomes coercive, never assumes absolute control over the material body of Redcrosse.[9]

Because, however, the Roman Catholics and Presbyterians were indeed seen as coercive in attempting to validate their viewpoints in the controversies of the moment, Spenser's false "Una" and Duessa attempt to do precisely this in their conversations with Redcrosse: they seduce him to alternative versions of history. Tracing their origins to the material rather than the transcendent body of Christ, their histories, quite literally, reveal their fallen, earthly origins. Through these dual representations, Spenser's first book can be seen to take a stand on the episcopal structure of the English Church, reinforcing in poetic terms Peter Lake's evaluation that this issue had "moved gradually towards the very centre of Protestant concerns." John King, then, is only partly right that "during Spenser's time a sharp cleavage had not yet emerged in the Church of England between conformists and separatists." Though no rupture had as yet occurred, the fissures were already starting to show in the vitriolic reactions of John Whitgift to the Presbyterian Thomas Cartwright, reactions so elaborate and detailed that Presbyterianism emerges, in Whitgift's writing, as a threat equal to Rome. As Whitgift puts it: "The papists and [the Presbyterians] jointly do, seek to shake, nay to overthrow, the self-foundations, grounds, and pillars of our

---

9. Spenser's portrait articulates a specific ecclesiastical and political agenda in which the popular voice has no place. As historian Peter Lake puts it, "the great advantage of rule by the Christian prince and the godly bishop was the exclusion of any popular voice from the process of government," since for conformists "tyranny was not a function of the presence or absence of consent or collective decision making, but of the relationship between the ruler's will and law. Neither man's propensity to sin nor Antichrist's power to delude fallen humanity left much hope that there was any safety to be found in numbers" ("Presbyterianism, the Idea of a National Church, and the Argument from Divine Right," 217).

church, although not by the self-same instruments and engines. Wherefore it is time to draw out the sword of discipline."[10]

Spenser's awareness that the two primary attacks on the church "are not by the self-same instruments and engines" leads him to chart the ecclesiastical exchanges of the moment in the dialogue of his characters, thereby clarifying the complexity, tension, and betrayal apparent in their individual representations of history. His brilliantly conceived "historicall fiction" can be seen to unveil how historical fictions themselves serve sometimes to divide, sometimes to unite the true church as it journeys across time and space.[11] In keeping with this, the dominant thread woven through each interior story of his "Legende of the Knight of the Redcrosse, or Holinesse" is that of historic recovery. His own method, too, is that of the epic poet, now clearly "historicized": "For the Methode of a Poet historical is not such, as of an Historiographer. For an Historiographer discourseth of affayres orderly as they were donne, accounting as well the times as the actions, but a Poet thrusteth into the middest, even where it most concerneth him, and there recoursing to the thinges forepaste, and diuining of things to come, maketh a pleasing Analysis of all."[12] Though Spenser does not say so, thrusting himself into the midst "where it most concerneth him" has the additional effect of catapulting a reading audience into a historical narrative already in progress, one that is ongoing, dynamic, and controversial. Puzzled by the uncertainty of origins that cannot be quickly discerned, confronted by contestatory voices with alternative versions of the past, his readers must discover—much as Spenser suggests—the pleasure of "Analysis."[13]

While "recoursing" and "diuining" in the present moment (always somewhere between past and future), Spenser's narrative discloses a prophetic assessment of history.[14] And, by making his readers attend to the voices in

10. Lake, *Anglicans and Puritans?* 1; King, *Spenser's Poetry,* 9–10; Whitgift, *Defence of the Answer,* 48:122.

11. Linda Gregerson argues that Spenser's poem as well as Milton's *Paradise Lost* "thematize and stage themselves as a series of specular recognition scenes" (*The Reformation of the Subject,* 6). But it is his observation and speculation that I believe Redcrosse must put behind him in learning how to listen, read, and interpret correctly.

12. Edmund Spenser, "A Letter of the Authors," in *The Faerie Queene,* 16–17.

13. For those critics emphasizing readers' responses, see Paul Alpers, *The Poetry of the Faerie Queene,* 152–59; and King, *Spenser's Poetry,* 73.

14. Harry Berger argues that "Spenser's vision makes no claims to being mystical or prophetic." Beyond this, he also notes that Spenser's references to history "are all secondary to the individual hero's experience" (*Revisionary Play: Studies in Spenserian Dynamics,* 83). I

the poem, to when they speak as well as why, he subtly reveals that history is always recovered during moments of temporary peace and supposed "rest," during moments in the poem when Redcrosse and Una take time off for physical or spiritual recovery. To some extent, such moments replicate the recovery of history evident in the work of Eusebius and Foxe, men who compose their histories during the peace ushered in by Constantine and Elizabeth. Yet the process is not entirely positive, as Spenser makes clear. Encoded in these recoveries is the alternative awareness that the time of peace is vulnerable to corrupt histories as well, to histories promoted as equally legitimate and definitive.

Redcrosse is particularly open to error along these lines. In fact, while returning from Error's Den, Una and Redcrosse encounter "an aged Sire" (1.1.29) dressed in black, one with a demeanor that replicates Redcrosse's own. Both men, we realize, seem "sad" (1.1.29; 1.1.2), but Archimago's "sage" sobriety clearly overmatches Redcrosse's "solemne" earnestness and suggests a calculating side to his character that may reach well beyond the Romishness that previous critics have cited.[15] In fact, Archimago dresses in a "habit" that Whitgift identifies as particularly Presbyterian: "They pretended great gravity; they sighed much; they seldom or never laughed; they were very austere in reprehending; they spake gloriously. To be short . . . they were great hypocrites."[16] Archimago's desire to wear his "booke" (1.1.29) in plain view while wandering the byways conflates his movement as a wandering minister with that of the monks, a blurring of Presbyterian and Romish referents that doubles the threat of ecclesiastical error.

Despite this ecclesiastical conflation, John King and D. Douglas Waters have focused primarily on the Romish dimension of Spenser's iconoclasm, King identifying Spenser's "double-edged" satire only in the later books of *The Faerie Queene* when the iconoclastic fury and multitongued discourse of the Blatant Beast uncovers Spenser's parodic attack on Presbyterianism.[17] I believe, however, that even very early in *The Faerie Queene* the Presbyterian threat emerges, a perception that Spenser's earliest readers came to quite easily: "Opinion dating back to Spenser's own age," John King

---

suggest that Spenser's playful re-vision and re-creation of Apocalyptic form (which Berger so elegantly reveals), actually blurs the boundaries between fiction and history, the individual and the church. Both exist within the same allegorical function, and neither is, in this sense, subordinate to the other.

15. D. Douglas Waters, *Duessa as Theological Satire*, 62–93; King, *Spenser's Poetry*, 73–77.
16. Whitgift, *Defence of the Answer*, 48:97.
17. King, *Spenser's Poetry*, 109, 237.

notes, "identifies him with the conservative attack on late Elizabethan radicals."[18]

It is hardly surprising, then, that in the initial encounter between Redcrosse and Archimago, the magician proves capable of being both "Presbyterian" and Romish, both militantly apocalyptic and monastically devotional. He continues to establish his link to the Presbyterians when he tells Redcrosse of a "straunge man" who is a product of "homebred euill." In this double-tongued way, Archimago both reveals and conceals himself, enabling Spenser to encode the "homebred" character of the "radical" attack on the church. As we might expect, John Whitgift makes the same point: "We of this church, in these perilous days, do see that we have a great number of hollow hearts *within this realm,* that daily gape for alteration of religion" (emphasis added).[19] Redcrosse is of course blind to the fact that this danger is far nearer than he knows and, rather ironically, asks for directions. To this Archimago responds in words that prove as shifty as the ground where he, only moments ago, located danger:

> Far hence (quoth he) in wastfull wildernesse
> His dwelling is, by which no liuing wight
> May ever passe, but thorough great distresse.
> (1.1.32)

Archimago's depiction of the "wastfull wildernesse" that awaits Redcrosse has, again, a range of possibilities. Christopher Hill has shown that the term was coopted by a variety of ecclesiastical and political parties throughout the next century to represent "a safe condition or a hiding place," "a time of testing and tutelage," and a place "of disorder, darkness, and death."[20] These same references appear in the wilderness motifs of the sixteenth century, evident not only in Bale's safe retreat into "desert" exile, but also, as we shall see, in the wilderness flight of the woman in Revelation.

Archimago has, however, changed not only the proximity and location of danger but also the marks of his ecclesiastical affiliation: now he is distinctly Romish. Calling himself a holy father praying with his "beades," he identifies his place of residence as a "hidden cell" (1.1.30). It is to this residence that he takes both Redcrosse and Una, and it is here that Redcrosse undergoes his first history test. Again, the test arises during a time of intended refreshment,

---

18. Ibid., 237.
19. Whitgift, *Defence of the Answer,* 48:5.
20. Hill, *The English Bible and the Seventeenth-Century Revolution,* 141–42.

a rest Una has recommended, Archimago has offered, and Redcrosse has accepted. As all retire to their bedrooms, we find Archimago busily at work, constructing, it turns out, an alternative "Una":

> Who all this while with charmes and hidden artes,
> Had made a Lady of that other Spright,
> And fram'd of liquid ayre her tender partes,
> So liuely, and so like in all mens sight,
> That weaker sence it could have rauisht quight:
> The maker selfe for all his wondrous witt,
> Was nigh beguiled with so goodly sight:
> Her all in white he clad, and ouer it
> Cast a blacke stole, most like to seeme for *Vna* fit.
>
> (1.1.45)

As John King has noted, John Dixon, an early reader of the text, saw Archimago as "a false profite" and "Antichrist."[21] A wielder of images that feign the truth, Archimago engineers the corruption of the church on seemingly holy ground, evident, as I have argued, in his Presbyterian and Romish attempts to replace the transcendent truth of Una with a false image of her, re-covering her by giving her a material body.[22]

Recognizing almost immediately that Redcrosse's solemn idealism leaves him open to the Presbyterian "dream" of a pure, visible church, Archimago seeks to shatter that dream and thus to bring about the very fragmentation that conformist divines such as Whitgift regarded as the end result of Presbyterian "fantasy." Conformist Matthew Sutcliffe in his *Examination of Cartwright's Apology* pushed this point even further, noting that the Presbyterian representation of the church as an innocent "Lady" was itself a fabrication, a carefully staged performance in which Cartwright himself was implicated. Cartwright, Sutcliffe asserted, was stripping himself "of his priestly ornaments" and taking on "a woman's attire to play innocencie, of whom now we must speak only in the feminine gender."[23]

---

21. John Dixon, *The First Commentary on "The Faerie Queene."* For an analysis of this commentary, see King, *Spenser's Poetry,* 72–75.

22. Perhaps because of Spenser's reformation leanings and the strength of his apocalypticism (evident in his commitment to provide military aid to protestants on foreign soil), he has not been interpreted as anti-Presbyterian in any way. These two positions, however, were not mutually exclusive, and Spenser takes a fairly standard conformist stance in both. For Spenser's politics, see Norbrook, *Poetry and Politics,* 109–56.

23. Matthew Sutcliffe, *Examination of Cartwright's Apology,* 15v, 16v. As Spenser's work and Sutcliffe's appeared in print at about the same time, it is difficult to tell who precedes who, but it may not matter. The ideas, in my view, are the result of an ongoing ecclesiastical dialogue.

Duplicating Sutcliffe's argument quite literally, Archimago's "fabricated" Lady appears in Redcrosse's bedroom, apparently seized with the desire to discuss her earlier history:

> Your owne deare sake forst me at first to leaue
> My Fathers kingdome, There she stopt with teares;
> Her swollen hart her speach seemd to bereaue,
> And then againe begun, My weaker yeares,
> Captiu'd to fortune and frayle worldly feares,
> Fly to your faith for succour and sure ayde:
> Let me not dye in languor and long teares.
> Why Dame (quoth he) what hath ye thus dismayd?
> What frayes ye, that were wont to comfort me affrayd?
>
> (1.1.52)

Here, too, "Una's" forced departure from her "Fathers kingdome" out of love retraces the historical and verbal lines of the Presbyterians who were similarly underscoring the church's break with royal authority and its temporary captivity. As Thomas Cartwright argued, the church, in carrying out this action, merely followed the example of Christ: "For seeing he, being Lord, took upon him to be a servant, and being Emperor and King of heaven and earth, was content to want all the glory and shew of the world (his ministry so requiring)."[24] Parroting and thus parodying Cartwright's arguments, "Una," an image of the invisible church, now appears as a "material" girl, urging Redcrosse to comfort her sexually by overcoming the final distance between them.[25] Spenser underscores through this all too fraudulent temptation the necessary separation of the visible and the invisible church, a union that must remain unconsummated in order for the true church to maintain its purity.

Unfortunately, Redcrosse is struck far more by "Una's" histrionics than by her history; if he were listening attentively, perhaps he would know better. The "perhaps" is of course significant, for this was not an evaluation that contemporary readers were necessarily capable of making. Because Spenser's "Letter to Raleigh" was the only point in time when readers were offered the "true" history of Redcrosse and Una's relationship before Una's revelation in Canto 7, and because the "Letter" was not prefatory material in the earliest versions of the poem, readers in fact had relatively

---

24. Cartwright's *Admonition,* quoted in Whitgift, *Defence of the Answer,* 48:149.

25. In *Anglicans and Puritans?* Peter Lake analyzes this Presbyterian tendency, focusing on "the body of the saving God" who, in descending, becomes one with his people (126).

little to go on.[26] Consequently, while they were aware that "Una's" history could not be trusted, only the extremely perceptive among them would be able to discern why.[27] And Redcrosse, who does indeed have a history with Una, appears oblivious to the fact that "Una" has just remembered a very different past in her panting bursts and pauses, has remembered it for what it never was. Though aware of "Una's" "doubtfull words," then, Redcrosse does not come to any deeper conclusions, any recognition of falsehood, any need for confrontation: instead, we are told, "no'vntruth he knew" (1.1.53). In this sense, the absence of narrative and historical origins leaves the reader on ground nearly as shaky as that of Redcrosse himself, for not knowing and not remembering amount to the same dilemma. To maintain an originary purity, Spenser hints, the past must be recovered *and* remembered correctly.

"Una's" historical fiction—though it does not immediately lead Redcrosse astray—nevertheless sows the seeds of doubt in his mind:

> Long after lay he musing at her mood,
> Much grieu'd to thinke that gentle Dame so light,
> For whose defence he was to shed his blood.
>
> (1.1.55)

In speculating on the "lightness" and faithlessness of his beloved, Redcrosse now believes that his standard for faith and truth is no longer error-free. By doubting Una's firmness, he also believes—on an allegorical level—in the infidelity of the true church. In short, he no longer believes.

Archimago quickly turns Redcrosse's psychological sense that the true church can err into a "reality": he enables Redcrosse to see what he has already suspected, and the impurity inflames Redcrosse in both senses, in "gealous fire" as well as "furious ire" (1.2.5). Engaging in the Presbyterian "sight and flight" syndrome, Redcrosse's inward attraction to "material" purity and his equally zealous hatred of visible error cause him to abandon Una, the invisible true church of the elect. Thus, Redcrosse's fascination with a material purity leads him away from rather than toward a deeper spirituality, much as the exclusionary tendencies of the Presbyterians caused

26. See Darryl J. Gless's comments regarding Spenser's "Letter" in *Interpretation and Theology in Spenser*, 48–49.

27. As Harry Berger puts this, "the darkness in which the hero moves is by no means balanced by the clarity of the reader's understanding . . . Because Spenser keeps us as well as the hero off balance, we are forced to follow the narrative more intently, and indeed we come to realize that the hero is our scapegoat" (*Revisionary Play*, 61).

them to miss, in their emphasis on a "material" discipline, the interior, spiritual realm that must exist in that dynamic tension between worldliness and otherworldliness.

In this sense, Spenser's revision of the Apocalypse is both illuminating and extremely subtle: Una, the invisible true church of the elect, does not "flee" into the wilderness to avoid corruption; she is abandoned.[28] Totally fearless, she makes the entire time of her exile a quest for Redcrosse, not a quest for purity: "She of nought affrayd, / Through woods and wastnesse wide him daily sought" (1.3.3).[29] Conversely, Redcrosse, Spenser's portrait of the visible church, does indeed take flight, his "Presbyterian" departure propelling him headlong into deeper error.

Redcrosse's readiness to put all his confidence in the visible and the material both undermines the very nature of faith and places him in immediate jeopardy with regard to Rome. A few stanzas later, he encounters Duessa, and her candid rehearsal of her immediate past provides yet another history of the church. She reveals that she

> Was, (O what now auaileth that I was!)
> Borne the sole daughter of an Emperour,
> He that the wide West vnder his rule has
> And high hath set his throne, where *Tiberis* doth pas.
>
> (1.2.22)

Duessa, unlike "Una," does not trace her origins to the Kingdom of the "Father," nor does she identify any time of captivity there. Rather, she is the product of an earthly emperor whose domain encompasses the entire West. Having lost her beloved she remains in mourning, seeking constantly to recover one whose body remains somehow hidden from her. In her origins and in her history of the missing "Mass," Fidessa/Duessa reveals her materiality and attendant Romishness, but Redcrosse's "dull eares" (1.2.26) cannot discern it, for the Word that has always guided him is absent.[30] His "quicke

28. Other critics have long acknowledged Spenser's representation of the woman clothed with the sun who flees into the wilderness (Florence Sandler, "The Faerie Queene: An Elizabethan Apocalypse; and Anthea Hume, *Edmund Spenser: Protestant Poet*, 84–85). They do not, however, notice how carefully Spenser revises *Revelation* in 1.3.3.

29. John E. Hankins notes that Spenser here combines the Apocalypse with the Song of Solomon, a transformation that is, in my view, political ("Spenser and the Revelation of St. John.")

30. Redcrosse's tendency to trust his eyes rather than his ears suggests the extent to which he has abandoned reformation values that always privilege the ear, the hearing of the Word, over

eyes" are accordingly busy on her face and dress, but despite his almost obsessive attentiveness, he fails to read her clothing as either dangerous or damning: neither the "scarlot red" (1.2.13) dress, the brilliant jewels, nor the multiple crowns. Indeed, it seems, the paradoxical combination of "her humbless low" and her "ritch weedes" (1.2.21) make her all the more appealing to him. With these words, Spenser encodes in his text the parable most often used in ecclesiastical controversy, that of the wheat and the tares.[31] Proving only too willing to allow tares to be sown in the visible church, Redcrosse accepts Duessa's "ritch weedes" and agrees to sustain her with his "earthly" protection. Overly lax and even blind, he now embraces the riches that so quickly corrupt the visible church.

Unlike the first two histories, Una's story is not revealed for some time. When we finally hear it, her personal history in Canto 7 has little in common with "Una's" or Duessa's, women who, in telling their stories in the bedroom and on the battlefield, reveal the sexually and militarily coercive origins of their historical fictions. In contrast, Una slowly unravels the earliest stages of her relationship with Redcrosse, a story that Arthur almost fails to wring from this most reluctant of storytellers. Only in a space entirely free of manipulation—originating out of the dynamic interplay of Faith and Reason—does Una finally commit her past to words.

For at least three stanzas, however, the reader must hear a debate over the relative merits of history, especially when history must "disclose the breach" (1.7.42), as Una puts it, must find its way around the silence. Here, Una's decision not to speak about the past, especially when it is a history of corruption, is especially revelatory:

> Such helplesse harmes yts better hidden keepe,
> Then rip vp griefe, where it may not auaile,
> My last left comfort is, my woes to weepe and waile.
>
> (1.7.39)

Una's assessment of "helplesse harmes" accurately locates those injuries to herself and to the invisible church, as well as to Redcrosse in his present powerlessness. To speak of either is to "rip vp griefe," to make a gaping wound of articulation itself. All that is "left" to Una, then, is to weep, yet even this "left comfort" becomes "right" as she is answered by the echoing

---

the eye, the visible icon. Waters analyzes in full detail the extent to which Duessa represents the Roman mass (*Duessa as Theological Satire,* 62–93).

31. See, for example, Richard Hooker, *Of the Laws of Ecclesiastical Polity,* 1:288 (3.1.8).

responses of the knight at her side. Spenser here rings the changes on Pauline doctrine as the "wondrous great griefe" (1.7.40) that leaves Arthur groaning in empathy echoes Christ's groaning on behalf of the suffering church.[32] Una's anguish is apparently answered before she finds the words, the self-isolating linguistic gap filled mysteriously by One who already knows and joins her there. Beyond Presence, of course, Arthur provides a justification for language as well as history:

> Mishaps are maistred by aduice discrete
> And counsell mittigates the greatest smart;
> Found neuer helpe, who neuer would his hurts impart.
>
> (1.7.40)

If history is a story of "mishaps," it is also a story of recovery, Arthur reminds her, and to locate where, why, and how things went awry provides access to mastery, counsel, and cure. In contesting Una's silence, Arthur forces her to abandon it as an inappropriate defensive gesture; and Una, in "willing" herself to respond, quite literally comes to life and finds herself in dynamic and engaging conversation. Only at this point does she begin to reveal her history, recovering her origins for the first time in the poem.[33]

Una thus "discloses the breach" in her relationship with Redcrosse and closes another breach in the narrative itself by returning to that time long before the beginning, a critical moment in the text that has been repeatedly withheld.[34] Una's story, the reader finds, originates out of public, redemptive action, not private desire. By representing this difference, Spenser removes Una from the individualistic and material passions of "Una" and Duessa and foregrounds instead "all the territories" on behalf of whom she journeys as well as the monarch's role in establishing her potential redemption: Una's longing to liberate her parents from captivity—both Adam and Eve, and more immediately, the suffering church abroad—takes her to the court of the

32. Here, the dialogue between Una and Arthur paraphrases Paul's entire argument in Rom. 8:18–27, perfectly echoing verse 26: "Likewise the Spirit also helpeth our infirmities: for we know not what we should pray for as we ought: but the Spirit itself maketh intercession for us with groanings that cannot be uttered."

33. Spenser constructs an Una that initially chooses to remain silent on the subject of abuse—doubtless the preferred feminine response. Arthur prompts her into speaking, but even here, her words locate no blame in Redcrosse's behavior. Rather, she faults the coercive feminine wiles that have entrapped him.

34. As I have suggested, the only other place it is located is in Spenser's "Letter to the Reader." Printed at the end of the 1590 edition, it was hardly prefatory.

Faerie Queene where political and ecclesiastical interests are united (1.7.43, 46).[35] There she discovers the Redcrosse knight.

Like all histories, Una's history necessarily involves chronological time, and it is here that we would expect the poet of numbers most clearly to show his hand.[36] He does. As Una begins to explain the details of her parents' imprisonment, she also notes the length of time they have been subject to the persecution of the dragon: "He has them now foure yeres besieged to make them thrall" (1.7.44). Here, Spenser adds to the "forty-two months" or "twelve hundred and sixty days" so obsessively analyzed in apocalyptic commentary an additional six months, a variation that eighteenth-century commentator John Upton could not help declaring "very remarkable."[37] As this prophetic number was believed to encode the emergence of the Reformation Church during the sixteenth century, Spenser's alteration is politically and hermeneutically charged. John Napier, in contrast, seeks the utmost accuracy: "Then after 1260 yeares darknesse, was that true Temple of God opened and made manifest, as is plainlie saide in the seventh trumpet or age." The "darknesse" of the intervening time is, like Duessa's corruption of Redcrosse, "popish" in implication, a point Napier is quick to make: the "first pope unmartyred received his three crowns and large patrimonies of the Emperour Constantin, as is alledged betwixt the yeere of Christe 300–316 to the year of God 1560 which time the notable decay of his kingdom began." Foxe becomes almost obsessed with the implications of the number itself:

> Thus, being vexed and turmoiled in spirit about the reckoning of these numbers and years; it so happened upon a Sunday in the morning, I lying in my bed, and musing about these numbers, suddenly it was answered to my mind, as with a majesty, thus inwardly saying within me: "Thou fool, count these months by sabbaths, as the weeks of Daniel are counted by sabbaths." The Lord I take to witness, thus it was. Whereupon thus being admonished, I began to reckon the forty-two months by

35. The fact that Spenser includes "all the territories" in Una's mission reflects his own commitment to Protestants outside of England and Elizabeth's role in that commitment, as Norbrook has argued in *Poetry and Politics*, 126–31.

36. No one has gone further than Alastair Fowler in demonstrating how precisely Spenser plays the numbers game; see his *Spenser and the Numbers of Time*.

37. In his *Notes on the Faerie Queene*, Upton says, "The poet elegantly uses a round number; the allusion is to Revel.xi.2" (1:258). Several pages later he says, "'tis very remarkable how our poet has varied the prophecy concerning the persecuted state of the church, exemplified in Una's parents, Una herself, and in this Christian knight" (1:275).

sabbaths: first, of months; that would not serve: then by sabbaths of years; wherein I began to feel some probable understanding.[38]

Here, Foxe recounts both the prophetic nature of his own interpretation and the temporal mysteries encoded in forty-two months, a numbers game, surprisingly enough, that Spenser chooses not to play. More than at any other point in Book 1, Spenser sets his creative and revisionary writing off against the work of his contemporaries. Modifying apocalyptic numerology according to the constraints of his own narrative rather than the other way around, Spenser provides time not only for the three and a half years that Una, as the hidden church, has been wandering in the wilderness but also for earlier portions of the story she tells: her parents' captivity, her journey to the Faerie Queene, and her initial travels with Redcrosse. But in departing so clearly from a number essential to contemporary interpretation, Spenser highlights as well the provisional and creative character of his own prophetic art.

Moreover, through the silence, stuttering, and ambiguous turns of phrase in which Una articulates her history, Spenser accentuates the tenuous nature of ecclesiastical history itself, the difficult, even vulnerable position in which the invisible church must necessarily locate itself because of its ties to the visible church. So much relies on an appropriate union between the two dimensions, Spenser suggests, that even Una appears destabilized by her loss:

> Be iudge ye heauens, that all things right esteeme,
> How I him lou'd, and loue with all my might,
> So thought I eke of him, and thinke I thought aright.
> (1.7.49)

As Una highlights her constancy, her thinking about Redcrosse's love causes her thinking to founder, prompting a series of reevaluations. Forced to recognize that Redcrosse has proved uncommitted, his love ephemeral, she begins to doubt her own judgment, though her love for him never wavers.

Spenser, however, refuses to close the canto with Una's fainthearted and fainting conclusion, leaving us instead with Arthur's promise of a happy ending:

> But be of cheare, and comfort to you take:
> For till I have acquit your captiue knight,

---

38. Napier, *A Plaine Discovery of the Whole Revelation of St. John*, 32, 43; John Foxe, *The Acts and Monuments of John Foxe*, 1:290.

Assure your selfe, I will you not forsake.
His chearefull words reuiu'd her chearelesse spright,
So forth they went, the Dwarfe them guiding euer right.

(1.7.52)

Again echoing Christ's promise to send the Spirit during times of suffering, One who will never forsake his own, Arthur hints at the redemption of the visible church to come. To make this a realistic possibility, Redcrosse must recover his own origins, must come to understand his place in history. Then and only then will he be ready to fight the dragon.

As we might expect, Redcrosse makes this discovery through Una's directive. At the House of Holiness located at the nexus between the invisible and the visible worlds, Redcrosse undergoes the necessary transformation of his inner life and undergoes education in how to transform his world. In this second stage, Mercy takes him up the Mount of Contemplation where his own life has been transcribed in two coalescing narratives: that of the blind visionary Heavenly Contemplation and that of Spenser himself.

Through Redcrosse's encounter on the mountain, Spenser reveals the prophetic forms that mediate across the gap separating the invisible from the visible world: the first is experienced through the prophet's private meditation with God, the second through his dialogue with the visible church. Heavenly Contemplation, however, almost refuses to shift from the first means of prophetic revelation to the second. He is so caught up in meditation when Mercy and Redcrosse arrive that he is "agrieued sore" at their interruption; we are even told that he "would not once have moved for the knight" but for Mercy's intercession (1.10.49). As Contemplation puts it,

Thou doest the prayers of the righteous sead
Present before the maiestie diuine,
And his auenging wrath to clemencie incline.

(1.10.51)

It is only as "righteous sead"—the visible church purified—that Redcrosse can hear the narrative of his origins. The son of "Saxon kings" and mighty conquerors, he has been brought to "Faerie lond" and hidden (we are told) "in an heaped furrow" (1.10.65–66). Recovered from this furrow is the "seed" that is Redcrosse's origin, the seed of the visible church. Again, Spenser ties his metaphor to the ecclesiastical controversies of the moment as well as to the good pastor of the past by allowing a plowman to locate this "good seed," nurture him, and finally name him:

As he his toylesome teme that way did guyde,
And brought thee vp in ploughmans state to byde,
Whereof *Georgos* he thee gaue to name;
Till prickt with courage, and thy forces pryde,
To Faery court thou cam'st to seeke for fame,
And proue thy puissaunt armes, as seemes thee best became.
(1.10.66)

Redcrosse's origins thus spring "out from English race," and firmly root him in "earthly conquest" (1.10.60), as the seed of heroes combines in him with the seed of the visible church. Called "Georgos," an earthworker, he must learn to distinguish the "ritch weedes" (1.2.21) from the wheat as he labors on behalf of the church. In the end, his name, Heavenly Contemplation reveals, will remain the same with a difference:

For thou emongst those Saints, whom thou doest see,
Shalt be a Saint, and thine owne nations frend
And Patrone: thou Saint *George* shalt called bee,
Saint *George* of mery England, the signe of victoree.
(1.10.61)

Capable now of seeing his eventual "victory"—a future contained not only in the name he is originally given but also in the "Redcrosse" under which he has traveled—the knight finally knows who he is. He also sees who he will be, for he will one day join Una and the other "Saints" in the invisible true church of the elect. Having seen this heavenly vision, Redcrosse does not want to return to earth:

O let me not (quoth he) then turne againe
Backe to the world, whose ioyes so fruitlesse are;
But let me here for aye in peace remaine,
Or streight way on that last long voyage fare,
That nothing may my present hope empare.
(1.10.63)

Redcrosse's awareness of his "fruitlesse" joys pinpoints rather tellingly the errant way he has repeatedly taken, but turning away from the challenge here is just as surely a refusal of the "streight way" assigned to him. His longing for peace before the appropriate moment would be a rejection, Contemplation tells him, of "that royall maides bequeathed care," for she has committed "her cause" into his hands and he will find his destiny only in fulfilling it (1.10.63). Because the visible church is also the militant church, Redcrosse must remain to combat evil across time and space.

In preparation for his return to earth, Redcrosse looks down and finds himself so dazzled by the brightness of his vision that for a time he cannot see. He is still very much a man of the earth, clearly separate from the transcendent and the holy: "So darke are earthly things compard to things divine" (1.10.67). Yet Redcrosse is no longer blindly stumbling along; in coming to the Mount of Contemplation, he has discovered himself at last, and it is on this note that Spenser concludes his journey to the House of Holiness:

> At last whenas himselfe he gan to find,
> To *Vna* back he cast him to retire
> Who him awaited still with pensiue mind.
>   (1.10.68)

It is fitting, too, that readers are confronted with Una's "pensiue mind," for her reflections and evaluations haunt the remainder of "The Legende of the Knight of the Redcrosse, or Holinesse" and resonate well beyond the conclusion of the poem itself.

Through Una, Spenser makes his readers face the need to recover a specific version of history that acknowledges the corruption and purification of the visible church, a message convincingly relayed through Redcrosse's "historicall fiction" composed immediately after his dragon fight. During Redcrosse's all too triumphant account, Una remains strangely silent, and it is not until Duessa's letter arrives that we understand why. Suddenly forced to compose an entirely different version of the history he has just told, Redcrosse stumbles over his words and finally pauses altogether:

> It was in my mishaps, as hitherward
> I lately traueild, that vnwares I strayd
> Out of my way, through perils straunge and hard;
> That day should faile me, ere I had them all declard.
>   (1.12.31)

Having withheld much of the narrative to which we (as readers) have been privy, Redcrosse now finds it almost impossible to acknowledge his corrupt past. As he poetically stutters over how Duessa and he came together, his linguistic and moral confusion merge in the ambiguity of his account:

> There did I find, or rather I was found
> Of this false woman, that *Fidessa* hight,
> *Fidessa* hight the falsest Dame on ground
> Most false *Duessa,* royall richly dight,
> That easie was t'inuegle weaker sight
>   (1.12.32)

Redcrosse's narrative falters on the issue of origins, naming, and history: he does not seem to know who found who, what her name really was, or why her clothing was so alluring; in short, he has mistaken the "name" of Faith for the meaning, the external sign for that mystery that can never be fully signified. Now unsure of how he lost his faith—in interpreting as well as in representation itself—Redcrosse's halting repetitions reflect in his discomfort with language an equal discomfort with his own history. Only Una can clarify the role of Duessa, but in doing so, even she must acknowledge her role as interpreter after the fact:

> And now it seemes, that she suborned hath
> This craftie messenger with letters vaine,
> To worke new woe and improuided scath,
> By breaking of the band betwixt vs twain.
>   (1.12.34)

Identifying what Duessa "seemes" to be doing—a duplicity Una cannot understand—Una nevertheless exposes the "letter" as a false claim, one forged after the "band" established between Redcrosse and herself. By returning to the origins of their relationship, the status of their initial agreement, Una displaces Duessa's account and Redcrosse's problematic history. Her speech thus breaks the seal of authority that Duessa's letter holds over Redcrosse by solidifying their own "band."

By first giving us Redcrosse's interpretation of Duessa's letter and then, of course, Una's, Spenser records two potential responses to the question of Protestant church history before Luther: on the one hand, the visible church that Redcrosse represents has been corrupted by its material entanglement with Roman Catholicism, with false loves and false riches, a fact that cannot be omitted, obscured, or selectively remembered; on the other hand, the visible church has been "sealed" to Una, the invisible, true church of the elect, and its origins, in this sense, are pure. It is on this basis that the church in both its dimensions can be called a legend of holiness.

Spenser's carefully modulated "historicall fiction" not only dramatizes the ecclesiastical debates in which the church was then engaged, but also acknowledges the repeated reconstruction of history itself. Yet the mysterious tension between the invisible and the visible church that Spenser weaves together so brilliantly through the protracted engagement of Una and Redcrosse quickly unravels in the early years of the seventeenth century, making the conformist perspective far more difficult to weave together again. As Peter Lake says: "It is perhaps one of life's little ironies that by the time the Church of England had acquired a self image so inclusively national as to suppress any trace of tension between the godly community and the national church, the effects of that ideology were so divisive as to split the English protestant tradition into its constituent parts for good and all."[39] Under the political pressures of the seventeenth century, the prophetic and ecclesiastical union found in Spenser's "Legende of the Knight of the Redcrosse, or Holinesse" would split into two opposing prophetic forms, one embodying a militant Una and the other a pacifistic Redcrosse. The Presbyterians, Fifth Monarchists, and Quakers would trace their origins to the woman in the wilderness who would come to represent the visible, uncorrupted community of the godly. Through her, they would proclaim the ultimate triumph of good over evil, a triumph culminating in that apocalyptic moment when all Romishness would be purged and episcopacy would no longer exist. In contrast, the English Churchmen would make no such claims to absolute purity. Instead, they would trace their origins back to the visible and peaceful temple of Constantine, a church that, they would acknowledge, had later fallen into Romish error but had since been purified. Sanctioning their episcopal hierarchy on the basis of the ancient histories of the church, they would develop a form of prophecy that was inward, pacifistic, and sacramental, one rendered into language by the priesthood of the English Church.

39. Lake, "Presbyterianism," 219.

2

War and Peace

Prophecy in Thomas Brightman and Lancelot Andrewes

The Church of God whiles it is in the way towards Canaan is still militant, but now more especially.

—S. B., *Great Dangers over Our Heads*

A MONG THE most popular commentaries on Revelation during the seventeenth century were those put forward by the nonconforming Puritan Thomas Brightman.[1] Translated into English soon after Brightman's death in 1607, *A Revelation of the Apocalyps* and *A Revelation of the Revelation* surfaced in the religious debates of the 1620s and 1630s and were reprinted under a variety of titles following the outbreak of the English civil war. By this time, Brightman's indictment of a corrupt clergy and his prediction that "some horrible calamity will straightwaies ensue" seemed to capture the moment perfectly. The "immeasurable gulfe, full of miseries already prepared," was yawning precipitously in the ecclesiastical and civil strife of war, enabling Brightman's sense that "we which live at this day doe stand on the very brink of it" to echo with all the force of prophetic pronouncement.[2]

While apocalyptic commentaries such as Brightman's were shaping the thinking of the literate public and the sermons of the preaching ministers, a number of English Churchmen were fashioning an alternative model of prophetic discourse in the early decades of the seventeenth century. Stuart historian Peter Lake has labeled this group "avant-garde conformists" to underscore the innovations in theology, ecclesiastical history, and biblical interpretation that those close to the crown were carrying out on the older

---

1. Peter Milward designates Brightman's work as the most popular of the commentaries (*Religious Controversies of the Jacobean Age,* 133–34). Christopher Hill, on the other hand, believes it was not widely available until the 1640s (*English Bible,* 266).

2. Brightman, *The Revelation of St. John,* A2v.

conformist model of the church.[3] The churchman who spearheaded this movement was Lancelot Andrewes.

Thomas Brightman and Lancelot Andrewes can therefore be seen to shape two opposing views of prophetic discourse that inform nearly all of the religious writing of the seventeenth century, from ecclesiastical controversy to sermons to poetry. Each, by "re-covering" Revelation, employs his interpretation to identify ecclesiastical differences in church history, politics, and forms of worship. It is hardly surprising, then, that Brightman's apocalyptic commentary resonates throughout Milton's oeuvre as well as the prose and poetry of the woman prophets. Like Brightman, Milton gives voice to the need for ongoing reformation and ecclesiastical change, though as Stephen Honeygoskey has thoughtfully demonstrated, Milton's theology is finally more ecclesial than ecclesiastical, more concerned with a people undergoing dynamic and continual transformation than with the restructuring of institutions.[4] Following Brightman as well, women prophets ring the changes on the woman in the wilderness, but they do so as much to authorize their gender as the institutional structure of the churches to which they belong.

In this chapter we shall begin to recognize just how radically both Brightman and Andrewes depart from Spenser's "conformist" model of the English Church as they equate the woman of the Apocalypse with the visible rather than the invisible church. In doing so, they dress Una in clearly marked "ecclesiastical" clothes: Brightman shows her declaring war on the corruption that inevitably ensues during times of peace as she seeks to strip away the trappings of episcopacy; Andrewes, on the other hand, reinforces her episcopal unity by equating all militancy with the voice of the false prophet who would destroy her. In making this point, Andrewes modifies the standard conformist line of thought evident in John White's *The Way to the True Church*, where, like Spenser, White openly acknowledges the trouble arising out of the time of peace occurring during the reign of Constantine: "As soon as ever Peace came to the Church, they fell to [quarreling] againe, that the good Emperor which brought this peace, had much ado with all his authority, to appease them." What ended this golden age of peace and prosperity, White asserts, was the division and dissension occurring within the church itself. And because this same error was now troubling the seventeenth-century church, White suggested that it "acknowledge the envy of Satan, who can set brethren at oddes in their father's own house, who

---

3. For Lake's careful delineation of Andrewes, see "Andrewes, Buckeridge, and Conformity."
4. Honeygoskey, *Milton's House of God*, 30–44.

are to be advised to reconcile themselves, and at length to embrace unity when they see Papists their enemies scorning them and clapping their hands at their bickering: lest all too late, when Gods judgment fall upon them, as they did upon the primitive Church for that same sinne, they learne by their own calamitie, to professe faith in unitie."[5] Invoking the apocalyptic vein of prophecy—standard procedure during the later years of Elizabeth's reign and the early years of James's—White predicts the fall that the English Church will undergo if it does not resolve its dissension peaceably. White focuses on the animosity arising on both sides of ecclesiastical and reformation issues, while Andrewes, in seeking so adamantly to contain the bellicose rhetoric of his Puritan opposition, refuses to acknowledge that he is implicated as well. Peace, for Andrewes, becomes the ultimate good, and apocalyptic rhetoric— particularly with militant overtones—is necessarily called into question.

Clearly, then, Brightman and Andrewes diverge over the ramifications of "peace" in Constantine's time and in their own, evaluating other aspects of ecclesiastical history in opposite ways as well. Once again, both men revise the conformist line of thought. As we saw in Chapter 1, John Foxe located the hidden Protestant church in the proto-protestant martyrs who had opposed Romish corruption throughout history, those who had repeatedly undergone persecution as a consequence. Thomas Brightman alters this line of the faithful by setting it apart more definitively: in his view, the true church had immediately distanced itself from Rome's ecclesiastical government and ceremonies, remaining hidden a thousand years and then emerging in full view in the Presbyterian discipline.[6]

Andrewes saw rather quickly that both of these interpretations gave radical reformers opportunities to identify their origins in a conveniently "hidden" past. In tracing the true church back to a persecuted minority, the first interpretation authorized the voices of those who claimed to be the "persecuted" minority in the present church; the second group was even more dangerous since it traced the true church back to the Presbyterian discipline itself. Sidestepping both points of view, Andrewes eradicated all conformist notions of a hidden church. He argued that the visible church under Constantine—not the persecuted one—was the "pattern" for the "days of peace" in which the present church now found itself: "But if be so happy as to find the days of peace, Moses and Constantine are patterns for the

---

5. White, *The Way to the True Church*, 143.
6. Brightman, *Revelation of the Revelation*, 407. Future references will be designated *Rev* and cited parenthetically within the text.

days of peace . . . In a word, none can seek to have the congregation so called as before Constantine, but they must secretly and by implication confess they are a persecuted Church as then was, without a Moses, without a Constantine."[7] As Andrewes now realized, the "peace" in which godly leaders reigned over a visible church provided the only possible model for the present church. In his view, the persecuted, hidden church that was known "secretly and by implication" was not only hermeneutically problematic but also potentially subversive.

Andrewes had to confront one additional problem, however. Nearly all commentators on the Apocalypse agreed that a final confrontation between the forces of Christ and a "Papal" Antichrist would eventually take place. In the first decade of his reign, King James had asked him to write on this subject, and Andrewes had responded in *Tortura Torti*, quoting King James as well as Robert Abbot and Thomas Brightman on the nature of this apocalyptic encounter. Yet, as Christopher Hill hints, while Andrewes provides "converging signs that the Pope may be Antichrist," he "leaves the substantive question open, which in the circumstances suggests that he may not have shared the King's opinion."[8] When speaking from the pulpit, Andrewes flatly rejected militancy against the Roman Catholics, stating that "in the way of christianity there is yet no difference between the papists and us" (6:57). He thus refused to find any separation between the visible and "hidden" church in Christian history, locating a visible church throughout time.

Because both Brightman and Andrewes interpret history to valorize the past and to confirm their understanding of prophecy, I wish to focus on those passages in Brightman's *A Revelation* where he uncovers the ecclesiastical history of the English Church and the political significance of Constantine. These same passages, we shall see, resonate in the prophetic discourse of Andrewes, Herbert, and Donne as they attempt to suppress Brightman's political and ecclesiastical interpretation and to respond with an alternative conception of prophetic form. Once heard in dialogue, the interchange between Brightman and Andrewes provides a way of locating two competing strands of prophecy and a whole range of prophetic discourse that derives, in innovative new directions, from them.

Central to Brightman's analysis is a firm belief in the reforming zeal that Protestantism demands, a zeal, Brightman contends, that fades all too

---

7. Andrewes, *The Works of Lancelot Andrewes,* 5:166. Future references will be cited parenthetically within the text.

8. See Lancelot Andrewes, *Tortura Torti,* 183; Hill, *Antichrist,* 33–34.

quickly when the church attains peace. The apocalyptic letter that God has called him to carry to the English Church is particularly incriminating in this regard, but it is a letter he cannot ignore: "I that by Gods prouidence had found theis Epistles cast abroad, and understoode by the inscriptions to what Churches they were sent, durst not but giue them unto yow, least by interceptinge, and keepinge them close to my selfe, I should both treacherously indanger your safetie, and also make my selfe worthily guilty of high treason against Gods Maiestie" (*Rev,* opening letter "To the Holy Reformed Churches of Britany, Germany, and France"). Brightman refuses to keep this correspondence "private," or as he puts it, "close to my selfe." In choosing to deliver this unwelcome mail—sealed with a clear "inscription" to the English Church—Brightman nevertheless recognizes the political fallout. But the charge of "high treason" against God is considerably more damning than the indictment of an earthly monarch, and Brightman accepts the political consequences. He does, however, attempt to mediate against royal disfavor by including several well-chosen words in praise of Queen Elizabeth immediately after indicting the English Church itself: "He hath giuen vs a most gracious Queene, so excellinge in all thinges that are praiseworthy, as the like to her age euer saw" (*Rev,* 127). Even the queen cannot forestall the inevitable judgment, however: "The Counterpaine (I say) of Laodicea, is the third reformed Church, namely: Our Church of England" (*Rev,* 125).

As Brightman spells out the English Church's errors depicted in the Apocalypse, chief among them is the church's rejection of a definitive Protestant position: "*I knowe* (saith he) *that thou art neither cold nor hott,* but some odde strange thinge moulten and compacted together of them both. So that this euill consisteth of certaine contraries strangely tempered and blended together" (*Rev,* 131). Gone is the celebratory beauty of the via media, in its place "some odde strange thinge." With just such phrasing, Brightman lashes out at the habit of mind that had come to characterize English Churchmen in their metaphysical embrace of opposing positions. "[C]ontraries strangely tempered and blended together," he asserts, are not an art form but an evil.

Brightman's most direct target, however, is the structure of the English Church itself:

> [The] outward regiment is as yet for the greatest parte Antichristian & Romish. In the degrees of cleargie men, in elections & ordinations, & the whole administration of the Church-censures. The which temperinge of pure doctrine and Romish regiment, maketh this lukewarmnes, whereby we stand iust in the middest betweene cold and hott, betweene the

Romish and the Reformed Churches; of both which we make a medley. (*Rev,* 132)

Clearly, Brightman contends, God chooses to not align himself either with a corrupt hierarchy or with those lukewarm servants who make it up. Rather, he chooses "hott," passionately committed personalities: "Hee calleth him hot, who boyleth with heate and feruency of Spirit, in his due and full regards of Gods worshippe. . . . with a certaine restles motion. For so doth the word *hott* in the Greeke signifie, to wit, such an one as can by no meanes indure superstitious and impious religions, but will hazard all hee hath, so farre as may bee, to effect a reformation" (*Rev,* 131). Brightman thus privileges the fiery, restless spirit that refuses to stop short of a full reformation over the spirit of moderation, for "heate," he asserts, is the outward manifestation of a deep and abiding passion for holiness: "Heate or zeale here is an affection, that doth pursue after the loue of holines with a great vehemency of minde, which is as it were a certaine holy violence" (*Rev,* 131). Barely submerged beneath Brightman's rhetoric of "holy violence" and vehemency is of course actual violence, a desire to act against betweenness itself. He therefore turns the inquiry and self-questioning apparent in the sermons and poetry of the English Churchmen against them with a vengeance:

> Therefore if Baal bee God followe him, why halt ye beetweene both? As if it were hard to determine, whether were more excellent. God abhorreth to come into such an inquiry. There is more sound judgment left in him, who beinge ignorant what is true, sticketh fast in his superstition, then in him, that beinge inlightened with some knowledge of the truth, wauers vp and downe, as vncertayne where hee should follow. The mediocritie therefore is worst of all, which indeed is honoured of the world, because of that shewe it maketh of a certaine moderation and peaceablenes. (*Rev,* 133)

Though the churchmen of the via media make an obvious show of peace, Brightman hints, this is merely a cover for their spiritual mediocrity. For this halfhearted, uncommitted self-absorption, they will be judged by God himself: "Certainly a great and shamefull judgment doth waite for these luke warme men, the feare whereof, though it doe not at all torment them, . . . yet howsoever all men bee husht and stilled; hee will not faile nor falsifie his word, who hath threatened that hee wilbe auenged of them" (*Rev,* 136). Breaking through the hush of history, God will judge the corrupt bishops that, in Brightman's view, have usurped the priestly function of the church by focusing more on titles, honors, and wealth than on divine truth.

The Apocalypse is, for Brightman, the ultimate means of decoding this truth, containing as it does the entire history of the church—its enigmatic past as well as its mysterious future:

> And nowe see how exceedinge acceptable this Booke of the Revelation ought to be unto thee, not onely because of theis euents of most great moment which are to come, but also in respect of the History of thinges past, unto which if thou wilt cast thine eyes, thou shalt see the perpetuall tracke in which thou hast sett thy footesteps euen from the Apostles tymes, so lively described that thou canst require no more lightsome & notable History. (*Rev*, opening letter)

Carefully following these "trackes," Brightman uncovers the historical, political, and spiritual "footsteps" that link the primitive church to the contemporary one. Believing that John describes the gradual corruption of the visible church in two overlapping metaphors—the metaphor of the temple in Rev. 11 and the metaphor of the woman clothed with the sun in Rev. 12— Brightman slowly unravels their implications in hopes of reforming his contemporary audience.

The metaphor of the temple encodes something of a political surprise as Brightman argues that Constantine's elimination of persecution and establishment of Christianity as the state religion were far from ideal. In fact, Brightman suggests, Constantine's open embrace of orthodox Christianity both corrupted the visible church and forced the true church into hiding and apparent heterodoxy: "When Constantine therfore came to the Kingdome, the Church began to hide it selfe in secret, by departing aside from the viewe of the world into a certaine secret, sanctuarye" (*Rev*, 351). Reading this dilemma into late-sixteenth- and early-seventeenth-century ecclesiastical politics, Brightman hints that the era of peace and plenty that the "new Constantines" Elizabeth and James have made possible are similarly open to question. They have only stepped up the corruption of the visible church and forced true believers to separate themselves from the rampant corruption of the episcopal hierarchy.

To understand what must be done, Brightman argues, contemporary readers only need consider the temple of the past: "The Company of inhabitans, of those that did flocke daily to the Temple, was huge, but howe fewe were the Priests, that were with in meane while, to that innumerable multitude that was without? The same proportion should there be of fained Christians, to the true and kindly Cittizens" (*Rev*, 353). Only by moving "within" the temple do the "kindly Cittizens" escape the corruption of the "fained

Christians" in the outer court. But what really distinguishes them is the reformation doctrine they embrace, a doctrine symbolized by the worship they engage in at the "Altar": "Nowe all the faithfull are said to worship in the Altar, because they place all their hope, and affiance in Christs death alone; which kinde of sacrifices belonge not onely to the Tribe of Levi; but aswell to euery truly godly one" (*Rev,* 352). This altar represents faith, not ceremonial activity, and since "euery truly godly one" sacrifices here, the priesthood in the temple proves to be far more egalitarian than the elitist priesthood in the orthodox church outside. In fact, Brightman argues, all class-based social, ecclesiastical, and educational privileges do not apply here: "And it was not the Temple onely that should be opened, but the holy of holies also, wherein the Arke of the couenant was set. . . . Nowe it should be alike common for all the Saints to goe into, seeing nowe all the mysteries of saluation were made so plaine, familiar and manifest vnto euery one as they were of old to the learned, whose whole studye was spent in them" (*Rev,* 393). Even the temple's interior spaces are no longer compartmentalized into rooms of increasing spirituality but are "alike common for all the Saints." Here, divine meaning is "manifest vnto euery one," an assessment that clearly displaces the long-standing ecclesiastical emphasis on languages and learning. Perhaps most important, the opening of this hidden "temple" points forward in time to that moment when the Presbyterian structure of the reformed church will be opened as well, when the purity of the primitive church will be restored to view. Prophetically, then, Brightman draws a sharp line between the past and the present, the outside and the inside, the visible church and the true church, thereby advancing a Presbyterian model for the present English Church.

While this initial metaphor enables Brightman to trace in architectural terms the distance between the corrupt, episcopal outer court of the temple and its Presbyterian interior, the metaphor of the woman clothed with the sun enables him to recapture the moment just prior to this separation when the visible church was still pure. In outlining the "woman's" characteristics, he gives her distinctly Presbyterian features: "There was one forme of gouern-ment in al Churches," her ministers were free "from ambition and the desire of honours," and she abhorred "the desire of riches, and contention about worldly dignity" (*Rev,* 399–400). Moreover, he asserts, these features are on record in *The Auncient Ecclesiasticall Histories* of Eusebius: "Howe plaine & simple is the History of this time in Eusebius? The Bishops are by name reckoned vp that were notable for life or doctrine, their combats, writings, sufferings are spoken of. . . . Neither had Satan brought in prelaticall pompe and pride into the sheepefold of the Lord" (*Rev,* 400). In short, early church history supports his interpretation.

Just as occurs in the careful unraveling of the first metaphor, the second enables Brightman to introduce a parting of the ways. It occurs when the woman clothed with the sun delivers a "son" who has tremendous political and ecclesiastical power: "The Church doth at length bringe forth this manlike and stout Champion, when she instructed Constantine the great in the Christian faith, howsoever the Dragon stroue to the contrary with all his might" (*Rev,* 404–5). But the woman's "labour" beforehand proves to be the ultimate prophetic activity and not the moment that she actually gives birth: "But why doth the woman flye awaye, when she is thus blessed & aduanced by meanes of so powerfull a Sone, who before this, when she was barren and was in so great paines of travelling in childbirth, did so valiantly beare of[f] the fury of the Dragon? Certainly it could not be the feare of the enemye that did thus putt her to flight, but rather an intollerable irkesomenes, by meanes of some home-bred evill" (*Rev,* 408). While she is in labor, Brightman argues, the woman as true church "valiantly" fights off satanic corruption in all its forms. Once she delivers Constantine, however, the very nature of her deliverance from political and spiritual tyranny paradoxically brings about another form of enslavement: "And so indeed it came to passe, that the security which she fell into by this birth of her Sonne, tooke away from her all care of true pietye. For nowe when the yoke of tyranny was driuen of[f] from her shoulders, she gaue her minde to increase and furder contentions and ambition" (*Rev,* 408). The visible church so recently "clothed with the sun" of spiritual purity and divine truth now undergoes a complete makeover; shedding one article of clothing after another, she dresses in new and altogether different clothes:

> That clothing made of the Sunne, which was wholy wouen out of the thrids of the most Holy truth, both woofe and warpe, began to be changed in the sanctity of our owne works. The Moone which before gouerned their steppes was taken away, and inuocation of Saints was set in the Roome of it in the publike worship of God, and the whole most Holy discipline was distained, and defloured. The Starres that glistered so like a crowne on her heade, were changed into honourable good Lords. (*Rev,* 408)

Lest, however, we assume that the true church has been "defloured" during this gradual alteration of the visible church, Brightman prevents that perspective by indicating that the woman herself has escaped into the wilderness:

> Which things the woman seeing could not endure the greife of it, but
> gate her selfe from thence presently vppon it, yea flewe away to some
> place, where she might at least want the torment of minde, which the
> beholding of these euills would have putt her to, that is, where no
> publike Assemblies were to be found, wherein the Ordinances of God did
> flourish in their integritye. For this woman doth not beare the person
> of the faithfull one by one, but of the whole assemblies of the faithfull.
> (*Rev,* 408–9)

Confronted by the grief and "torment" of sin, the woman abandons the
visible church and its "publike Assemblies," choosing rather to meet in
private where the truth is preserved in its integrity. As in the metaphor
of the temple, her withdrawal—in this case to the wilderness—ensures her
purity. This metaphor of wilderness wanderings takes form throughout the
seventeenth century in a variety of sermons, political tracts, and ecclesiastical controversies analyzed by Christopher Hill.[9] In these other versions, it
is occasionally equated with chaos, darkness, and death, being frequently
juxtaposed with the "hedge" of safety and the "garden" of promise. The
"wilderness" was thus a resonant metaphor, accessible for use by churchmen
and Separatists alike, depending on which way they wanted to view it.

In concluding his analysis of Rev. 12, Brightman summarizes his points
with a damning historical evaluation of what inevitably occurs when the
monarch establishes the peace of the church: "Thus we see that the womans
sonne brought more mischeife to her, then her enemye, not with any desire
or purpose he had to hurt her, but by meanes of the wickednes of men,
who did abuse this happy peace in so foule a fashion, to worke all manner
of iniquity with it" (*Rev,* 409). While refusing to implicate Constantine, and
through him, Elizabeth and James, Brightman nevertheless suggests that the
result of political and ecclesiastical security is just as damning as if actual
hurt were intended; corruption inevitably occurs both as a result of the
monarch's authority and as a function of those in the ecclesiastical hierarchy
who abuse the peace of the church for their own profit.

Nevertheless, the corruption of the visible church is temporary, Brightman
argues. Collapsing the boundaries between his two metaphors, he suggests
that the true church's time of separation and lurking in the wilderness is
almost over: "The space of time wherein she should liue thus in obscurity,
and want her publike liberty, is that space of a thousand two hundred and
threescore dayes, the same wherein those two witnesses should Prophecye

---

9. Hill, *English Bible,* 142–45.

clothed in sackcloth, Chapt. 11.3. The agreement of al which things doth teach vs that this wildernes is that Temple, and that this continuance of banishment in the wildernes is that abode that was made in the Temple" (*Rev,* 407–8). During this interim, the true church as temple and woman both engages in prophetic speech—here, the rhetoric of lament. But she is shortly to experience her final deliverance:

> For after this storme blowne over there shall followe presently gawdy dayes, and most greatly to be wished. For what can be more joyfull to a most chast spouse, that is thrust out of dores by the whore of Rome (which yet boasteth herselfe as if shee were Christes true wife) that hath bene for so many ages vexed with all manner of iniuryes and reproaches by her, then to see this impudent harlot at length slit in the nostrills, stript of her garments . . . consumed with fire? (*Rev,* letter)

In the complete destruction of the Romish whore and all her political and episcopal accouterments, the true church of the elect will become visible at last.

Brightman's prophetic analysis of the corrupting effects of peace and prosperity may have caused some spiritual and political reverberations when, less than two years after this work came out, James published *The Peace-Maker* to underscore the pacifistic character of his reign and to reinforce his decision not to pursue war with Catholic Spain. Addressing his reading audience as "truth-loving and peace-embracing subjects," James included them in the flight of Noah's dove, which, he argues, seeks to avoid "the perpetuall deluge of blood and enmity" that has now flooded the world.[10] This "dove" finds an olive branch in England, the country to which James has brought peace "full Sixteene yeeres" (sig. A4).

The churchman who had an active hand in James's writing of *The Peace-Maker* is thought to have been Bishop Lancelot Andrewes. Moreover, as tensions deepened and Protestant anger escalated during the remaining years of James's reign, the king turned increasingly to Andrewes for an alternative conception of prophecy, one that was pacifistic, lyrical, and interior rather than militant, apocalyptic, and politically charged.

Long before the Bohemian revolt and the ill-fated Spanish Match, Lancelot Andrewes was already articulating the difference between two modes of prophetic discourse in his court sermons on Whitsunday. Using the feast of Pentecost and the Holy Spirit's descent on the apostles as the biblical basis for

---

10. King James I, *The Peace-Maker,* sig. A3v. Future references will be cited parenthetically within the text.

his understanding, he drew a sharp line between the spirit of peace inspiring the apostles of the early church and the apocalyptic militancy increasingly dividing the church of the seventeenth century. In leaving behind the spirit of the dove and taking for themselves "the beak and claws of a vulture" (3:254), Andrewes suggested that contemporary prophets such as Brightman were becoming heretical. They were in fact disclosing their affinity with Montanus who, inspired by "private revelation," had, in the early days of the church, first split the church asunder. For Andrewes, their militant response signaled a clear departure from the terms of primitive Christianity: "The Dove, they tell us, that was for the baby-Church, for them to be humble and meek, suffer and mourn like a dove. Now, as if with Montanus they had yet *parocletum alium,* 'another Holy Ghost' to look for, in another shape, of another fashion quite, with other qualities, they hold these be no qualities for Christians now" (3:254). In rewriting the divine text, Andrewes suggested, the prophets of his time were printing a very different gospel, and reproducing, as a consequence, proud and violent "Christians": "But the date of these meek and patient Christians is worn out, long since expired; and now we must have Christians of a new edition, of another, a new-fashioned Holy Ghost's making" (3:254). For Andrewes who had presided over the King James translation of the Bible, such "new editions" of the Gospel were clearly unauthorized. They bore a "spirit" markedly different from the spirit of peace informing the divine original and sanctioned by the king of peace himself. Against such false texts and false prophets Paul had issued a strong warning: "But though that we, or an Angel from heaven preach any other gospel unto you than that which we have preached unto you, let him be accursed" (Gal. 1:8). To expose how thoroughly these "Christians of a new edition" had strayed from the pristine form of the Bible, Andrewes placed both versions side by side. This, he indicated, made it all too evident that "lying men may change—may and do; but the Holy Ghost is *unus idemque Spiritus,* saith the Apostle, changes not, casts not His bill, moults not His feathers. His qualities at the first do last still, and still shall last to the end, and no other notes of a true Christian, but they" (3:255). For Andrewes, the "notes" of a true Christian were not only eternal but also "still" and pacifistic. They bore no resemblance to the violent drumbeat of a "new Holy Ghost" bearing a "match-light in her beak or a bloody knife" (3:255).

In reviewing these "new editions" of the Gospel, Andrewes recorded other significant changes, including attempts to cancel ceremonies, to institute alternative forms of church government, to privilege preaching, to universalize interpretation, and to predict the end of history—all under the auspices of prophetic revelation. By returning to the same biblical passages employed by his contemporaries to arrive at these positions, Andrewes enters into dialogue with them for the express purpose of containing their interpretations. He thus counters national reproof and apocalyptic prediction with a prophetic form designed to unify, edify, and uphold the church rather than to call it into question.

In Andrewes's sermons on Whitsunday, then, the wind and tongues of Pentecost are a visible manifestation of the spirit descending upon a visible church, one that remains public rather than private and open rather than closed. Clearly contesting the viewpoint of Brightman, Andrewes asserts that the line of episcopal succession continues intact, passing from the apostles of the primitive church to the Episcopalian priesthood and so "derived from them to us, and from us to others, to the world's end" (3:277). It is in this sense no "voluntary calling," taken up by "mock-apostles" sprinkling "their own heads with water" (3:273). It is a sacramental ceremony designating a priesthood first instituted by divine authority in the primitive church:

> We may be sure, Christ could have given the Spirit without any ceremony; held His breath, and yet sent the Spirit into them without any more ado. He would not; an outward ceremony he would have, for an outward calling He would have. For if nothing outward had been in His, we should have had nothing but enthusiasts—as them we have notwithstanding; but then we should have had no rule with them; all by divine revelation: into that they resolve. (3:273)

This ceremony is the business "in hand" at the "imposition of hands" celebrating "the giving of Holy Orders" (3:262–63), for the outward anointing of Episcopalian priests, as at Pentecost, conveys "what is invisibly done within" (3:264). Such a ceremony rejects out of hand the unmarked, invisible, and suspect "inspiration" of the "enthusiasts."

Moreover, Andrewes argues, taking a "calling" to which one has not been appointed comes with a price: Uzzah was struck dead when he attempted to steady the ark of God, only because he went "beyond his degree," did "more than a Levite might do" (3:390). What happened to him provides an ominous example to those outside of the church as well as to those within it: ministers must never presume to have any authority for functions they have not been ordained by the ecclesiastical hierarchy to perform.

But the "wind" of Pentecost manifests more to Andrewes than the visible presence of the priesthood. It reveals the character and quality of divine "breath" and contrasts sharply with the "breath" issuing from the false prophets of the period. Now, of course, Christ's ability to speak "by the Prophets" takes form in the utterance of his apostles and their successors. They are "as trumpets, or pneumatical wind-instruments" (3:266), a simile that allows Andrewes to reveal their prophetic art in the articulated wind of musical form. The expressive notation of their music is not forte, however, but pianissimo, not loud and discordant but soft and lyrical. It is precisely to this point, Andrewes notes, that the prophet Elisha speaks: "There came first 'a boisterous whirlwind,' such an one as they wish for—but no God there. After it, a rattling 'earthquake;' and after it, crackling flashes of fire:—God was in none of them all. Then came a soft still voice:—there comes God. God was in it, and by it you may know where to find him" (3:267). While contemporary prophets locate God in apocalyptic "flashes of fire," and revolutionary "earthquakes," God makes himself known in the "soft still voice" that can be discerned only by the most attentive of listeners. Refusing to be known in the roaring and crying of "them and their novices, that will needs bear his name" (3:267), God turns down the volume, choosing an increasingly quieter voice. It is doubtless for this reason, Andrewes suggests, that contemporary prophets cannot hear him: "The waters of Shiloh run too soft for them. Well, the waters of Shiloh though the Prophets commend to us; and to them Christ sends us, and it is they, when all is done, whose 'streams shall make glad the City of God'" (3:268). The prophets of the Bible as well as Christ himself would have their listeners drink from the waters of peace. Thus, true prophets choose Christ's method at his postresurrection appearance, breathing softly and gently upon those who hear them, rather than asserting authority in the gale-force winds of condemnation and judgment.

The spirit of the true prophet is, accordingly to Andrewes, distinctly different from the spirit of the false prophet who is motivated either by a "private spirit" or by the "spirit of this world." Both of these "spirits" are ultimately destructive since they seek to control their recipients by throwing them into spiritual and political turmoil. Moreover, in asserting their own authority, those guided by such "spirits" reveal their egotistic, revolutionary designs: "And are there not in the world somewhere, some such as will receive none, admit of at no hand no other Holy Ghost but their own ghost, and the idol of their own conceit, the vision of their own heads, the motions of their own spirits, and if you hit not on that that is there in their hearts, reject it, be it what it will; that make their breasts the sanctuary?" (3:275). Andrewes here takes aim at those advocating extraordinary prophetic gifts by calling attention to the self-assurance and pride at the core of their revelations. In their unwillingness to receive any other forms of knowledge or to submit to alternative viewpoints, such prophets make an "idol" of their own interpretations, turning their visions into divine truth. Even their seemingly egalitarian desire to eliminate ecclesiastical callings and to have "all equal, all even at least" (3:289) is an intentionally deceptive ploy to obtain a position of absolute authority over all who have preceded them, from the prophets of the Bible to the Spirit of God himself: "Their spirit not subject to the spirit of the Prophets, nor of the Apostles neither, if they were now alive; but bear themselves so high . . . as if this Spirit were their underling, and their ghost above the Holy Ghost" (3:289). Rather than conveying the submissive and responsive attitude of true prophets, these "prophets" refuse to understand their role as "subjects" and thus their subordinate relationship to political, ecclesiastical, and spiritual authority. For Andrewes, such people are merely inflated with their own breath as they assume for themselves an authority belonging only to the church.

In similar fashion, those driven by the "spirit of the world" employ the "Holy Spirit" to advance their interests in the houses of Parliament, and in this sense to make false profit. Blown about not only by the will of the people but also by economic advancement, they legislate on ecclesiastical affairs with an eye to extending their wealth: "As if Christ's mouth were stopped and His breath like to fail Him, the world begins to fare as if they had got a new mouth to draw breath from; to govern the Church as if *spiritus Praetorii* would do things better than *Spiritus Sanctuarii,* and man's law become the best means to teach the fear of God, and to guide religion by. In vain then is all this act of Christ's; He might have kept His breath to Himself" (3:276). As in his assessment of a "new edition" of the Gospel, Andrewes here suggests that contemporary fascination with a "new mouth" and a new mode of prophetic utterance in Parliament has silenced Christ's voice and choked his breath.

This breath is restored, of course, in the speech of true prophets who draw their breath from Christ, received at "the door of the sanctuary" (3:195–96). Turning away from the political controversies of the moment, they engage their parishioners in spiritual scrutiny by making the focus of their prophecy the inner life: "If of our well-doing God's will be the centre, and His glory the circumference; we do it, not that our will, but His be done; not our name, but His be hallowed; the act is holy and the Spirit is of the same kind. Otherwise, philosophical, politic, moral it may be; theological, religious, holy, it is not" (3:196). For Andrewes, the crucial difference between the wind blowing through the church and the wind blowing through Westminster Hall is the absence of "self" and self-representation apparent in it, an absence calling attention to the presence of God.

Just as the movement of the wind reflects the spirit that drives it, two very different tongues distinguish the false prophet from the true one. The former speaks in a "common" tongue, "common" of course hinting at the limited education, lower economic status, and mediocre verbal skills apparent in the "common" preacher. The method of this prophet is "common" as well, for in "common phrases and terms well got by heart" (3:132), he takes aim at political and ecclesiastical institutions with inflammatory zeal. Such prophets, Andrewes notes, are "ever mending churches, states, superiors—mending all, save themselves" (3:133).

Beyond being "common," the "tongue" of these prophets is "forked," Andrewes states, for these men have an ability, like the devil's, "to speak that which was contrary to his knowledge and meaning" (3:122) and so to subvert God's Word. Rejecting the quiet unity of divine speech, their tongues "fly up and down all over the world, and spare neither Minister nor Magistrate, no nor God himself" (3:122). This feverish willingness to tongue-lash those in political and ecclesiastical positions indicates for Andrewes a desire to undermine all authority, and thus "God himself" who upholds these institutions.

Not surprisingly, Andrewes identifies the tongue of the true prophet as "learned" rather than "common." Asserting that Chrysostom, Oecumenius, and all the interpreters identify prophetic speech as "no slight, or light word, but *verbum talenti,* 'a word of weight, of a talent-weight' " (3:140), Andrewes contrasts the "talent" of the true prophet with the worthless speech of the rabble: "Not the crudities of their own brain, idle, loose, undigested gear, God knoweth; no, but pithy and wise sentences" (3:141). It is this weighty, proverbial style, this "speech according to learning," Andrewes suggests, that conveys the spiritual profit so clearly audible in the words of Old and New Testament prophets: "So St. Peter, such speech as may seem, or beseem the very 'oracles of God,' as may fashion light in the understanding, or fervour in the affection; those two shew it fire. The fire of the Old Testament, 'the burning coal,' wherewith the Seraphim touched Esay's mouth, and gave him as he saith, *linguam eruditam,* 'a learned tongue;' not only a tongue, but 'a learned tongue.' As the fire of the Old, so of the New" (3:141). Noting that this "tongue of fire" does not "speak chaff" but consumes it, Andrewes does away with the false prophecies of the ignorant in one telling conflagration. Then, by shifting into Latin, he characterizes the illumination of the "flaming tongue" in its ability to increase understanding as well as fervor rather than in its destructive potential. Unlike those who are continually increasing the volume and straining their tongues in "passionate delivery," this speech, though quiet, is branded forever on the memory. The reason, Andrewes indicates, quoting David in Ps. 119:93, is that such speech is like "the nail red-hot, that leaveth a mark behind, that will never be got out" (3:142).

True prophecy, then, can best be discerned in its lack of self-representation, its learning, its pacifism, its multilingual skill, its talented, proverbial style, and its double motion, best captured, by Andrewes's account, in the Greek word *nxos:* "You know what sound an echo is; a sound at the second hand, a sound at the rebound. *Verbum Domini venit ad nos:* 'The Word of the Lord cometh to us:' there is the first sound, to us; and ours is but the echo, the reflection of it to you" (3:117). Through doubling and internal rhymes, Andrewes aligns himself with the ancient prophets who first heard "the Word of the Lord" and echoed it to others. The prophet, in this sense, is God's translator—chosen to repeat him, word for word, across human and divine languages. Andrewes calls attention to the process as he utters God's Word in Greek, in Latin, in Hebrew, in English, in proverbial doublets and catchy phrases, becoming increasingly conversational as he passes from one language to another and increasingly dialogic as he echoes a full range of human and divine voices. His movement from verbatim repetition to the illumination of interpreters merely multiplies the field of semantic and divine play. Divine mystery is everywhere, Andrewes hints, but particularly in the intricacies of divine language: "*Moreh,* the word in Hebrew for rain, is so for a preacher too, that it poseth the translators which way to turn it" (3:305). For Andrewes, of course, the "turn" is itself significant, linking the "rain" with the preacher's heavenly and life-sustaining art.

Consequently, for Andrewes, the apostles who reversed "the curse of Babel" (3:123) by supernaturally speaking all tongues provide the spiritual model for a priesthood with the same linguistic competence, the same ability to restore divine truth to its original, unfallen form: "And indeed, it was not meet one tongue only should be employed that way, as before but one was. It was too poor and slender, like the music of a monochord. Far more meet was it that many tongues, yea, that all tongues should do it; which as a concert of many instruments, might yield a full harmony" (3:139). The heteroglossic music of the first Pentecost—a chorus of different voices—typologically prefigures the prophetic art of the bishops in the church: "In which, we behold the mighty work of God; that the same means of divers tongues, which was the destroying of Babel, the very same is here made to work the building of Sion; that means that scattered them from the tower of confusion, the very same to reduce them to the fold of unity" (3:139). Where once "tongues" were a curse bringing about division, they now build the church, bringing all peoples and all nations into the fold of God.[11]

For Andrewes, true prophets continue to reverse the curse of Babel and thus the dissension in seventeenth-century society by allowing the organ of the Holy Ghost its fullest musical—and dialogic—play. Distinctly different from the "common," autonomous tongue of the false prophet, the heteroglossic organ of the true prophet incorporates a range of voices and languages as it recollects divine truth from all of time. Basic to its form is a recovery of texts, for as Andrewes is overwhelmingly aware, the Spirit is not the same as it once was:

> I shall not need tell you, the Spirit comes not upon us now at our conception in the womb, to anoint us there. No; we behove to light our lamps oft, and to spend much oil at our studies, ere we can attain it. This way come we to our anointing now, by books; this book chiefly, but in a good part also, by the books of the ancient Fathers and lights of the Church, in whom the scent of this ointment was fresh, and the temper true; on whose writings it lieth thick, and we thence strike it off, and gather it safely. (3:287)[12]

To reproduce a prophetic text, another kind of "oil" must now be spent, an oil far different from that anointing in the womb that occurred at the incarnation of the Word. For Andrewes, the light of that virginal "conception" now glimmers only in "books," first in the Bible and then in the "oil" of the Spirit that "lieth thick" on the writings of the Fathers. Only by reading can one recapture that moment "when the sent of this ointment was fresh, and the temper true," a time, signaled by Andrewes's sudden lyricism, when the Word was rendered in its fullness. Only by this "light," this "scent," this music "struck off" in harmony, can one find inspiration, now through a distinctly intertextual and heteroglossic prophetic form.[13]

---

11. Such a mission is completely in keeping with Andrewes's skill as a translator of the Word, a skill so vast, according to a fellow churchman, that Andrewes could have "served as an interpreter-general at the confusion of tongues" (Thomas Fuller, *The Church History of Britain*, 3:391).

12. Trevor Owen discusses the fact that Andrewes's attitude toward the church fathers and their interpretation of Scripture was at first skeptical, but quickly became wholehearted as is clear in this passage (*Lancelot Andrewes*, 64–65).

13. In a sermon on Saint Jude, prefixed to the first edition of his *Works*, Richard Hooker combined the images of writing, music, and honey in describing the prophetic act: "Which books were so often delivered [the prophets] to eat, not because God fed them with ink and

By highlighting the increasingly dialogic and intertextual nature of his own prophetic discourse, Andrewes sets it off against the work of the populist prophets of the age who know few books and fewer languages. Their rejection of the "Word" in favor of visions and dreams, he makes clear, is the stock-in-trade of false prophets:

> Now in this latter pouring on His "servants," which only concerns us, "visions" and "dreams" are left out quite. If any pretend them now, we say with Jeremiah, "Let a dream go for a dream," and "let My word," saith the Lord, "be spoken as My word. *Quid paleae ad triticum?* What, mingle you chaff and wheat? We are to lay no point of religion upon them now; prophecy, preaching is it, we to hold ourselves unto now. As for "visions" and "dreams," *transeant,* "let them go." (3:313)

Andrewes here dismisses the claims of contemporary prophets in his own analysis of Acts 2:16–21, the passage most often cited by the radical fringe.[14] Recasting these dreams and visions as pretense and deception, he echoes Jeremiah as he recalls a now forgotten "Word." At the same time, he exposes the corrupt intentions of those who make such claims: "Behold I am against them that prophesy false dreams, saith the Lord, and do tell them, and cause my people to err by their lies, and by their lightness; yet I sent them not" (Jer. 23:32).[15] Dramatizing this confrontation with falsehood by quoting Jeremiah's question verbatim, *"Quid paleae ad triticum?"* Andrewes quickly translates it into the very parable capturing the controversies of the moment: "What, mingle you chaff and wheat?" To place dreams and visions on a par with the Word is to corrupt the truth and to pervert the

---

paper, but to teach us, that so often as he employed them in this heavenly work, they neither spake nor wrote any word of their own, but uttered syllable by syllable as the Spirit put it into their mouths, no otherwise than the harp or the lute doth give a sound according to the discretion of his hands that holdeth and striketh it with skill. . . . I opened my mouth, saith Ezekiel, and God reached me a scroll saying Son of man, cause thy belly to eat, and fill thy bowels with this I give thee. I ate it, and it was sweet in my mouth, saith the prophet. Yea, sweeter, I am persuaded, than either honey or the honeycomb" (*The Works of that Learned and Judicious Divine, Mr. Richard Hooker*, 2:756).

14. Acts 2:27 (based on Joel 2:28) was often employed by the later prophets of the seventeenth century, though Andrewes's sermon (preached on Whitsunday, May 24, 1618) suggests the prevalence of radical prophetic discourse in the early decades as well. A similar attempt to quell popular prophecies is signaled by the reprinting in 1620 of Henry Howard Northampton's tract *A Defensative against the poyson of supposed prophesies*. Keith Thomas traces the rise in radical prophetic discourse both before and during the Interregnum (*Religion and the Decline of Magic*, 128–46).

15. The King James version of the Bible, 1611. Future references will be cited parenthetically within the text.

divine message. "Now," he says, repeating the temporal adverb four times, is the time for preaching or prophesying, for illuminating the Word with well-informed and careful analysis. Again, however, Andrewes limits those capable of prophesying to a select few:

> But then, for prophecy in this sense of opening or interpreting Scrip-
> tures, is the Spirit poured upon all flesh so? Is this of Joel a proclamation
> for liberty of preaching, that all, young and old, men-servants and maid-
> servants may fall to it? Nay, the she sex, St. Paul took order for that
> betimes, cut them off with his *nolo mulieres*. But what for the rest? May
> they? . . . "drunken" Prophets then indeed; howbeit "not with wine," as
> Esay saith, but with another as heady a humour, and that doth intoxicate
> the brain as much as any must or new wine; even of self-conceited
> ignorance, whereof the world grows too full. But it was no part of Joel's
> meaning, nor St. Peter's neither, to give way to this phrensy. (3:313–14)

Andrewes slowly whittles away all who seek to engage in the "liberty of preaching" by calling upon biblical authority. First, he "cuts off" women prophets with one knifelike Pauline stroke, slicing away other contenders almost as easily. Then Andrewes highlights the irrational behavior and the "self-conceited ignorance" of the prophets who tender their revelations in the streets. Emphasizing the error and divisiveness that they have introduced, he slams the door on radical discourse: he will not "give way to this phrensy."

In form and technique, Andrewes then maps out the appropriate pro-phetic terrain. Separating two strands of prophetic discourse found in the biblical text, he divides them historically; the prophets in the Old Testament foretold the future, while the apostles in the New Testament "disclose[d] the hidden things of 'the Oracles of God'" (3:313): "But not in the sense of foretelling things to come . . . That indeed was the chief sense of it in the Old Testament; and well, while Christ was yet to come. Christ, He was the stop of all prophetical predictions. Then it had his place, that. But now, and ever since Christ is come, it hath in a manner left that sense, at least in a great part, and is not so taken in the New" (3:312). Using the dramatic pause, Andrewes breaks time into two dispensations, giving priority to Christ as he ushers in the new order. But as Christ unites the two eras, he also draws a firm line between the "Old" sense of prophecy and the "New."[16] In the Apostles and New Testament writers, Andrewes locates this "New"

---

16. As Andrewes continues, however, his qualifying phrases begin to erode his stance, suggesting what only "in a manner" has taken place. His parenthetic "at least in a great part" reveals his inability to close the door on contemporary prophecy altogether.

manner of prophecy: "How prophesied St. Peter? He foretold nothing; all he did was, he applied this place of the Prophet, to this feast" (3:313). Peter's prophecy, Andrewes notes, was not predictive. In fact, Peter showed how Old Testament prophecy foreshadowed Christ, making the "feast" of Pentecost into a moment of temporal fulfillment. With this distinction, Andrewes cleverly revises apocalyptic prophecy out of existence, turning it into an old and predictive form that is no longer sanctioned.

Moreover, this predictive, apocalyptic strand of prophecy, Andrewes argues, goes directly against the Word of God: " 'it was not for them to know all, not the times and seasons,' and such other things as 'the Father had put into His own power' " (3:328). Echoing Acts 1:7, Andrewes makes it clear that to stray into prediction is to usurp an authority God never intended men to have and so to participate in Romish error: "I speak it for this, that even some that are far enough from Rome, yet with their new perspective they think they perceive all God's secret decrees, the number and order of them clearly; are indeed too bold and too busy with them. Luther said well that every one of us hath by nature a Pope in his belly, and thinks he perceives great matters" (3:328). Through this stunning inversion, Andrewes argues that those engaged in apocalyptic prophecy participate in the very error they seek to eradicate. Their "new perspective" designed to foresee the fall of Antichrist is itself a "popish" lens, causing those who look through it to become what they behold. Consumed by the enemy outside of them, they fail to recognize the enemy within.

Their emphasis on prophecy and preaching, Andrewes notes, perpetrates a similar error:

> Is the pouring of the Spirit to end in preaching? and preaching to end in itself, as it doth with us? a circle of preaching, and in effect nothing else,—but pour in prophesying enough, and then all is safe? No; there is another yet as needful, nay, more needful to be called on, as the current of our age runs, and that is, "calling on the name of the Lord."
> This, it grieveth me to see how light it is set; nay, to see how busy the devil hath been, to pour contempt on it, to bring it in disgrace with disgraceful terms; to make nothing of Divine service, as if it might be well spared, and *invocaverit* stricken out. (3:318)

Calling attention to what has been "stricken out" of this new edition of the Gospel, Andrewes seeks to recover the original message and to reinstitute "Divine service." In the earlier and, for him, pristine version of the Gospel, the prayers that occur in the church, not the preaching, are essential: "Two errors there be, and I wish them reformed: one, as if prophesying were all we had to do, we might dispense with invocation, let it go, leave it to the choir. That is an error. . . . The oratory of prayer poured out of our hearts shall save us, no less than the oratory of preaching poured in at our ears" (3:318). What must be reformed, in Andrewes's view, are the "reformers'" attempts to shorten prayers and lengthen sermons, a case Andrewes makes by noting that this new emphasis on prophesying and preaching obscures the role of the audience, turning them into passive nonparticipants: "To make religion nothing but an auricular profession, a matter of ease, a mere sedentary thing, and ourselves merely passive in it; sit still, and hear a Sermon and two Anthems, and be saved; as if by the act of the choir, or of the preacher, we should so be, (for these be their acts,) and we do nothing ourselves, but sit and suffer" (3:319). Instead, Andrewes would have his listeners join their voices with the human and divine voices of the text, a musical "concord" that can take place only if their spirits are one with the divine spirit received at the first Pentecost. To achieve this kind of harmony, the unity of that originary moment must be recovered: "And there is not a greater bar, a more fatal or forcible opposition to His entry, than discord, and dis-united minds, and such as are 'in the gall of bitterness,' they can neither give nor receive the Holy Ghost. *Divisium est cor eorum, jamjam interibunt,* saith the Prophet; 'their heart is divided,' their 'accord' is gone, that cord is untwisted; they cannot live, the Spirit is gone too" (3:113). In Andrewes's translation of the prophet's words, discord signals the death of the spiritual community. The work of the true prophet is thus to encourage accord, unity, and harmony in the church by building upon the gifts of individual members: "High shall be his reward in Heaven, and happy his remembrance on earth, that shall be the means to restore this 'accord' to the Church" (3:113).

Nevertheless, "unity" of spirit is not enough. Quoting the words of the Separatists, Andrewes foregrounds their desire to depart from the "one place" specified in the text: "If our minds be one, for the place it skills not; it is but a circumstance or ceremony; what should we stand at it?" (3:113). Giving voice to the Separatist assertion that locations, ceremonies, and rites of worship were not dictated by Scripture, and so as "things indifferent" need not be followed, Andrewes seeks to contain this response, arguing once again that the Holy Spirit who informs the church has a contrary view: "The same Spirit, That loveth unanimity loveth uniformity; unity even in matter of circumstance, in matter of place. Thus the Church was begun, thus it must be continued" (3:114). Using the Word to establish a precedent—a perfect strategy for nonconforming Puritans—Andrewes suggests that gathering "in one place" is not after all an "indifferent" matter, nor indeed are the "arteries" through which the Spirit now moves through the body of the church. These, Andrewes states, are "Prayer," the "Word," and the "Sacraments" (3:128). Again, however, Andrewes cautions his listeners against prescribing one particular way in which the Spirit comes. If one privileges preaching over prayer or prayer over the sacraments, Andrewes hints, one may miss the mysterious anointing that God seeks to confer: "For many times we miss, when we use this one or that one alone; where, it may well be God hath appointed to give it us by neither, but by the third. It is not for us to limit Him, how, or by what way, He shall come unto us" (3:128). Asserting that conformity and openness provide the basis for spiritual fulfillment, Andrewes strikes a mediating pose against any attempt to privilege a single means of grace.

In a final sermon on Pentecost, one Andrewes intended to preach in 1622, he turns to the pun on profit to articulate the prophet's intentions and to distinguish between the true prophet and the false one for a final time. Again rejecting the violent rhetoric of his contemporaries, he argues that God never provides gifts "to destruction" or to do others harm, but only "to edification," to build others up. This "ever argues a community; a profit redounding to more than ourselves" (3:400). Such an analysis allows Andrewes to provide his own brief model of edification, one conveyed through an ecclesiastical structure in which "Every one confers his several gift, office, and work, to the general benefit of the whole" (3:400). At the same time, however, Andrewes refuses to turn these "benefits" toward the economic or social profit of the spiritual community, nor does he envision any redistribution of wealth: "For the common salvation is the 'profit' here meant. The Apostle himself saith it plainly; 'Not seeking mine own profit or benefit, but the profit of many.' And how? that they may have lands or leases? No, but 'that they may be saved.' Which is the true profit, redounding of all these, and which in the end will prove the best profit; which if any attain not, 'what will it profit him, if he win the whole world?'" (3:400). Turning away from the social inequities of the moment in which leases were being raised and land owners were increasingly expelling the poor, Andrewes chooses to concentrate on spiritual salvation alone. The world might well be lost, he suggests, for salvation is the only profit worth achieving. As a result, his concluding words rhythmically echo—in poetic fashion—his transcendent prophetic vision, even as they circumscribe his ideological limits: "If we the profit, They the praise: the rather, for that even that praise shall redound to our profit also, the highest profit of all, the gaining of our souls, and the gaining of them a rest in the Heavenly kingdom with all the Three Persons" (3:401). In Andrewes's view, the community of singers who raise their voices in praise of the Trinity will increase the musical range of the true prophet, investing his "talent" for divine harmony toward greater and higher ends. The concord that he achieves will at last turn all to rest, his ecclesiastical and royal "interest" conveying precisely what he can and cannot offer: internal spiritual change perhaps, but no sociopolitical or economic redemption.

3

Subverting Paul
The True Church and the Querelle des Femmes in Aemilia Lanyer

And then the world by womans hands shall rul'd be and obey
But when the widow over all the world shall beare the sway
And cast into the sea the gold and silver with disdayne
And cast the brass of brittle man and yron into the main
Then shall the worldly elements all desolate remain.
—Thomas Brightman, *A Revelation of the Apocalypse*

I N *A REVELATION of the Apocalypse,* written in 1611, Thomas Brightman appropriates a passage from the "Sybyll's Books" to reveal the triumph of the bride of Christ at the end of time, a triumph represented through a stunning inversion of seventeenth-century economic and gender relations. As we have already seen, Brightman establishes the fact that the woman of the Apocalypse is not a woman at all but the "excellent brightness and purity" of the primitive church, at last restored. Her "disdayne" of wealth, he argues, bears witness to the fact that the primitive church "abhorred the coveting of riches, and contention for dignity" that now characterizes a power-hungry episcopacy. Consequently, what she "casts away" as the "brass of brittle man" is the corrupt hierarchy of the English Church.[1]

For Brightman, this reversal of power relations called attention to the "right rule" of Presbyterianism—only metaphorically a marginalized woman. Inevitably, however, Brightman's language prepared the way for women prophets of the period as his metaphor was translated into far more immediate terms. And the prophetic discourse of Lancelot Andrewes performed a similar function. Because he identified the Eucharist, the church, and the act of prophesying with "virginal conception," his language disclosed

---

1. Thomas Brightman, *A Revelation of the Apocalypse that is, the Apocalyps of St. John,* 698.

a Christian gospel that was, for all intents and purposes, feminine in orientation.

The fact that God chose a woman in which to "become flesh" was not, for Andrewes, a moment of female privilege but rather a moment of divine debasement. In his view, God "takes" woman, "the lowest and basest part of man" in order to incarnate in the feminine gender the very Word woman once refused: "Besides, from the flesh, as from Eve, came the beginning of transgression—longing after the forbidden fruit, refused the Word quite; so, of all other, least likely to be taken. The Word not refusing it, the rest have good hope" (1:89). The divine Word overcomes female transgression both by accepting her and by uniting with her to revise the whole of human history. First, of course, Christ must transform human origins by altering the reproductive process itself, an act he performs in the virgin's womb: "He was not idle all the time He was an embryo—all the nine months He was in the womb; but then and there He even eat out the core of corruption that cleft to our nature and us" (1:141). What Christ consumes in "eating out the core of corruption" reverses the cycle of death that Eve initiates in eating down to the "core" of the apple.

Yet, Andrewes concedes, Mary just as actively conceives Christ. Far from becoming a passive, merely receptive "vessel," she gives her own flesh and blood to the making of God:

> To conceive is more than to receive. It is so to receive as we yield somewhat of our own also. A vessel is not said to conceive the liquor that is put into it. Why? because it yieldeth nothing from itself. The blessed Virgin is, and therefore is because she did. She did both give and take. Give of her own substance whereof His body was framed; and take or receive power from the Holy Ghost, whereby was supplied the office and the efficacy of the masculine seed. (1:140)

The Holy Ghost fulfills the "office" of the "masculine seed," but it is Mary who "conceives" the Christ child, framing "His body" out of "her own substance" and delivering him to the world.

Andrewes pursues the implications of this transformation taking place in the "flesh" of woman by making Mary's activity central to the Eucharist: "That flesh that was conceived and this day born, *(Corpus aptasti Mihi,)* that body that was this day fitted to Him. And if we be not with Him thus, if this His flesh be not 'with us,' if we partake it not, which way soever else we be with Him, we come short of the *Im* of this day" (1:151). In switching to passive voice, Andrewes eliminates Mary from view, thereby obscuring the moment when Mary's "body" provides the clothing "fit" for Christ and thus the moment when her flesh becomes "His." But the logic of the sermon calls attention to her presence, even as her activity provides insight into the union of "flesh and word" taking place in the audience: "This then I commend to you, even the being with Him in the Sacrament of His Body—that Body that was conceived and born, as for other ends so for this specially, to be 'with you'" (1:151–52). In Andrewes's view, God places his Word in human flesh through a series of steps, moving from the "flesh" of a woman to the "flesh" of Christ, and now, through the "Sacrament of His Body," to the "flesh" of his people. Consequently, the gender issues that Andrewes foregrounds at the outset become increasingly submerged when divine love crosses all boundaries. As we have seen in Chapter 1, Andrewes relied heavily on Pauline authority and a range of voices from Christian tradition to firm up the contemporary exclusion of women as speakers and authors. Only in this way could he confine women prophets—and all female reproductions of the *logos*—to past history, indeed to the text of biblical narrative itself.

Nevertheless, both radical prophets like Brightman and conservative prophets like Andrewes unwittingly empowered women by foregrounding the reversal of gender relations apparent in the metaphoric language of the Apocalypse and the literal language of the Annunciation. The women of the seventeenth century turned this biblical language to political, poetic, and spiritual ends, identifying the woman not only with Mary and the true church but also with Elizabeth's chaste rule. On the basis of a developing prophetic awareness and recent history, they began to locate an originary purity in the feminine metaphors of biblical prophecy. Literalizing these metaphors, they turned them into sacramental and redemptive autobiography that sanctioned their own writing by locating it within a feminist, biblical tradition. At the same time, they openly contested the Pauline mandate as it was repeatedly represented to them in Renaissance sermons.

The text cited in the sermons, tracts, and arguments of the seventeenth century was the unequivocal pronouncement of the apostle Paul: "Let the woman learne in silence with all subjection. I permit not a woman to teach, nether to usurpe autoritie over the man, but to be in silence. For Adam was first formed, then Eve. And Adam was not deceived, but the woman was deceived & was in the transgression" (1 Tim. 2:11–14).[2] If women were

---

2. Suzanne W. Hull discusses the influence of Pauline authority on women (*Chaste, Silent, and Obedient*, 106–26), and a wide range of criticism offers the same assessment. See, for example, Margaret Ezell, *The Patriarch's Wife: Literary Evidence and the History of the*

to find a place for themselves as speakers and writers, they must first call into question Paul's interpretation of Genesis; they must first overturn his assessment of Eve.[3] Among those who took up this task, no woman did so with more art, authority, or skill than Aemilia Lanyer in *Salve Deus Rex Judaeorum*. Yet, despite the recent surge in scholarly criticism of Lanyer's work, we have not yet analyzed the revision of Paul that informs Lanyer's passion narrative, nor have we identified the subversive hermeneutic method that provides Lanyer with the impetus for this revision.[4]

What we have identified are the questions that puzzle us. Barbara K. Lewalski, for example, closes each of her articles with an awareness of how much we do not know, particularly about Lanyer's feminism: "How should we account for the feminist thrust of [Lanyer's] volume, which re-writes patriarchy by revising the fundamental Christian myths: Eden, the Passion of Christ, the Communion of Saints, with women at their centre?"[5] At the same time, Lewalski's work on Aemilia Lanyer suggests the beginning of an answer: she identifies the remarkable feminism of *Salve Deus Rex Judaeorum* with the *Querelle des Femmes,* a genre popular with Medieval and Renaissance writers.[6] The authors of the *Querelle* repeatedly attack

Family, 16; Margaret Patterson Hannay, ed., *Silent But for the Word: Tudor Women as Patrons, Translators, and Writers of Religious Works;* Constance Jordan, *Renaissance Feminism,* 22–33; Betty Travitsky, ed., *The Paradise of Women,* 5; Elaine Hobby, *Virtue of Necessity: English Women's Writing, 1649–1688,* 5–11. The quote is from *The Geneva Bible: A Facsimile of the 1560 Edition.* I refer to this translation throughout the article, as the *Geneva Bible* was the biblical text most often used until 1640. The King James Bible was printed the same year as Lanyer's work.

3. For an analysis of Paul's influence on Renaissance texts in general, see John S. Coolidge, *The Pauline Renaissance in England: Puritanism and the Bible.* Coolidge argues that Pauline authority led the Puritans to "feel the old modes of presentation as a form of bondage" (xiii). As I will demonstrate here, a number of writers felt that Paul had not gone far enough. Because Paul placed women under the "law," he put them in the very "bondage" from which Christ came to liberate them. If women were to gain a voice, the prophetic reading had to be given authority: "I will pour out my Spirit upon all flesh; and your sons and your daughters shall prophesy" (Joel 2:28), the Pauline reading suppressed.

4. Aemilia Lanyer's lengthy passion poem *Salve Deus Rex Judaeorum* has had a checkered literary history. First emerging under the editorial direction of A. L. Rowse in 1974 and called *The Poems of Shakespeare's Dark Lady,* Lanyer's text became a footnote to Rowse's thesis— that he had located the Dark Lady of Shakespeare's sonnets. For the range of criticism now available, see Esther Gilman Richey, "To Undoe the Booke: Cornelius Agrippa, Aemilia Lanyer, and the Subversion of Pauline Authority," 107.

5. Lewalski, "Re-writing Patriarchy and Patronage: Margaret Clifford, Ann Clifford, and Aemilia Lanyer," 106; Lewalski, "Of God and Good Women: The Poems of Aemilia Lanyer," 224.

6. Lewalski cites Lanyer's final epistle "To the Vertuous Reader" as a "remarkable contribution to the *Querelle des femmes*" in "Of God and Good Women" (212), and she analyzes

the Pauline interpretation of Genesis, contesting both his analysis of the Fall and his subordination of women.[7] Among these, Cornelius Agrippa's *Of the Nobilitie and Excellencie of Womankinde* offers the most striking parallel to the revision of Paul found in Lanyer. A book first entering the English imagination as an affirmation of Mary and Elizabeth's right to ascend the throne, *Of the Nobilitie* is, according to Constance Jordan, the "most explicitly feminist text to be published in England in the first half of the century."[8] Its popularity would increase during the reign of Elizabeth, a time when the works of Agrippa were being widely read by Sidney, Bacon, Nashe, and Marlowe and when the debate about women was culminating in the pamphlet wars.[9]

Before turning to Lanyer, then, I shall first illustrate how Agrippa rereads the Genesis account to undermine Pauline hermeneutics, thereby overturning the very authority that underwrites Renaissance gender relations. By writing the Pauline subjugation of Eve and her daughters not only out of the

---

this epistle more completely in "Rewriting Patriarchy and Patronage" (102). Elaine Beilin sees the *Querelle* as a much larger influence, noting that Lanyer "accomplished her task" by drawing upon the "traditional debate material on the women question"; she makes a direct connection to the early defenses of women, citing Cornelius Agrippa in particular (*Redeeming Eve*, 179, 323). The *Querelle* itself has been much discussed. A bibliography of primary texts participating in this tradition is available in Francis Lee Utley's *The Crooked Rib*. For an analysis of it, see Katherine Usher Henderson and Barbara F. McManus, eds., *Half Humankind*, 3–46; Hull, *Chaste, Silent, and Obedient*, 106–26; Joan Kelly, "Early Feminist Theory and the *Querelle des Femmes*, 1400–1789"; Betty Travitsky, "The Lady Doth Protest: Protest in the Popular Writings of Renaissance Englishwomen"; and Linda Woodbridge, *Women and the English Renaissance*.

7. In *Renaissance Feminism,* Jordan says that the argument over woman's postlapsarian status "fueled feminist responses" throughout the sixteenth century (23). These arguments emerge in a number of texts of the *Querelle*. See, for example, the work of Jane Anger and Esther Sowernam in *Half Humankind*, ed. Katherine Usher Henderson and Barbara F. McManus, 172–88, 217–44. William Heale in his *An Apologie for Women* also offers a compelling reinterpretation of Genesis (60–66).

8. See Jordan, *Renaissance Feminism*, 122–26. For critical commentary on Agrippa and the Querelle, see also Linda Woodbridge, *Women and the English Renaissance*. Agrippa's text is, for her, a "personal favorite," but she "cannot believe it was meant to be taken seriously" (40). Whether or not it was, Agrippa's radical revision of Paul fueled the intellectual debate on the woman question, influencing other writers in the *Querelle* tradition, among them Aemilia Lanyer.

9. Agrippa's influence in the Renaissance is documented by Charles G. Nauert Jr., who notes that Erasmus, Vives, Rabelais, Sidney, Nashe, Marlowe, Bacon, and Vaughan read his works (*Agrippa and the Crisis of Renaissance Thought*, 325–26). That Agrippa was recognized as subversive by Renaissance readers is also true. John Harington cites Agrippa as calling the authority of court, priests, lawyers, and physicians into question (Ludovico Ariosto, *Orlando Furioso in English Heroical Verse*, sig. iij2-iiij).

Old Testament but also out of the epistles of Paul himself, Agrippa indicates that Eve and the women who follow her reproduce an open, more generous New Testament—a Renaissance version of *ecriture feminine.*[10] I will argue that it is this hermeneutic process—visible most clearly in Agrippa and available to Lanyer in the general milieu of the *Querelle des Femmes*—that becomes the "feminist" framework for *Salve Deus Rex Judaeorum.*

As Agrippa analyzes Genesis, then, he quite literally starts over, providing an altogether different "genesis" for women:

> Thus blessyng was gyven for the woman, and law for the man: The lawe I say, of anger and of cursynge. For why, the fruyte of the tree was forbydden to the man, but not to the woman: which was not than created. For god wolde her to be fre from the begynning. Therefore the manne sinned in eatynge, not the woman. The man gave us deathe, not the woman . . . And we take orygynalle synne of oure father the man, not of our mother the woman.[11]

In his thorough rereading of Gen. 2:15–17, Agrippa explores the gaps in the chronology of the biblical narrative: God plants a garden, places Adam within it, and issues a command not to eat the forbidden fruit. Immediately afterward God says, "It is not good that the man shulde be him selfe alone: I wil make him an helpe mete for him" (Gen. 2:18). God's statement, according to Agrippa, calls attention to Eve's absence: she "was not than created." Consequently, Adam alone is under the "Law" of the Father; Eve is free, subordinate neither to the "Law" nor to Adam and therefore the conduit of divine "blessyng." In making Eve's absence the locus of divine presence, Agrippa undoes the patriarchal assessment that Paul's interpretation reinforces: thus, Adam fathers the discourse of law, judgment, and death (as he writes the Old Testament), while Eve gives birth to Christ and the freedom of the Gospel.

Agrippa continues to link the feminine gender with the incarnation as he rewrites the order of creation. Revising Paul's argument that God affirmed Adam's dominant role by making him first, Agrippa suggests that God affirmed Eve's nobler role by making her second, in this way perfecting

---

10. I refer specifically to Luce Irigaray's description of the feminine union with the divine on the basis of a "free offering of the self" (*Speculum of the Other Woman,* 196) and to Helene Cixous's awareness that "the question a woman's text asks is the question of giving" ("Castration or Decapitation").

11. Henricus Cornelius Agrippa, *Of the Nobilitie and Excellencie of Womankynde,* sig. CV1. Future references will be cited parenthetically within the text. A modern edition, *Declamation on the Nobility and Preeminence of the Female Sex,* is also available.

his work of redemption. And Agrippa refuses to describe woman in Pauline terms as the image and "glory of Man" (1 Cor. 11:7), identifying her instead as the "simylitude of Christ" (Cv4), the one who most adequately reflects the *logos*. Even in taking flesh, Christ refuses to be the "sonne of man," choosing a "womanne" to reproduce him: "Yet for all that I say, that he beynge verye God (I speak of Christe) wold not be the sonne of man, but of a woman, the whiche he so hyghly honored, that of a womanne onely he toke fleshe and bloudde" (sig. Cv5). Agrippa's Christ circumvents patriarchal "Law," taking his descent "of a womanne onely." It is thus in the "fleshe and bloudde" of a woman that Christ observes his first communion, receiving the "fleshe and bloudde" from Mary that he will offer to the world.

This communion between Christ and women, in which women reflect and reproduce him, continues to predominate in Agrippa's interpretation of a women-centered New Testament. At the same time, he identifies the men who judge and crucify Christ with the fallen patriarchal "Law" they attempt to perpetuate over time: "Christe was boughte and solde, accused, condemned, scourged, hanged on the Crosse, and at the last putte to cruell deathe onely by men" (sig. Cv7–8). Even the men who are part of Christ's inner circle, the disciples whom he calls and trains, abandon him in his hour of need. In the midst of this absence, women fill in the gap, becoming Christ's only supporters: "Yea, he was denyed of his owne Peter, forsaken of his other disciples, and only accompanied wayted upon and folowed of women unto the crosse and grave. Also the very wyfe of Pylate, an hethen woman, went aboute, and laboured more to save Jesus than any man, yea, any of these men, that beleved in hym" (sig. Cv7–8). Here, too, a woman "incarnates" and delivers the *logos*: the wife of Pilate "labours" to save Christ more than any of his disciples, becoming the single person at Christ's trial committed to correctly representing him. Unfortunately, Agrippa notes, the truth to which she and others like her bear witness is repeatedly suppressed: "Also they be repelled frome preachynge of goddes worde, against expresse and playn scripture, in whyche the holy gost promised unto them by Johel the prophet saieng: And your daughters shall prophecie and preache: lyke as they taught openly in the tyme of the apostles" (sig. G). Highlighting Joel's prediction of women prophets, Agrippa notes that "later Lawe-makers" suppress this truth and so break "goddes commaundemente, to stablyshe theyr owne traditions" (sig. G). Because they "prove theyr tyranny by holy scripture" (sig. Gi4-Gii), by, in fact, quoting Paul's injunction to female silence, they actually reveal their carnal way of reading: "these thynges," Agrippa notes, "be not repugnant but in the rynde" (sig. Gii). The Spirit resides in the kernel of truth that such interpreters overlook, a truth that Agrippa uncovers in the words of Christ: "But whan men commytte offence and erre, the women have power of Judgement over theym. . . . And that quiene of Saba shall judge the men of Jerusalem" (sig. Gii1). Citing Christ's revolutionary statement about female awareness in Matt. 12:41, Agrippa offers Christ's words to justify his "spiritual" reading of the text. For Christ, the Queen of Sheba's ability to search out the truth puts the present generation to shame: "The Quene of the South shall rise in judgement with this generation, and shall condemn it: for she came from the utmost parties of the earth to heare the wisdom of Solomon: and beholde, a greater than Solomon is here" (Matt. 12:41). Holding up the Queen of Sheba as an ideal, Christ notes that her wisdom contrasts sharply with the ignorance and blindness of his age. Though separated from him by religion (she was a heathen), by gender (she was a woman), and by time (she lived during the reign of Solomon), she nevertheless will receive the right to judge in the Apocalypse, illuminating, by way of contrast, the very wisdom that the "present generation" has missed.

Agrippa takes Christ's affirmation of women still further, however, locating it within the Pauline allegory of "Law" and "Grace" in Gal. 4. Paul, of course, argues that Hagar, Abraham's bondwoman, gives birth to Ishmael and the Law of Mount Sinai, while Sarah, Abraham's wife, gives birth to Isaac and the Grace of "Jerusalem which is above" (Gal. 4:25–26). Agrippa glosses this allegory more completely by incorporating into it the fact that God privileges Sarah's voice in the Old Testament account: "In all that Sarah shall saie unto thee, heare her voice: for in Isak shall thy sede be called" (Gen. 21:12). By combining the two texts, Agrippa arrives at a completely alternative reading of Paul: "Therfore they, whyche beynge iustifyed by fayth: are become the sonnes of Abraham, the chylderne I say of promyssion, be subdewed to a woman, and bounden by the cõmandement of god, sayenge to Abraham: what so ever Sara saith unto the[e], folow it" (sig. Gii1). Using God's Word to revise Paul's word, Agrippa reveals that those "iustifyed by fayth" are typologically prefigured in Abraham who is "bound" to hear the "cõmandement of god" spoken by his wife. Because Sarah provides access to divine truth and because she conceives the son that brings in the New Covenant, she initiates, through speech and bodily action, the "freedom" available only by faith. As a result, the human race is no longer subject to patriarchal Law "which gendereth to bondage" (Gal. 4:24), but lives instead under the covenant of Grace. On this basis, Agrippa informs us, Abraham and all men after him must listen to women if they are to hear the Spirit of God.

Through this cunning reinterpretation of Paul, Agrippa locates a spiritual reading of the biblical text that transforms gender relations and displaces the Pauline reading of Genesis. Beneath the "rynde" of the "Law" so often employed by carnal interpreters to silence women, he finds the Spirit of the New Covenant that authorizes women to speak and to justify all who believe. Those who fail to listen, he suggests, do far more than oppress women; they silence the liberating message of the New Testament.

Applying what becomes available to her through the work of Agrippa and other writers of the *Querelle,* Aemilia Lanyer creates *Salve Deus Rex Judaeorum* to recover the status that Christ assigns women. In fact, each point Agrippa makes—his reinterpretation of Genesis, his awareness of feminine incarnation and communion, his christological foregrounding of Matt. 12 to displace Pauline hermeneutics, his understanding of feminine insight and vision—reappears in *Salve Deus Rex Judaeorum.* Beneath Lanyer's pen, however, these points are transformed into a feminist theory of reading and writing that is both visionary and poetic. Deeply aware, like Agrippa, that the feminine body contains the *logos,* Lanyer shows that Paul himself employs metaphors of female reproduction, gender-coding the revelation of Christ as specifically feminine.[12] Reappropriating this discourse for women where, in her view, it originates, Lanyer writes her New Testament to give women a voice.

Similar to Agrippa, Lanyer recovers her New Testament from the gaps in biblical narrative. Consequently, at the very margins of her text, in her subtitles, and in her concluding letter "To the doubtfull Reader," Lanyer locates the female visionaries of Scripture.[13] Linked to the title and to one another by the word *containing,* these women reproduce Christ in a variety of ways, from cogently argued defense to divine incarnation. Not surprisingly, Lanyer places herself among these female prophets in her final words, indicating in closing that her title was "delivered unto me in sleepe many yeares before I had any intent to write in this maner" (139). This dream is now a "significant token," an indication that she, like the female bearers

12. Elizabeth Harvey traces the cultural preoccupation with birth metaphors during the sixteenth and seventeenth centuries and the way they informed the writing of male poets, creating "a strange transvestism" (*Ventriloquized Voices: Feminist Theory and English Renaissance Texts,* 79). Aemilia Lanyer not only recognizes this gender coding in the language of Paul but also employs it to authorize her feminist reproduction of the *logos.*

13. Aemilia Lanyer, *Salve Deus Rex Judaeorum,* in *The Poems of Aemilia Lanyer,* 139. Future references to Lanyer's poetry will be cited parenthetically within the text and will include page and line numbers where appropriate.

of the *logos,* is "appointed to performe this Worke" (139). Consequently, she assigns the "title" as received.[14]

But what Lanyer receives is subversive to men in positions of power as the title she delivers immediately indicates. The words *Salve Deus Rex Judaeorum* ("Hail God, King of the Jews") are the words of the men who crucify Christ, a "title" they assign him on the cross. Written in Latin and ironic in implication, the title indicates not only what men do with Christ but also what they do with power and knowledge. For Lanyer, the words reveal them better than they know.

When Lanyer turns to the body of her text, the epistolary dedications and *Salve,* she demonstrates that the epistolary form participates in the virgin's incarnational act. To reinforce this perspective, Lanyer replaces Paul's epistolary instruction with John's apocalyptic letters and Passion narrative,[15] a move that allows her to subsume the Pauline oppositions of flesh and spirit into an incarnational theology where the flesh no longer opposes the spirit but in fact gives it form.[16] On this maternal and material basis, Lanyer offers her patron, Margaret Clifford, "Jesus himselfe":

> I present unto you even our Lord Jesus himselfe, whose infinit value is not to be comprehended within the weake imagination or wit of man: and as Saint *Peter* gave health to the body, so I deliver you the health of the soule; which is this most pretious pearle of all perfection, this rich diamond of devotion, this perfect gold growing in the veines of that excellent earth of the most blessed Paradice, wherein our second *Adam* had his restlesse habitacion. (34)

By emphasizing what she "offers," and "delivers" as well as what "grow[s] in the veines" of women, Lanyer calls attention to her epistle as a reproductive

14. The name of her prophetic text—like the names of John the Baptist and Christ—is assigned in a dream. See Matt. 1:23 and Luke 1:13.

15. John Donne comments on the epistolary nature of the New Testament, perhaps illuminating Aemilia Lanyer's choice of this form for *Salve Deus Rex Judaeorum:* "They erre not much, that call the whole new Testament Epistle. For, even the gospells are *Evangelia,* good messages, and that's proper to an Epistle, and the booke of the Acts of the Apostles is superscrib'd by Saint Luke, to one person, *Theophilus,* and that's proper to an Epistle; and so is the last booke, the booke of Revelation, to the several Churches" (*The Sermons of John Donne,* 1:285).

16. In this respect, Aemilia Lanyer's understanding—though far more radical—reflects that of Christian humanists such as Erasmus who fused the separate strands of Pauline and Johannine Christianity. For a brief account of this theological position, see Florence Sandler, "The Faerie Queen: An Elizabethan Apocalypse," 152–53.

act.[17] She thus identifies Paul's metaphoric "travail in birth again until Christ be formed in you" (Gal. 4:19) as distinctively feminine, noting with some irony that the "infinit value" of reproducing Christ "is not to be comprehended within the weake imagination or wit of man." But Lanyer also acknowledges the fact that the "black soyle" that reproduces Christ has little value in itself:

> For as a right diamond can loose no whit of his beautie by the blacke soyle underneath it, neither by beeing placed in the darke, but retaines his naturall beauty and brightnesse shining in greater perfection than before; so this most pretious diamond . . . can receive no blemish, nor impeachment by my unworthy hand writing; but wil with the Sunne retaine his owne brightness and most glorious lustre, though never so many blind eyes looke upon him. (35)

Having clothed the "Sunne" in her "unworthy" handwriting, Lanyer pauses over the possibility of hiding what she intends to reveal, of darkening what she intends to illuminate.[18] She finds, however, no impairment of divine beauty; Christ shines "in greater perfection than before," unaffected either by the darkness of her "hand" or the blindness of a readership.[19]

What Lanyer learns about representing Christ through handwriting becomes the primary message of her feminist epistle: women must continue to convey Christ to the world, in their words as well as in their actions. Beginning by reflecting Christ to nine different noblewomen, Lanyer engages them in the same art: that of endlessly reflecting the beauty of the "sun/son." As Elaine Beilin and Lynette McGrath have suggested, she takes her metaphoric mirror from Paul, but she moves beyond the "dark mirror" of 1 Cor. 13:12 to identify women with the ever increasing radiance of 2 Cor. 3:17–18: "Now the Lord is the Spirit, & where the Spirit of the Lord is, there is libertie. But we all behold as in a mirrour the glory of the Lorde with open face, and are changed into the same image, from glorie to glorie, as by the Spirit

17. George Herbert similarly describes Mary as the "holy mine whence came the gold," in "To all Angels and Saints" (*The Works of George Herbert*, 77–78).

18. I echo George Herbert's "Jordan (II)." The impure desires of the poet—inextricably woven into their representations of Christ—are mentioned in the works of Donne, Vaughan, and Marvell, to name a few.

19. Here, Aemilia Lanyer's "hand writing" as the OED suggests, is "the action of the hand in writing and its product." At the same time, Lanyer's "hand" is infinitely reproduced in the darkness of print, a color with which Lanyer associates the feminine reproduction of Christ. See Lorna Hutson, "Why the Lady's eyes are nothing like the sun," for a similar point (155). Because "darkness" generally signifies the flesh, Herbert describes the Incarnation of Christ as the divine willingness to be "wrapt in nights mantle" ("Christmas," in *Works of Herbert*, 81).

of the Lord."[20] Emphasizing the liberation that the Spirit provides, Lanyer writes reflection and refraction into every aspect of female behavior: women "re-present" the divine image in all their interaction, mirroring the "glory of the Lorde" and becoming, as Agrippa argues in his text, "the simylitude of Christ." Lanyer thus revises out of existence Paul's doctrinal assertion that "[Man] is the image and glorie of God: but the woman is the glorie of the man" (1 Cor. 11:7).

Because women not only reflect Christ but also reproduce him, the female delivery of Christ is metaphorically present in Paul's description of communion. Paul had written, "For I have received of the Lord that which also I delivered unto you, *to wit* That the Lord Jesus in the night that he was betrayed, toke bread. And when he had given thanks, he brake it, and said, Take, eat: this is my bodie, which is broken for you: this do ye in remembrance of me" (1 Cor. 11:23). In connecting the Passion of Christ with his "flesh and blood" delivery by a woman, Lanyer highlights the basic doctrine of the Church of England put forward by Bishop Jewel: "For they are sacraments of Christ's body and blood; therefore whoso receiveth the same confesseth thereby that Christ of the virgin received both body and blood."[21] As we have seen, Lancelot Andrewes pushes Mary's material communion with Christ still further, and Lanyer embraces his awareness; for her, receiving the "body and blood" has less to do with the Pauline "confession" and more to do with the feminine reception and delivery of Christ's suffering—the desire to participate in the same betrayal, marginality, and brokenness that Christ undergoes. As she directs this understanding to noblewomen, then, Lanyer invites Queen Anne to participate in the Passion in a surprisingly unconventional way:

> Here may your sacred Majestie behold
> That mightie Monarch both of heav'n and earth,
> He that all Nations of the world controld,
> Yet tooke our flesh in base and meanest berth:
> Whose daies were spent in poverty and sorrow,
> And yet all Kings their wealth of him do borrow.
> (5.43–48)[22]

---

20. Beilin, *Redeeming Eve,* 186; Lynette McGrath, "Metaphoric Subversions: Feasts and Mirrors in Aemilia Lanier's *Salve Deus Rex Judaeorum.*"

21. John Jewel, *The Works of John Jewel,* 258.

22. Ann Baynes Cairo takes the radical dimension of Lanyer's epistolary address to nobility much further by analyzing the sociopolitical dimension ("Writing in Service: Sexual Politics and Class Position in the Poetry of Aemilia Lanyer and Ben Jonson").

Lanyer requests the queen to find herself in a Christ who surrenders "Monarchy" to assume "*our* flesh," one who relinquishes power to accommodate the lowly. Choosing the "meanest berth" among the lower classes, this Christ bridges the gulf between divine sovereignty and human suffering, taking his form finally from a woman. And it is in this "meane attire"—the text before us—that he continues to appear:

> In the meane time, accept most gratious Queene
> This holy worke, Virtue presents to you,
> In poore apparell, shaming to be seene,
> Or once t'appeare in your judiciall view:
> But that faire Virtue, though in meane attire,
> All Princes of the world doe most desire.
>
> (6.61–66)

Because Christ makes no claims to outward power, authority, or status, Lanyer suggests for the queen the same willing renunciation.[23] Indeed, she invites "all vertuous noblewomen" to embrace Christ's marginality, to find themselves in a reading of the Passion:

> Come like the morning Sunne new out of bed,
> And cast your eyes upon this little Booke,
> Although you be so well accompan'ed
> With *Pallas,* and the Muses, spare one looke
> Upon this humbled King, who all forsooke,
> That in his dying armes he might imbrace
> Your beauteous Soule, and fill it with his grace.
>
> (17.8–14)

Identifying her readers as "the morning Sunne," Lanyer reveals them to be the mirror image of the "mourning Son" whose dying arms embrace them in a still more perfect union. Christ's Passion becomes the ultimate passion, wedding each woman to the fairest of lovers: "And in his humble paths since you do tread, / Take this faire Bridegroome in your soules pure bed (20.41–42). Lanyer thus associates her female audience with the bride of the Song of

23. Perhaps this advice is a subtle critique of Anne's love of fine things. According to Beilin, "art historians have vindicated the results of [Anne's] extravagant spending" (*Redeeming Eve,* 322). Cairo notes a "sustained critique" reflecting at least some resentment ("Writing in Service," 367).

Solomon and the woman clothed with the sun of the Apocalypse.[24] Because women are really "one" with Christ, Lanyer invites "all vertuous Ladies" to re-present him, to wear Christ's clothing even as she does: "Let all your roabes be purple scarlet white, / Those perfit colours purest Virtue wore" (12.15–16). In this way, Lanyer encourages her entire audience (from the queen to "the Vertuous Reader") to reproduce Christ by giving up, as he does, status, life, and authority. In her New Testament, color, class, and gender become meaningful only through a complete inversion of the standard hierarchies since Christ identifies with the dark, the poor, the feminine.[25]

Near the end of her dedicatory epistles, Lanyer opens her text to a still wider readership. Offering her work "for the generall use of all virtuous Ladies and Gentlewomen of this kingdome" (48), she seems to envision a readership beyond the immediate one: "And this have I done, to make knowne *to the world,* that all women deserve not to be blamed" (48; emphasis added). Aware of the constant defamation to which women have been subjected, Lanyer calls such libelous discourse into question by subtly adopting Christ's own term for this abuse; the "Vipers" who "deface the wombes wherein they were bred" (48) have already been judged by Christ: "O generations of vipers, how can you speake good things, when ye are evil? For of the abundance of the heart the mouth speaketh" (Matt. 12:34). Because Christ links scurrilous speech with the satanic perversion of divine truth, he confirms for Lanyer a further parallel: men who defame women and deny them the right to speak take the same strategy as the persecutors of Christ and the murderers of the prophets. Like Agrippa, Lanyer identifies their attempt to silence women with the intentional suppression of divine truth: "Such as these, were they that dishonoured Christ his Apostles and Prophets, putting them to shamefull deaths" (48–49). The only way

24. Lanyer here draws on Rev. 12:1: "And there appeared a great wonder in heaven; a woman clothed with the sunne, & the moone was under her feete, and upon her head a crowne of twelve starres." She may be also incorporating apocalyptic commentary like that of John Bale by revising his metaphoric position on women into a literal recognition of their value: "Not Mary Christes mother is this woman, though many hath so fantasyed in ther commentaries. But it is the true Christen church of whom Marye is a most notable member" (*Image of Bothe Churches,* Dv2).

25. Aemilia Lanyer may be writing her own "dark" appearance into her representation of Christ. That Lanyer was "dark" has been argued by A. L. Rowse, ed., in *The Poems of Shakespeare's Dark Lady,* 13–14; and contested by Paul Ramsey in "Darkness Lightened: A. L. Rowse's Dark Lady Once More." Neither writer discusses the extent to which Lanyer refers to her own darkness in *Salve.*

to escape the corrupt influence of these interpreters is to recover biblical narrative in its purest form and to interpret it anew; this is all the more necessary, Lanyer argues, because women are beginning to forget who they are: "though some forgetting they are women themselves, and in danger to be condemned by the words of their owne mouthes, fall into so great an errour, as to speake unadvisedly against the rest of their sexe" (48). As she echoes Christ's statement in Matt. 12:37, Lanyer returns to the same passage that Agrippa uses to justify the speech of women. Here, Christ's "For by thy wordes thou shalt be justified, and by thy wordes thou shalt be condemned" establishes a new precedent: women's speech, not their silence, will ultimately condemn or justify them. Moreover, Lanyer suggests, if we give attention to male and female ways of representing Christ, we will discover that Christ who was "borne of a woman, nourished of a woman, obedient to a woman" (49) will continue to take form in the words of women. Recommending on this basis that men "speake reverently of our sexe" (50), Lanyer closes by submitting her words to the judgment of a readership: "To the modest sensures of both which, I refer these my imperfect indeavours, knowing that according to their owne excellent dispositions, they will rather, cherish, nourish, and increase the least sparke of virtue where they find it, by their favourable and best interpretations, than quench it by wrong constructions" (50). Having underlined the difficulty of correctly interpreting the *logos,* Lanyer makes the "dispositions" of her readers the ultimate test: those who have learned to read in a way that nourishes and sustains will extend the prophetic act, refusing to "quench it by wrong constructions." Again appropriating Paul's injunction, "Quench not the Spirit. Despise not prophecying" (1 Thess. 5:19–20), Lanyer subtly turns his own words against him: in silencing the woman prophet he has broken his own rule.

In *Salve Deus Rex Judaeorum* Lanyer gives form to the feminist theory she develops in her opening epistles by illustrating the difference between masculine and feminine ways of reading. Consequently, Christ offers himself as a text to a series of people, first, to his disciples (who fail to stay awake), and then to those who come to arrest him:

> When loe these Monsters did not shame to tell,
> His name they sought, and found, yet could not know
> *Jesus* of Nazareth, at whose feet they fell,
> When Heavenly Wisdome did descend so lowe
> To speake to them: they knew they did not well,

Their great amazement made them backeward goe:
Nay, though he said unto them, I am he,
They could not know him, whom their eyes did see.
(73.497–504)

Lanyer underscores the breakdown of interpretation as these men "name" the one they seek, ironically find, and fail to know; in their skewed relationship to the *logos,* Lanyer pinpoints the failure of Adamic "naming" and the limits of masculine knowledge. Christ's self-revelation ("I am he") only compounds their hermeneutic difficulties, forcing Christ to "descend" still lower. In pursuing their redemption, he must now write the Passion, must turn his body into a book, willingly being "bound" to "loose" his disciples and all future readers:

And he alone is bound to loose us all,
Whom with unhallowed hands they led along,
To wicked *Caiphas* in the Judgement Hall,
Who studies onely how to doe him wrong.
(78–79.633–36)

"Bound," handled, and finally "studied" by men who preside over a corrupt legal system, Christ is repeatedly misread as his words are twisted to serve the worst of human motives: "They tell his Words, though farre from his intent, / And what his Speeches were, not what he meant" (79.655–56). According to Lanyer, these powerful men cannot represent Christ, revealing instead their fallen way of reading; for them the *logos* remains cryptic, incomprehensible, mysterious. In the face of their failure, Christ remains silent, speaking only when he is charged "in his glorious name" by Caiaphas himself. Then he echoes Caiaphas's words back to him, suggesting the extent to which all meaning has been deferred. Caiaphas reacts, however, by choosing to distance himself still further: he sends Christ to Pilate.

Having shown how men misread, mishandle, and abuse Christ in attempting to preserve their power, Lanyer now focuses on women's interpretations. Here, she enters the gaps in New Testament narrative to recover the voices that have been suppressed, recording for the first time the words of Pilate's wife.[26] It is at this point that Lanyer draws most clearly on Agrippa, artistically

---

26. W. Gardner Campbell discusses the fact that a positive and a negative version of Pilate's wife exists in the literary and theological tradition available to Lanyer ("The Figure of Pilate's Wife in Aemilia Lanyer's Salve Deus Rex Judaeorum").

linking in the wife's speech Agrippa's rereading of Genesis with his "spiritual" interpretation of Paul. By having Pilate's wife speak precisely when men have committed the greatest of spiritual errors, Lanyer indicates that Christ has authorized women under just such circumstances—"when men commit offense and err." By having her speak in defense of Eve, Lanyer underscores the intimate connection between the Passion of Christ and the suppression of the female voice. Moreover, Lanyer suggests, if one is to rectify the simultaneous misrepresentation of Christ and women so long perpetrated by those in power, one must begin at the very beginning; one must analyze the political implications of the first story.[27]

Thus, for Lanyer as for Agrippa, Eve is not present when God creates Adam and utters the prohibition; Pilate's wife underscores Eve's absence: "For he was Lord and King of all the earth, / Before poore *Eve* had either life or breath" (85.783–84). Despite the fact that Eve is not yet created, Pilate's wife does not assert Agrippa's interpretation by arguing that the divine command does not apply to Eve; instead, she notes that Eve comes later and so receives the command in mediated form. I believe Lanyer revises Agrippa in this instance to make the distinction between woman's interpretation of what happened and the "canonical" interpretations that have arisen more explicit: she does so by tracing patriarchal authority back to creation, to the "breath" of knowledge and power moving between two males, God and Man: "And from Gods mouth receiv'd that strait command, / The breach whereof he knew was present death" (85.787–88).[28] The command comes to Adam in fully integrated form, making his knowledge of life and death complete. But Adam does not use his knowledge when the moment arrives: he fails to tell Eve what he has learned, fails to stop her at the crucial moment: "He never sought her weakenesse to reprove, / With those sharpe words, which he of God did heare" (86.805–6). Forgetting what he knows in the heat of a merely physical longing, Adam takes the fruit because it is "faire" (86.798), and he takes it for himself alone. Eve, in contrast, takes the apple

27. Predating Christine Froula by several centuries, Lanyer unravels the political implications of the Fall by identifying its relationship to canonical interpretation. For Froula's version, see "When Eve Reads Milton: Undoing the Canonical Economy." Lanyer provides a renaissance version of Elaine Pagels's argument in *Adam, Eve, and the Serpent*.

28. Froula would have found a candidate for her rewriting of the text—her "blank page"—in Aemilia Lanyer, who gives voice in her own text to the fact that "an all powerful *male* Creator . . . soothes Adam's fears of female power by Himself claiming credit for the original creation of the world, and further, by bestowing upon Adam "Dominion" (332). In Aemilia Lanyer's text, however, God shifts from male to female representation after Adam's failure—a response, Lanyer indicates, that has been suppressed in Christian tradition.

only after God's Word has been corrupted by Satan, a process perfectly captured in the serpentine twisting of her speech: "For she alleadg'd Gods word, which he denies, / That they should die, but even as Gods, be wise" (85.775–76). Though Eve's knowledge of the command is partial, Pilate's wife argues that she still defends God's Word when Satan challenges her. But she is no match for the hermeneutics of this "Viper" and eventually succumbs to his plot. Her motives, however, are nobler than Adam's. She eats the fruit "for knowledge sake" (86.797), a knowledge that—denied her by God and Adam alike—makes her far more susceptible to deception. And, acting out of generosity rather than selfishness, she gives the apple to Adam so that his knowledge too might "become more cleare" (86.804). Unfortunately, Pilate's wife contends, Eve's desire to share knowledge has been skewed by male interpreters, becoming the very reason it is now withheld: "Yet Men will boast of Knowledge, which he tooke / From *Eves* faire hand, as from a learned Booke" (86.807–8). Switching into future tense, Pilate's wife reveals the real fruit of the Fall. It is not to be found in "Eves faire hand" but in that "boasting" associated with male knowledge and control.

Yet God, according to Pilate's wife, gives women the last word. Choosing to circumvent masculine authority, he now offers himself to women in visions and dreams. On the basis of her own revelation—a knowledge she shares with her husband—Pilate's wife warns Pilate not to go through with the murder of Christ, prophesying a sin of such magnitude that worlds cannot contain it:

> Whom, if unjustly you condemne to die,
> Her sinne was small, to what you doe commit;
> All mortal sinnes that doe for vengeance crie,
> Are not to be compared unto it:
> If many worlds would altogether trie,
> By all their sinnes the wrath of God to get;
> This sinne of yours, surmounts them all as farre
> As doth the Sunne, another little starre.
> (86–87.817–24)

Because the unjust trial of Christ exposes the corruption of men and the institutions they represent, Pilate's wife asks her husband to surrender his "Sov'raigntie," to recognize her, not as his inferior, but as his equal: "Then let us have our Libertie againe, / And challendge to your selves no Sov'raigntie" (87.825–26). Pilate, of course, does not listen, assuming control in the trial while refusing to hear the truth his wife has spoken. Lanyer will not let him off so easily. Standing on the same ground with the Queen of Sheba and Pilate's wife, Lanyer openly judges men who fail to acknowledge divine truth:

> Canst thou be innocent, that gainst all right,
> Wilt yeeld to what thy conscience doth withstand?
> Beeing a man of knowledge, powre, and might,
> To let the wicked carrie such a hand,
> Before thy face to blindfold Heav'ns bright light,
> And thou to yeeld to what they did demand?
> Washing thy hands, thy conscience cannot cleare,
> But to all worlds this staine must needs appeare.
>
> (91.929–36)

Because Pilate ignores the promptings of the Spirit and dismisses the revelation of his wife, his "knowledge, powre, and might" perpetrate the greatest injustice the world has ever seen, leaving the "staine" of patriarchy before the eyes of all.

But what appears equally clear in Lanyer's narrative is the way women respond to Christ's suffering; while men blaspheme in a further abuse of the *logos,* the women cry:

> Yet these poore women, by their pitious cries
> Bid moove their Lord, their Lover, and their King,
> To take compassion, turne about, and speake
> To them whose hearts were ready now to breake.
>
> (93.981–84)

Calling to Christ in terms that reveal the intimacy of their union, the women of Jerusalem reflect the Passion they too undergo. The Virgin Mary suffers along with them, and as she does, Lanyer introduces into her narrative a lyrical interlude that records how Mary's "faultless fruit," delivered to a woman and through a woman, redeems the world:

> What wonder in the world more strange could seeme
> Than that a Virgin could conceive and beare
> Within her wombe a Sonne, That should redeeme
> All Nations on the earth, and should repaire
> Our old decaies.
>
> (98.1097–1101)

Lanyer locates in the womb of the Virgin the "Sonne" who "repaires" fallen language, one who takes form in women to write the liberating truth of the New Testament.

Lanyer concludes her New Testament, much as the New Testament itself concludes, with John's visionary and apocalyptic marriage; Christ returns for the church who is his bride, prefigured in the loving union of the Canticles and described again in Revelation. Recording this shift generically, Lanyer's Gospel narrative gives way to Epithalamium, but it also revises Canticles as, beneath her pen, the speech of the bridegroom merges with that of the bride; both discover that their "lips" drop the sweetness of the "honey comb" (Song of Sol. 4:11) as they reveal divine truth:

> His lips like skarlet threeds, yet much more sweet
> Than is the sweetest hony dropping dew,
> Or hony combes, where all the Bees doe meete;
> Yea, he is constant, and his words are true.
> (107.1314–17)

By this means Lanyer's New Testament discloses the "hony" of prophecy that she receives from Christ in the same way as does the beloved disciple John: "Then I toke the litle boke out of the Angels hand, and ate it up, and it was in my mouth as swete as honie: but when I had eaten it, my bellie was bitter. And he said unto me, Thou must prophecie againe among the people and nations, and tongues, and to many Kings" (Rev. 10:10–11). In Lanyer's book Christ and women offer themselves in the bitter sweetness of the prophetic act, offer themselves to be read and interpreted anew.

As Lanyer concludes her poem, then, she returns to the origin of her inspiration, the countess of Cumberland. And what the countess reproduces—in her life and in Lanyer's text—is Christ:

> Therefore (good Madame) in your heart I leave
> His perfect picture, where it still shall stand,
> Deepely engraved in that holy shrine,
> Environed with Love and Thoughts divine.
> (108.1325–28)

As Lanyer represents the life of Margaret Clifford, she shows her asserting no authority over others. Surrendering her status as Christ does, the countess joins the poor and suffering, recognizing that it is as "the least of these" that Christ appears in this world:

Sometime imprison'd, naked, poore, and bare,
Full of diseases, impotent, and lame,
Blind, deafe, and dumbe, he comes unto his faire,
To see if yet shee will remain the same.
                              (109.1353–56)

The countess finds in the broken and suffering masses the Beloved whom she seeks, offering "all paines, all cost, all care" (109.1359) to restore the masses to health. In the process she receives a spiritual vision: her "eyes are op'ned" (109.1365), allowing her to look upon the one whose image she reflects. Lanyer's feminist Gospel has come full circle, the life of the countess reproducing the text of Christ himself.

In the final passages of her book, Lanyer reveals that Clifford's representational act surpasses all previous feminine texts, even women in Scripture. Because Margaret Clifford reproduces Christ, she reveals greater love than *Cleopatra,* deeper piety than *Hester,* more constancy than *Joachim*'s wife, higher wisdom than the Queen of Sheba. In the course of revealing this last portrait, however, Lanyer pauses to illustrate the reciprocity of the Queen of Sheba's desire for wisdom:

Spirits affect where thy doe sympathize,
Wisdom desires Wisdome to embrace,
Virtue covets her like, and doth devize
How she her friends may entertaine with grace;
Beauty sometime is pleas'd to feed her eyes,
With viewing Beautie in anothers face:
Both good and bad in this point doe agree,
That each desireth with his like to be.
                              (119.1593–1600)

Through an artful doubling of subject and object Lanyer reveals that the queen desires Solomon because she is like him; she is his mirror image. But she is also a luminous "star" who guides the countess to reflect the divine "Sonne" and, like John the Baptist, to bear witness to his light:

No travels ought th'affected soule to shunne
That this faire heavenly Light desires to see:
This King of kings to whom we all should runne,
To view his Glory and his Majestie;
He without whom we all had been undone,
He that from Sinne and Death hath set us free.
                              (120.1625–30)

It is finally the "Son" within Margaret Clifford who comes to liberate women by unraveling all patriarchal ways of speaking and writing, a willingness perfectly summed up in Christ's willingness to "undoe the Booke":

> He onely worthy to undoe the Booke
> Of our charg'd soules, full of iniquitie,
> Where with the eyes of mercy he doth looke
> Upon our weakeness and infirmitie,
> This is that corner stone that was forsooke,
> Who leaves it, trusts but to uncertaintie:
> This is Gods Sonne, in whom he is well pleased,
> His deere beloved, that his wrath appeased.
> (122.1657–64)

Because, as Saint John reveals, "no man in heave nor in earth . . . was able to open the Boke, neither to loke thereon" (Rev. 5:3), Christ alone can provide this new way of reading; he alone can undo the book. Submitting to the judgment of the Father and the "plots" of men in order to "undoe" them, he discloses himself only at the margins of discourse, in the prophetic and visionary utterances of women. Thus, it is precisely at this moment that he turns his attention upon the Queen of Sheba, granting her the grace and authority that women have been denied:

> Of whom that Heathen Queene obtain'd such grace,
> By honouring but the shadow of his Love,
> That great Judiciall day to have a place,
> Condemning those that doe unfaithfull prove;
> Among the haplesse, happie is her case,
> That her deere Saviour spake for her behove;
> And that her memorable Act should be
> Writ by the hand of true Eternitie.
> (123.1681–88)

Christ validates feminine speech not only by allowing this "Heathen Queene" —a clearly marginal figure—to judge the unfaithful but also by representing her love of wisdom with his own hand. Again following Agrippa, Lanyer foregrounds Matt. 12:41 as the kernel of truth about female speech and writing that patriarchy has suppressed. To all assertions of masculine power and authority, she discloses Christ as the redemptive countertext:

> The Pilgrimes travels, and the Shepheards cares,
> He tooke upon him to enlarge our soules,

What pride hath lost, humilitie repaires,
For by his glorious death he us inroules
In deepe Characters, writ with blood and teares,
Upon those blessed Everlasting scroules;
His hands, his feete, his body and his face,
Whence freely flow'd the rivers of his grace.

(124.1721–28)

It is only by reducing himself that Christ can "enlarge our soules," only by coming in humility that he can restore "what pride hath lost," only by writing in the feminine language of "blood and teares" that he can redeem the book. From this divine communion with human suffering, Lanyer's inspiration flows, spilling over her lines in a lyrical recovery of prophetic truth:

Sweet holy rivers, pure celestiall springs,
Proceeding from the fountaine of our life;
Swift sugred currents that salvation brings,
Cleare chrystall streames, purging all sinne and strife,
Faire floods, where souls do bathe their snow-white wings,
Before they flie to true eternall life:
Sweet Nectar and Ambrosia, food of Saints,
Which, whoso tasteth, never after faints.

(125.1729–36)

Lanyer's language here approaches the apocalyptic, her "currents" carrying redemption and offering the receptive reader a heavenly vision. The concluding stanzas of her poem move progressively toward this glimpse of the eternal as Christ's "hony dropping dew of holy love" (125.1737) enters the mouths and takes form in the words of men who have embraced the same understanding of the Passion. Thus, Stephen, Saint Laurence, Andrew, and John the Baptist, like the women of this text, are completely receptive to divine truth, willing to confront political and religious institutions in prophetic power and even to die at their hands: "Not sparing Kings in what they did not right; / Their noble Actes they seal'd with deerest blood" (128.1813–14). Enacting Christ's passion in a similar willingness to undo patriarchy, their words record the sweetness of the vision they attain. Lanyer closes *Salve* with a portrait of John the Baptist, the greatest, according to Christ, "among them which are begotten of women" (Matt. 11:11). Because he stands up to a corrupt political system, he dies just as Christ does, "for speaking truth according to Gods Word" (128.1820). But his willingness to justify the divine text by speaking from the margins of society reveals a communion he shares with women, one for which he gives his very life.

In form as well as content, *Salve Deus Rex Judaeorum* embodies Agrippa's subversive rereading of Paul, but it goes one step further: it records the voices of women who have been silenced in the pages of the New Testament and it uncovers the politics of that suppression. Behind these voices Lanyer's own voice can also be heard, a voice that becomes deeply personal only in her final poem "To Cookeham." Then, in a last rewriting of Genesis, Lanyer takes us to the "tree" where Margaret Clifford led her "by the hand" (136.162), where Clifford offered the Passion to her in the fruit of her own life. To speak in this way, Lanyer reveals, is to be bound in order to liberate, to be "undone" in order to undo. Consequently, Lanyer closes her work by acknowledging the rich chains "tying" her to the countess—tying her to redeem women and the book.

4

Admitting Adultery
Donne's Versions of the True Church

If any Ragges or Reliques of that Whore have been patched to our Mothers
Robe, we ought to rip it off, and strippe our selves of it.
—Henry Burton, *A Tryall of Private Devotions*

I N 1608, John White, chaplain to King James, published *The Way to the*
True Church, explaining that his work would help readers "find the truth
in every controversie."[1] To give a sense of the ecclesiastical debate in progress,
White introduced the ideas of the Jesuit John Fisher into the margins of
his book, setting them off in darker, smaller print.[2] But he warned his
readership before he did so, telling them that the Romish writer was akin to
the Serpent in the Garden: "But seeing the author thereof, under colour of
directing you in controversies, goeth about to make another Eve of you,
by seducing your mind from the simplicitie that is in Christ, you have
little cause to thanke him, and the lesse to rejoyce in his labour."[3] White
hints that his readers might become an ecclesiastical version of Eve if they
allow this marginal viewpoint to override his own authorized position. And
this is a particularly resonant possibility, White suggests, since the story of
the Fall is not only the story of Adam and Eve but also the story of what
happens to the church in the absence of true government: "Thus the Church
is like a woman fallen from her ancient happinesse, and retaining only some
signes thereof. She has the sheathes and caskets where her ornaments lay,
but the goods themselves she is spoiled of. Not through his carelessness
and negligence that first enriched her, but through their naughtinesse that

---

1. White, *Way to the True Church,* 3.
2. The work was *A Treatise of Faith,* and the Jesuit was really John Percy. Milward traces
the spate of texts responding to the question of the true church in *Religious Controversies,*
143–47.
3. White, *Way to the True Church,* 1.

governed not things as they should have done." Adopting a strategy similar to Aemilia Lanyer, White implicates neither God nor the woman in this ecclesiastical "fall" from "ancient happinesse." It is instead the "government" that has allowed the church to be "spoiled" of her goods, and it is the government that must restore her: "If this be wanting, that God be not pleased, but sinne increase, and so much superstition remaine still in the land unreformed, No humane wisdome can keepe out Gods judgements, but they will come at the last upon us." White therefore highlights the necessary separation of the true church from Rome to foreground the importance of the reformation government now operating in England, a move little different from Spenser's fusion of Una with Elizabeth. At the same time, he recognizes the need for vigilance, even militancy: "we rather wil pul [peace] to us with violence," he states, "so that the true faith withal may be confessed."[4]

As White's text suggests, the purgation of Romish corruption was, for the conformists of the earlier seventeenth century, often conceived in terms of violent and aggressive political action against Spain, France, and other Catholic countries. Consequently, Francis Trigge's lyric preface to his work *A Touchstone, whereby may easelie be discerned the true Catholike faith* reveals the "Woman of true faith" preparing for battle against the "Whore of Babylon."[5] Unlike Spenser's Una, however, Trigge's Woman of Faith wears next to nothing:

> She cloathed is with vile attire,
>> Not pleasant to the eie,
> Her shoulders naked are, her haire
>> Doth out of order lie.
> Her tender armes unarmed are
>> They stand in steede of shield
> Her naked body to defend
>> Not weapons for to yeeld.

As "naked Truth," she needs only faith to protect her. Attacking the crested whore who is clothed with "maine and might," Truth's bare arms prove weapon enough, enabling her to attain victory through the strength of her own hands:

---

4. Ibid., "The Epistle Dedicatorie."
5. Trigge, *A Touchstone, whereby may easelie be discerned the true Catholike faith,* prefatory poem, n.p.

But faith amounting to the skies
   Doth wound her crested head,
Her face she dashes on the ground
   And mouth with blood beraide,
Her eies she putteth out, her winde
   She stoppeth and her breath
Thus Gentilisme, wanting winde:
   Doth see no way but death.

Gone is the eloquent exposé in which Una interprets and contains the epistolary machinations of Duessa. Trigge's naked woman quite literally strangles the life out of her female opponent in the bloodiest of apocalyptic triumphs.

But just how seriously was one to interpret the struggle between the true church and the false represented in the diametrically opposed women of the Apocalypse? And how was a complete reformation to be effected? Despite the argumentative clarity with which White and Trigge attempt to contain their Roman opposition, the prophetic discourse on the subject was unquestionably murky. It was a murkiness John Donne was more than willing to admit in the early decades of the seventeenth century when he replaced White as chaplain to King James.[6]

When Donne also takes up the question of the "true church" in Holy Sonnet 18 (Shawcross 179), he emphasizes the problematic hermeneutics involved in all such interpretations of the Apocalypse. Rather than offering to "direct" readers toward the "truth," he opens his sonnet by making the demand of God himself: "Show me deare Christ, thy spouse, so bright and cleare."[7] Donne's simple request calls attention to the absence of the "spouse" and the absence of that brightness and clarity associated with her. The solutions so frequently offered, he hints, are far from satisfactory. He accordingly highlights their controversial status as potential misinterpretations by turning the "answers" of his time into a series of questions:

6. R. V. Young calls attention to Donne's "ecumenical" inclination, noting that he prefers a "unity based on the form of *any* of the principal churches—Roman, Genevan, or Anglican—to the disunity prevailing in his day" ("Donne's *Holy Sonnets* and the Theology of Grace," 24). Jeanne M. Shami also traces Donne's political discretion ("Donne on Discretion") as do Dave Gray and Jeanne Shami ("Political Advice in Donne's Devotions").

7. Claude J. Summers has provided a convincing interpretation of the relationship between Una, Donne's Holy Sonnet 18, and Herbert's "The British Church" in "The Bride of the Apocalypse and the Quest for True Religion: Donne, Herbert, and Spenser." Quote is from Donne, *The Complete Poetry of John Donne*, 349.1. Future references will be cited parenthetically within the text and will include page and line numbers.

> What, is it she, which on the other shore
> Goes richly painted? or which rob'd and tore
> Laments and mournes in Germany and here?
>
> (349.2–4)

Far from pitting the two women against one another in hand-to-hand combat, Donne calls attention to the representations themselves. While she who goes "on the other shore" is geographically separate from the "rob'd and tore" woman who resides "here," both echo in opposite ways the "whore" who dare not speak her name. At issue, it seems, are their histories—the time, place, and purity of their origins—and it is here that Donne's questions proliferate in a series of broken rhythms:

> Sleepes she a thousand, then peepes up one yeare?
> Is she selfe truth and errs? now new, now'outwore?
> Doth she, 'and did she, and shall she evermore,
> On one, on seaven, or on no hill appeare?
>
> (350.5–8)

In four brief lines, Donne manages to encapsulate hundreds of pages of ecclesiastical controversy. Initially, he calls into question the response that many Protestant writers gave to the history of the church before Luther. In accounting for the thousand-year gap between the apostolic church and the Protestant church in the sixteenth century, John White along with Patrick Forbes, John Napier, Thomas Brightman, and countless others argued that the thousand-year disappearance and reappearance of the true church had been foretold in the Apocalypse.[8] Donne's well-turned question reconceives this time of darkness as a period when the true church "sleepes," and finally "peepes" out upon the world, highlighting an all too obvious lack of vigilance in the true church's behavior.

The alternatives to this line of reasoning, however, prove no more satisfactory. Thus, in the next line Donne dismantles the Catholic claim that they, as the "true church," are the pure original by questioning whether anything concerned with "selfe truth" can be free of error. The Genevan church's

---

8. For example, Napier notes, "Then after 1260 yeares darknesse, was that true Temple of God opened and made manifest, as is plainlie saide in the seventh Trumpet or age. So then, this Temple, the opening, closing, and opening againe thereof agrees so well with the Ecclesiasticall historie in all points after the former senses, that we must conclude, by this temple of God in heaven, to be meaned his holie Church among his heavenly elect upon earth" (*Plaine Discovery*, 32).

position is similarly suspect. In attempting to cover herself historically, her "now new, now'outwore" clothing signals a break with an impure past, but only by refashioning that past. In analyzing the "true church" through this series of questions, Donne bares to public view the very issues that make each ecclesiastical position so untenable.

Thus, in the second set of questions, Donne begins to consider the multiple ways the Roman Catholics, English Churchmen, and Presbyterians are now affirming their unfallen origins by identifying themselves with the bride of the Apocalypse. In seeking to pinpoint the bride's emergence in time and space, their interpretations have turned her actual presence into the ultimate mystery: "Doth she, 'and did she, and shall she evermore, / On one, on seaven, or on no hill appeare?" Finding her becomes impossible in this geographic and hermeneutic quest as the "one" hill of England blurs into the "seaven" of Rome and the "no hill" of Geneva.

Donne, as he begins to question his very mode of questioning, suggests in the sestet that perhaps such overdetermination is itself inappropriate. Perhaps we are not to circumscribe the time and place of the true church's appearance, but to make our search a function of the answer: "Dwells she with us, or like adventuring knights / First travaile we to seeke and then make love?" (350.9–10).[9] With this question, Donne returns to the apocalyptic narrative of Spenser, now approaching it in an inclusive rather than an exclusive way.[10] All "we" who interpret, he suggests—the Roman Catholics, English Churchmen, and Presbyterians—are "traveling/travailing" seekers, each motivated by the same labor to reproduce ourselves; indeed, our desires prompt the refashioning of "truth" articulated here. To this dilemma, the

9. Anthony Low argues that Donne here "substitutes the Church for God as an intermediary in the usual trope" and so creates a ménage à trois involving Christ, the speaker, and the spouse, as both become rivals for her affection ("The Holy Ghost Is Amorous in His Metaphors," 214–15). I believe that while the speaker addresses Christ throughout, he maintains his focus on how the "spouse" might be known to men here, questioning at this point whether she is already present or to be revealed at the end of the quest (like Una in Spenser's poem). As both bride and elect "body," she is joined to Christ and men both. This, however, is no ménage à trois, her transcendent union purifying all human error.

10. Claude J. Summers, like James Nohrnberg, evaluates the nature of this interconnection between Spenser and Donne. Nohrnberg says that the "paradox of the errant unity of the faith lies behind Donne's *Holy Sonnet 18*. Donne threatens the bride with the commonness of Duessa, and doubtless he would say that Redcrosse has not yet 'known' Una. In the meantime, like errant Israel, Una is likened to a harlot" (*The Analogy of the Faerie Queene*, 212). I believe, however, that Donne rewrites Una as "open" and therefore "known" to all who will embrace the "dove" of peace, a position that revises Claude Summers's position only slightly. Summers argues for a transcendent, invisible consummation.

speaker foresees one possible answer: "Betray kind husband thy spouse to our sights, / And let myne amorous soule court thy mild Dove" (350.11–12). Cognizant now that his opening "Show me" can never resolve the question, the speaker requests a universal disclosure. Built into this demand are major ironies, however. Would a "kind husband" reveal his "spouse" to those who would seduce her? Would he "betray" her to "our sights" if our only purpose were to shoot down the "Dove"? The sexual and social potential for violence within the request must be contained if the true church is to emerge—if the "Dove" is to brood anew. Consequently, Donne's final couplet, echoing the Song of Solomon, suggests precisely how the "dove" might best be "known": "Who is most trew, and pleasing to thee, then / When she'is embrac'd and open to most men" (350.13–14). As Donne has been hinting throughout, the "whore" echoing beneath each ecclesiastical position (and paradoxically contained in each church's version of the Antichristian "Other") is, in fact, the bride of Christ. This true church can be known only when the violence and antipathy of each ecclesiastical position is itself contained, when, as Donne hints, each courts the "Dove" in all her mildness. He thus suggests that the "way to the True Church" is found in an open embrace of Otherness and difference rather than in the exclusionary purity so often foregrounded in the controversial works of the time.[11]

Through this shocking elision of "whore" and "bride," Donne unites the true church with the bride in Song of Sol. 1:5 who is "black, but comely," erring but beloved.[12] At least initially in his sermons, however, Donne takes a far more traditional stance. Then, like his family friend George Herbert, he identifies the English Church as noteworthy for avoiding the seductive extremism of the churches on either side of her. She refuses to find herself "Either in a *painted Church,* on one side, or in *a naked Church,* on another; a Church in a *Dropsie,* overflowne with *Ceremonies,* or a Church in a *Consumption,* for want of such Ceremonies, as the primitive Church found usefull, and beneficiall for the advancing of the glory of God, and the

11. Donne's critique of his contemporaries as problematic lovers of the "true church" is similarly illuminated in "Satire III," believed to be written much earlier. Richard Strier offers a thorough analysis in "Radical Donne: Satire III." I see Donne as less radical, however, agreeing with J. B. Leishman that Donne's commitment, like Spenser's, is to the "laborious process of historical or semi-historical research" (*The Monarch of Wit,* 116).

12. William R. Mueller suggests that because Donne's poetry was probably not motivated by extraneous considerations like political advancement in his early career or a court audience during his deanship of St. Pauls, it may be closest to his "real" position (*John Donne, Preacher,* 18).

devotion of the Congregation."[13] Here much closer to the typical evaluation, Donne nevertheless employs the metaphors of sex and food to distinguish the visible body of the true church from her erring sisters. Deriving her clothing and ceremonies from the primitive church of the past, she avoids in her spiritual communion both the sensual appetite of Rome and the anorexia of Geneva. Through these metaphors, Donne also articulates his own perspective in the divisive debate over the rejection or use of ceremonies then occurring in the Stuart church; he argues that the English Church neither flatly rejects ceremonies nor accepts them whole cloth, but employs them moderately—for the glory of God and the benefit of the congregation.

Gradually over time, however, Donne begins to admit in his sermons the radical position he sketches in Holy Sonnet 18. What I will examine in the remainder of this chapter is how ecclesiastical and royal politics eventually lead Donne to reveal his hand and, in the process, to rewrite the very nature of prophetic discourse. Moving away from the dominant concerns of prophecy at the close of the Elizabethan age—the threat of the "Roman" Antichrist and the necessary purity of the true church—Donne focuses on the inclusive nature of the visible church instead. His prophetic discourse thus reflects the gradual erosion of what had been, up to the early seventeenth century, a conformist and Puritan consensus. But even the members of this consensus, Peter Lake has shown, disagreed over the issue of the Antichrist.[14] Briefly, the terms of the argument can be described as follows.

In the late sixteenth century, Whitgift of the conformist wing and Whitaker of the Puritan wing had taken opposing stands on the threat of Antichrist when Whitaker invoked it to support further reforms in the English Church. As Lake notes, the Puritan position had become international, an "amalgam of the opinions of a whole series of European Protestant divines between whom an effective doctrinal consensus was assumed." The conformist position, in contrast, involved only the English Church; consequently, Whitgift and the conformist divines who succeeded him did not allow the threat of Antichrist to influence their decisions regarding contemporary affairs, especially those involving foreign policy. Unlike their Puritan counterparts, they did not believe it was necessary for Protestant countries to go to war to prevent fellow Christians from being forced into idolatry.[15]

13. Donne, *Sermons of John Donne*, 6:284. Future references will be cited parenthetically within the text and will include volume and page numbers.
14. Lake, "Significance of the Elizabethan Identification."
15. Ibid., 174, 176.

By the seventeenth century, this distinction drove a stake through the heart of the Protestant consensus as King James's foreign policy forced the issue into the limelight. Not only did James refuse to send troops on behalf of his daughter, Elizabeth, and Protestant son-in-law, Frederik of Bohemia, who were facing Spanish opposition, but he also attempted to bring peace in the matter by wedding his son Charles to the infanta, Maria, of Spain. Neither of these actions was acceptable to the Puritan wing of the English Church, for its membership believed in the militant conquest of the "Whore," not marriage to her.

By downplaying militant apocalyptic interpretation in his own prophetic discourse, Donne seeks to realign the political and spiritual sympathies of the English nation, to alter the perspectives of those brought up believing in the necessary destruction of the Romish whore. Almost by necessity, he chooses not to identify with the revolutionary prophet of the Apocalypse but rather with the Prophet Hosea who, in order to incarnate the love of God for his erring people, marries an adulterer to reveal the depths of divine love.

And the reasons for this choice are obvious. By the 1620s, according to Christopher Hill, Presbyterian, Anabaptist, and Separatist ministers were locating the Roman Antichrist in the English Church, visible to them in the renewed emphasis on vestments and ceremonies, the persecution of godly preachers, and the ambition of worldly bishops occupying seats of judicature.[16] In responding to these attacks, Donne "internalizes the enemy," much as Debora Shuger suggests, but less, I think, to direct "aggression against the self" than to redefine the very nature of prophecy.[17] In seeking to reform the apocalyptic mode of interpretation that had demonized Rome as the corrupt and seducing "Other," Donne gradually turns his focus on the enemy within and on scapegoating itself. The process of sitting in judgment, he argues, may be the real source of Antichristian error. Thus, while his prophecy continues to have a social and political edge, Donne turns that edge increasingly against those who foster division within the church and

---

16. Quoting Thomas Taylor's *Christ's Victorie over the Dragon* (1633), Christopher Hill clarifies the extent to which people began to apply the Romish threat to the bishops in the ecclesiastical hierarchy (*Antichrist*, 55; see also Paul Christianson, *Reformers and Babylon*, 246). The upsurge in this kind of thinking continued through the civil war, but as Anthony Milton, Christopher Hill, and others have noted, very few books were licensed on the subject of Antichrist from 1633 to 1640 while Laud was Archbishop of Canterbury (Hill, *Antichrist*, 38–39; A. Milton, *Catholic and Reformed*, 120).

17. While I find Shuger's analysis of Donne intellectually compelling, I have trouble accepting her political and psychological evaluation of Donne (*Habits of the Thought*, 183–84).

within the state.[18] Choosing scriptural texts that are particularly relevant to this purpose, Donne comments in subtle ways on the troubled ecclesiastical politics of his time.

A clear example can be found in his sermon on Esther 4:16, a text in which Queen Esther, in the hope of protecting her people and herself, declares a fast and, against the law of the land, enters the king's presence unrequested. To contain the subversive potential of this text, Donne differentiates Esther's actions from the Separatists of his time. First of all, he argues, Esther acts legally when she orders a public fast: "All Conventicles, all Assemblies, must have this character, this impression upon them, That they be *Legitima,* lawful. . . . And onely those are lawful which are made by the Authority of the State" (5:218). Donne is of course using a loaded term in speaking of "Conventicles," the word commonly deployed to describe the private meetings of Romans Catholics and Puritans. That there are exceptions to this "law," he also grudgingly admits: "In times of persecution, when no exercise of true Religion is admitted, these private Meetings may not be denied to be lawful" (5:218). This, however, puts Donne in the problematic situation of designating where to locate "true Religion." He locates it, much as he does in Sonnet 18, in terms of its policy of open admission as he focuses on the inclusive "taste" of the people of God. Through the metaphor of eating, Donne hints that food, like sex, involves the entire ecclesiastical Body in loving communion. Consequently, members of the true church eat their spiritual food in the orderly Eucharistic ceremonies of the Church of England. Those who go elsewhere "steal" their spiritual food in private because it is "not so dressed, so dished, so sauced, so served in, as we would have it; but accompanied with some other ceremonies then are agreeable to our taste." In this evaluation of culinary separation, Donne momentarily mocks the theological gourmands of his time while still managing to include them in his corporate "we." To move away from the church for reasons of taste, he argues, is to "steal" from it in both senses of the word, and this "is an inexcusable Theft" (5:218).

To reveal the nature of the communion he advocates, Donne tests those contemporary prophets who advise separation against the actions of the prophet Daniel. Daniel, he notes, chose not to "induce any new manner

---

18. Early on Whitgift had dubbed Thomas Cartwright "the tail of Antichrist," using Cartwright's own words against him. Cartwright of course inveighed against the "tail" of Antichrist present in episcopacy, while Whitgift located the "tail" in Cartwright's promotion of schism (Hill, *Antichrist,* 44). Quite naturally, the Laudians make the same move several decades later, turning the Separatists into the Antichrist.

of worshipping God" (5:219), even when an inappropriate law was enacted and worship was suppressed. Behaving instead in a public and open way, Daniel set "open his windows," and "prayed in his Chamber." In contrast, the prophets who now pray and preach do so with subversive, even seditious intention:

> So when these men pray in their Conventicles, for the confusion, and rooting out of Idolatry and Antichrist, they intend by their Idolatry, a Cross in Baptism; and by their Antichrist, a man in a Surpless; and not onely the persons, but the Authority that admits this Idolatry, and this Antichristianism. As vapors and winds shut up in Vaults, engender Earth-quakes; so these particular spirits in their Vault-Prayers, and Cellar-Service, shake the Pillars of State and Church. (5:219)

Such private prayers—prompted by openly subversive interpretations of the Apocalypse—are, in Donne's view, capable of undermining the entire power structure of England.

By 1620, with the Spanish Match in complicated negotiations and James moving daily closer to an international peace, Donne briefly returned to earlier apocalyptic interpretation to buoy up flagging confidence in the nation's Protestant commitments. In a sermon titled "I judge no man," Donne traces the distance between Christ and the pope in the latter's willingness to excommunicate, judge, condemn, and "Massacre" (2:328) millions. Because Donne's primary concern is with error closer to home, however, he concludes by attacking two other errors in judgment along with the pope's: those who "judge out of humane affections and passions, by detraction and calumny" and those who "judge so as that our condemnation should be irremediable in this life" (2:334). Slander and predestination to damnation make it into the same problematic category. At the same time, however, Donne reflected on the Spanish Armada of 1588 and the Gunpowder Plot of 1605 to assure his listeners that King James had forgotten neither the recent past, nor the subversive potential of the "Roman" Antichrist: "He that by Gods mercy to us, leads us, is as sure that the *Pope* is *Antichrist*, now, as he was *then*; and we that are blessedly led by him, are as sure, that their doctrine is the doctrine of *Devils*, now, as we were then" (3:124). Framing his analysis with a reminder that God has sanctioned King James's rule, he also affirms, for those less convinced, that "we are blessedly led by him." Despite the king's recent political maneuvers, Protestant spirituality, he underscores, is very much alive.

As negotiations continued, however, this position became more problematic. By 1621, Donne was stressing peace in an almost incantatory way—in a futile attempt to assuage English fears: "Peace in the Church, peace in the State, peace in thy house, peace in thy heart, is a faire Modell, and a lovely designe even of the heavenly Jerusalem which is *Visio Pacis,* where there is no object but peace" (4:49). To redirect the attitudes of his listeners, Donne makes a politically astute choice. He moves away from international policy and progressively closer to home, his rhetoric gradually downshifting from the politics of the church to those of the state, to those of the family, to those of the individual: "*Antichrist* alone is enemy enough; but never carry this consideration beyond thy self. As long as there remaines in thee one sin, or the sinfull gain of that one sin, so long there is one enemy, and where there is one enemy, there is no peace" (4:51). With one deft maneuver, "never carry this consideration beyond thy self," Donne turns the political fear of Antichrist into a private matter, the international threat of Romish invasion into that creeping "sin" within the self. Donne thus contains the fear of Antichrist by reconceiving the foreign in domestic terms, and placing it, through his psychological sleight of hand, under the control of his listeners. Here is a battle they can fight. Here—on the most intimate ground—is a victory they can win.

But the politics involved in the Spanish Match would not vanish into thin air, and Donne had to convince his listeners that King James had not gone over to the enemy. In a sermon preached at Paul's Cross at the height of the controversy over James's behavior—just after James had issued in 1622 "Directions on Preaching" to silence his growing opposition—Donne found it necessary to carry out more damage control. Now he had to argue that James was right to suppress zealous Protestant ministers who, in their outspoken interpretations of apocalyptic prophecy, hoped to stave off the Romish corruption of the English nation.

Speaking directly to these fears, Donne immediately acknowledges the difference between making peace in temporal affairs and making peace in spiritual affairs: "Now, though there be a *Beati Pacifici,* a blessing reserved to *Peace-makers,* to the *Peace-maker, our Peace-Maker,* who hath sometimes effected it in some places, and always seriously and chargeably, and honourably endeavoured it in all places, yet there is a *spirituall Warre,* in which, *Maledicti Pacifici;* Cursed bee they that goe about to make Peace, and to make all one, The warres betweene *Christ and Beliall*" (4:192–93). James has the right to make peace, he acknowledges, noting that James does so in admirable fashion. But does he have the right to force ministers, preachers of the Gospel engaged in "spiritual warfare," to do the same? Does he not risk quenching the Spirit of God that Paul had expressly warned against?

So a Man may quench the spirit in himselfe, if hee smother it, suffocate it, with worldly pleasures, or profits, and he may quench it in others, if he withdraw that favour, or that helpe, which keepes that Man, who hath the spirit of Prophesie, the unction of Preaching, in a cheerefull discharge of his duty. Preaching then being *Gods Ordinance,* to beget Faith, to take away preaching, were to disarme God, and to quench the spirit; for by that *Ordinance, he fights from heaven.* (4:195)

Temporal profit can quench the voice of the prophet; denying a prophet a livelihood can strip him of spiritual power, and both are potential outcomes of the king's recent "Directions." Punning on "ordinance," Donne even hints that royal "ordinance" can, in its bid for peace, be misdirected, and end up "disarming" God himself. Yet this is precisely what preachers must guard against: "That warre *God* hath kindled, and that warre must bee maintained, and maintaind by his way; and his way, and his *Ordinance* in this warre, is Preaching" (4:194). Donne leaves in suspense his response to the possibility of royal error and establishes greater rapport with his audience by concentrating on the importance of preaching itself. Turning back to the Apocalypse, he notes that God calls his ministers "stars" and ordains them to preach in order: "Not with a peace, and indifferencie to contrary Opinions in fundamentall doctrines, not to shuffle religions together, and make it all one which you chuse, but a peace with persons, an abstinence from contumelies, and revilings. . . . A perfect hatred is that which a perfect, that is, a charitable man may beare, which is still to hate *Errors,* not *Persons*" (4:196–97). Gradually, Donne begins to reconceive the nature of prophecy by rejecting altogether the apocalyptic strategy of demonizing the "Other." Indeed, he argues, to hate "Persons" and to misrepresent them through name-calling is not to preach Christ at all. Paul had, for this reason, informed the entire Thessalonian congregation that they must withdraw themselves *"from all that walke Inordinatè"* (4:197). Donne glosses the passage in terms particularly relevant to the seventeenth-century church and King James's "Directions" of 1622: "from all such as preach *suspiciously,* and *jealously.* And be the garden never so faire, wil make the world beleeve, there is a *Snake* under every leafe, be the intention never so sincere, will presage, and prognosticate, and predivine sinister and mischievous effects from it" (4:197). No longer is Rome the "seducer" in the margins, for the problem is now at the center of the church. What must be subjected to scrutiny, then, is the "*Snake* under ever leafe," brought into frightening existence by the "prediviners" who foresee a "sinister" end for England.

But does King James have the right to suppress preaching itself, to direct his "ordinance" at the church? By way of answer, Donne refers his listeners to the second canon where the British people had given *"the King the same authoritie in causes Ecclesiasticall, that the godly Kings of Iudah, and the Christian Emperors in the primitive Church had"* (4:199). Moreover, Donne argues, James's "Directions" are not so much a "suppression" of preaching as a renewed emphasis on the kind of preaching revealed in the primitive church: "to reduce Preaching neerer to the manner of those Primitive times, when God gave so evident, and remarkable blessings to mens Preaching" (4:201). It is this ordinance—and this emphasis—that Donne quite willingly embraces: "I was not willing only, but glad to have my part therein, that as, in the feare of God, I have alwayes preached to you the *Gospell of Christ Iesus,* who is the *God* of your Salvation; So in the testimony of a good conscience, I might now preach to you, the *Gospell of the Holy ghost,* who is the *God of peace,* of unitie, and concord" (4:201–2). The "ordinance" and the threat of a "Spiritual War" have been defused and contained in the course of the sermon. By carefully rereading James's "Directions," Donne reconceives his "Ordinance" as a pacifistic, nonmilitant charge, aimed at fostering "unitie" rather than blowing up Protestant commitment.

In fact, Donne argues, the "Directions" are intended to accomplish this peace by disclosing a method validated by history: King James requires his preachers to be "conversant in *Antiquitie*" (4:202), since, the king now recognizes, ecclesiastical history holds the key to the ongoing reformation of the church: "His Majesty therfore cals us to look *Quid Primum,* what was first in the whole *Church?* And againe, *Quid primum, when we received the Reformation in this Kingdom, by what meanes,* (as his *Majestie* expresseth it) *Papistry was driven out, and Puritanisme kept out, and wee delivered from the Superstition of the Papist, and the madnesse of the Anabaptists"* (4:202). King James here directs preachers to return to their origins, to the church in antiquity as well as the church "delivered" during the Reformation. Only with these models clearly in view will they discover the means to the middle way and find the appropriate foundation for a truly reformed church.[19]

But it was not quite that simple, especially since recent reformation history, encoded in Bale's *Image of Bothe Churches,* Foxe's *Acts and Monuments,* Spenser's *Faerie Queene,* and countless other Protestant texts, advocated the

---

19. Throughout his sermons, Donne follows this mandate, looking back to the fathers of the early church as well as to the fathers of the recent reformation to discern his prophetic style and to trace the church of the "middle way" that always navigates between erring extremists.

complete annihilation of the Romish whore in the most humiliating and destructive of political acts. As I have argued here, King James's repeated efforts to establish peace placed court preachers in the position of revising the militant nature of apocalyptic interpretation, an agenda even more important after 1625 when Prince Charles married Henrietta Maria.

The Protestant reaction to this marriage was less than favorable. Employing the apocalyptic awareness of Spenser, Henry Burton hinted at his opinion by drawing an example from Old Testament history. King Asa, he stated, chose to root out all "Antichristian Idolatry" rather than give it a place in the kingdom. With one powerful swing of his political sledgehammer, he took aim at the new queen: Asa "spared not his own mother Maachah, removing her from being Queene, because she had made an idol in a grove."[20]

Those closer to the court advocated no such drastic measures. In a work titled *The True Church Shewed to all men that desire to be members of the Same,* Griffith Williams reconsidered the history of the true church to identify the visible church with the Prophet Hosea's wanton wife. He thus reinforced the fact that the true church, despite her adultery, remains wedded to and claimed by God:

> Though in time she should forsake her first faith, and disloyally turne her eyes and her heart after other lovers, yea most shamelessly play the harlot in the sight of the world, and bring up many children of fornication unto her husband; yet till there passeth a publike renouncing and divorcing the one from the other, shee is still publikely accounted and taken for the wife of him, whose wife she publikely professeth her selfe to be; even so it is betwixt God and his visible Church: while it retaineth the seales and pledges of his covenant.[21]

Early in 1627, in a sermon titled "Take heed what you heare," Donne chooses to make his own comments on the king's marriage. Employing the words of Christ to contain the gossip and slander now rampant throughout the kingdom, Donne establishes the difference between the Roman Church and the English Church while acknowledging a certain amount of adultery in both. Initially, he focuses on the visibility of God's church and the power of its ministry, deploying the same "ordinance" he uses in 1622: "He hath constituted a *Church,* in a Visibility, in an eminency, *as a City upon a hill;* And in this Church, his Ordinance is Ordinance indeed; his Ordinance of preaching batters the soule, and by that breach, the Spirit enters; His

---

20. Burton, *Israel's Fast,* 32.
21. Williams, *True Church Shewed,* 26.

Ministers are an *Earth-quake,* and shake an earthly soule" (7:396). Donne here returns to the ambiguous terrain of Sonnet 18, becoming far more specific in terms of contemporary ecclesiastical politics. He now identifies the "true church" with the "City upon a hill." Emphasizing its visibility as well as its "eminence," he places it above the activities of Separatists and Roman Catholics, distinguishing it on the one hand from those who meet in secret, and linking it on the other to the kings who empower it.

In developing the importance of the true church's visibility, Donne highlights the fact that a "Conventicle Schismatick" refuses the divine exercise of "publique prayer," choosing rather to be heard "in his Pamphlets" and "in his disciples" (7:397). Rejecting the communion of the saints, he writes subversive texts and even calls his own disciples. In developing the importance of the true church's "eminence," Donne argues that since "Christ hath made you *Regale Sacerdotium,* Kings and Priests, in your proportion, *Take heed what you hear,* in derogation of either the State, or the Church" (7:407). The Holy Spirit, Donne argues, "imprints" a text quite different from that of the heretical "Schismatick." "Declaring ill affections towards others" as themselves "cursed," "God," he asserts, "hath imprinted in thee characters of a better office, and of more dignity, of a Royall Priesthood; as you have sparks of Royaltie in your soules, Take heed what you hear of State-government; as you have sparks of holy fire, and Priesthood in your soules, Take heed what you heare of Church-government" (7:408–9). Those who speak against this "government," this "priesthood," Donne suggests, speak in effect against themselves as well as against the divine order God has established.

Having broached this point, Donne focuses once again on the true church as the spouse of Christ, but this time his words have immediate political relevance, given recent prophetic diatribes against Henrietta Maria:[22]

> The Church is the spouse of Christ: Noble husbands do not easily admit defamations of their wives. Very religious Kings may have had wives, that may have retained some tincture, some impressions of errour, which they may have sucked in their infancy, from another Church, and yet would be loth, those wives should be publikely traduced to be Heretiques, or passionately proclaimed to be Idolaters for all that. A Church may lacke something of exact perfection, and yet that Church should not be said to be a supporter of Antichrist, or a limme of the beast, or a thirster after the cup of *Babylon,* for all that. From extream to extream, from east to west, the *Angels* themselves cannot come, but by passing the middle way between. (7:409)

22. See the editors' introduction to Donne, *Sermons of John Donne,* 7:41.

Writing the nasty apocalyptic evaluations of contemporary prophets into his sermon to articulate what "should not be said," Donne establishes a striking connection between the marriage of King Charles and the marriage of Christ to his people. Displacing the Spenserian paradigm in which Duessa's "beast" and "cup" require her exposure as "heretique," Donne foregrounds the "Noble husband" who claims his beloved "spouse" despite her adulterous past. Even as he admits the fact that the spouse of the king and the spouse of Christ "may lacke something of exact perfection," he makes the very betweenness of their progress the sign that they are engaged in reform. Nevertheless, Donne's somewhat tactless allusion to Henrietta Maria immediately put him in disfavor with King Charles, though he was subsequently forgiven by William Laud's account: "His Majesty King Charles forgave to Doctor Donne certain slips in a sermon preached on Sunday, April 1."[23] Donne's intention, of course, was to trace a middle way that was becoming, even for Donne, increasingly difficult to maintain:

> He that is come to any end, remembers when he was not at the middle way; he was not there as soon as he set out. It is the posture reserved for heaven, to sit down, at the right hand of God; Here our consolation is, that God reaches out his hand to the receiving of those who come towards him; And nearer to him, and to the institutions of his Christ, can no Church, no not of the *Reformation,* be said to have come, then ours does. (7:409)

Between setting out and arriving, Donne argues, is the "middle way" that the true church must always take toward Christ.[24] Rejecting those ends that provide easy closure or final answers, this spouse makes her way onward, awaiting only the "hand of God" who receives all.

But Donne also finds it necessary to respond to those who claim that the English Church would be at last purified if she adopted the discipline of the reformed churches on the Continent. Here, Donne cleverly snags his opposition in their own trap: "It is an ill nature in any man, to be rather apt to conceive jealousies, and to suspect his Mothers honour, or his sisters chastity, then a strange womans. It is an irreverent unthankfulnesse, to think worse of that Church, which hath bred us, and fed us, and led us thus far

---

23. Laud, diary entry for April 4, 1627, in *The Works of the Most Reverend Father in God, William Laud, D.D.,* 3:204.

24. Anna K. Nardo traces John Donne's playful habit of mind in continually articulating a "middle way," but this had its serious side as well, apparent in Donne's handling of controversy ("John Donne at Play in Between").

towards God, then of a forein Church, though *Reformed* too, and in a good degree" (7:409). Setting the English Church as Mother against a "strange woman," Donne hints at the adultery such foreign allegiances indicate. The "illness," he suggests, is not in the purity of the home church but in the mind of the maligners. Yet thankfulness would be the more appropriate response to a "Mother" who has done so much for "us" he cautions, his internal rhymes echoing with each resounding "bred," "fed," and "led" the maternal love of the true church.

In this sermon, Donne does not turn his prophetic edge only against the words of "Schismatick" pamphleteers and Roman Catholics, however. That would leave the greater part of his audience in an overly comfortable "middle." He also calls attention to the rationalizing inner speech in which high-placed members of his congregation daily engage: "This voice may bring great officers, to transfer their inaccessiblenesse, upon necessary State, when it is an effect of their own lazinesse, or indulgence to their pleasures; and this voice may bring rich landlords to transfer all their oppression of tenants, to the necessity of supporting the charge of wives and children, when it is an effect of their profusenesse and prodigality" (7:412). Here, the point of his prophetic edge touches issues very close to home, the "lazy" state official, the hard, uncaring landlord. And visible reform—in the social, economic, and spiritual realms—becomes the requirement. Throughout this sermon, then, Donne turns repeatedly to the "print" metaphor, first the printing of scandal, then the "imprint" of the Holy Spirit, and finally the "printing" of the divinely transformed life as a visible text: "He that desires to *Print* a book, should much more desire, *to be* a book; to do some such exemplar things, as men right read, and relate, and profit by" (7:410). The scandal-mongering prophets of the present moment are here supplanted by the "profit" to be found in the private and public life as a divine text.

Given this focus, it is hardly surprising that when Donne takes up the question of prophecy, he defines it as a textual act conveyed in epistolary form: as a letter, written and delivered by God to a reading audience. His awareness of the power of letters as units of social exchange capable of admitting the writer to a vast network of relationships is accordingly transferred to the power of the divine exchange: "All comes from Gods hand; and from his hand, by way of hand-writing, by way of letter, and instruction to us. And therefore to ascribe things wholly to nature, to fortune, to power, to second causes, this is to mistake the hand, not to know Gods hand" (8:305).[25] Divine messages, Donne suggests, are implicit in all social, political, and natural events, yet we fail to read them as such, even though these "letters" have our own names upon them. At the same time, Donne asserts, whenever we see God's handwriting, we must be extremely careful to read no one's mail but our own:

> In every judgement, God writes to the King; but it becomes not me to open the Kings letter, nor to prescribe the King his interpretation of that judgment. In every such letter, in every judgement God writes to the State; but I will not open their letter, nor prescribe them their interpretation of that judgement; God, who of his goodnesse hath vouchsafed to write unto them in these letters, of his abundant goodnesse interprets himselfe to their religious hearts. (8:306)

Donne relegates the interpretation of prophecy to a particular readership, in this case, to those engaged in political activity, whether that be the king or Parliament. God who has written them, he argues, will interpret his particular meaning to them, will inform them what must be done. In essence, then, Donne declines the political dimension of the prophet's role, refusing to interpret divine letters to officials of state; he affirms instead a series of private readings that involve his listening audience: "But then, in every such letter, in every judgement, God writes to me too; and that letter I will open, and read that letter; I will take knowledge that it is Gods hand to me, and I will study the will of God to me in that letter; and I will write back again to my God and return him an answer, in the amendment of my life, and give him my reformation for his information" (8:306). What each reader is responsible for, Donne indicates, is not the king's actions nor the state's actions nor even the church's actions; what he or she must understand is "Gods hand to me," and to such mail God demands a correct and deeply personal response. In this way, Donne manages to deny authority to recent sociopolitical interpretations of the Apocalypse— certainly a political maneuver—by forcing his listeners to focus on their responsibilities only.

Moreover, Donne argues (perhaps thinking back to Sonnet 18), the Apocalypse is an enigmatic, largely indecipherable letter: "So, many particulars, concerning the calling of the Jews, concerning the time, and place, and person, and duration, and actions of Antichrist, concerning the generall

---

25. Jonathan Goldberg comments extensively on the power of "letters" in Donne's life in *James I and the Politics of Literature* (211).

Judgement, and other things, that lye yet, as an Embryon, as a child in the mothers wombe, embowelled in the wombe of prophecie, are yet but as clouds in the eyes, as riddles in the understandings of the learnedst men" (8:302). Employing the imagery of conception for prophetic revelation as the woman prophets do, Donne argues in opposition to them that prophetic truth has not yet taken visible form—has not yet been reproduced. In fact, he notes, accurate prediction is impossible since Christ "enwraps not onely his Apostles, but himselfe in a cloud" (8:302), seeing no further into times and seasons than they do. The Apocalypse remains impossibly obscure and enigmatic.

By moving the epic contest between Christ and Antichrist from the geographical terrain of Rome or England to the heart of each individual and by turning the threat inward, to that division occurring within the self, Donne meets his more zealous Protestant listeners on the very ground they understand best: the adultery-prone realm of the human heart. Deflecting attention away from foreign policy, the new queen, and suspect royal "ordinances," Donne seeks to advance the Stuart king's desire for peace at home and abroad. Moreover, his focus on the inner life, particularly his emphasis on the importance of preaching the Word to facilitate transformation, enables him to engage those of strong Calvinist sympathies, and, in the process, to suppress radical, separatist strands of Puritanism. In essence, Donne negotiates his way across a prophetic minefield by linking private reformation spirituality with the ceremonies of "Antiquity," dressing the bride in what many later came to see as the "Whore's" clothes.[26]

As I have argued here, Sonnet 18 allows us to understand this inclusive habit of mind as it is gradually revealed in the political and prophetic choices Donne makes as a preacher. Hints of this habit of mind appear in "A Litanie," and Holy Sonnet 14 (Shawcross 171) as well, offering new insights into Donne's prophetic politics regarding the nature of the true church.

"A Litanie" is, like many of Donne's sermons, a text that negotiates the boundaries between the personal and the political by using as a model the individual and corporate prayers of an entire congregation. In seeking to

---

26. As Milton puts it quite eloquently in *The Reason of Church Government:* "Do not, ye church maskers, while Christ is clothing upon our bareness with his righteous garment to make us acceptable in his Father's sight, do not, as ye do, cover and hide his righteous verity with the polluted clothing of your ceremonies to make it seem more decent in your own eyes" (*John Milton: Complete Poems and Major Prose,* 673–74).

reform both realms, the voice of the poem attempts to find those lingering in that middle state between divinely offered gift and human transformation. Consequently, when Donne considers "The Prophets" in this work he distinguishes them from the schismatic prophets of his time by associating them with "harmony"—in fact, with "Church Organs," the very instrument that some Puritans and Separatists refused to hear. Here, the prophets' insight, rendered in divine poetry, brings people of the Word together, since it has the power to "unite, but not confound" (359.67). Nevertheless, the speaker notes as his voice turns self-critical, the poetry of the prophets must not become an excuse for personal excesses; the speaker too must find the middle way between "seeking secrets" and "Poetiqueness" (359.72).

As he turns to the nature of the church in "A Litanie," Donne acknowledges its corruption. The Virgins, he suggests, now speaking in a communal voice,

> have not obtain'd of thee,
> That or thy Church, or I
> Should keep, as they, our first integrity;
> Divorce thou sinne in us, or bid it die,
> And call chast widowhead Virginitie.
> (361.104–8)

Here, Donne comes to terms with the error in the present church, and thus with the need for radical reform. Taking a firm Protestant stance, he leaves the strength to carry out such purification to the justifying and sanctifying power of God. Only God, he hints, can reform ecclesiastical waywardness and give her a new, virginal name.

It is in Sonnet 14, however, that Donne develops this aspect of the church most fully. Here the speaking voice might well be associated with the voice of the church and, as I have hinted here, with the voice of Hosea's erring wife. Donne gives dramatic form to her predicament in order to underscore the traumatic nature of the reform that the church must undergo. Clearly under siege, as indeed the seventeenth-century church was, this woman as errant church directs her words to Christ, requesting that divine force that can alone liberate her: "Batter my heart, three person'd God; for, you / As yet but knocke, breathe, shine, and seeke to mend" (344.1–2). Initially, she acknowledges the limitations of Old as well as New Testament prophecy in what God "as yet" carries out. It would appear that the gentle "knock" of Christ in Rev. 3:20, the "breathing" of the Spirit in John 20:22, the "shining" features of God himself in Rev. 1:16—focused as they are on seeking "to mend" the House of the Lord (2 Chron. 24:12)—are not enough.[27] His woman as true church has far more drastic measures in mind: "That I may rise, and stand, o'erthrow mee, 'and bend / Your force, to breake, blowe, burn and make me new" (344.3–4). Again drawing on prophecy, the speaker focuses on the violent activities of a God in the process of remaking his beloved: consequently, he "breaks the yoke" off of her as Jeremiah prophesies, "blowing" down walls, and "burning" up the last vestiges of idolatry.[28] The purpose, as she suggests, is to "make me new," an echo of the most profound change effected in Old Testament prophecy: "Then will I sprinkle clean water upon you, and ye shall be clean: from all your filthiness, and from all your idols, will I cleanse you. A new heart also will I give you, and a new spirit will I put within you; and I will take away the stony heart from out of your flesh" (Ezek. 36:25–26). The remaining ten lines of the sonnet trace precisely how this occurs, now given dramatic form in the militant language of war and sexual conquest. Unaided by "Reason," empowered only by her capacity to recognize the knots of the "enemy" who has bound her to him in a parody of "betrothal," she requests God to liberate her from her present corruption:

> Divorce mee, 'untie, or breake that knot againe,
> Take mee to you, imprison mee, for I
> Except you'enthrall mee, never shall be free,
> Nor ever chast, except you ravish me.
>
> (344.11–14)[29]

If the church is to be liberated, she suggests (and Donne through her), it will occur through the paradoxical tension of a God going to extremes— imprisoning and enthralling, ravishing and purifying. Indeed, it is only when God joins himself to the "true church" in the end that he effects a final

27. In these genteel movements is quite possibly a veiled critique of the pacifistic prophetic strategies advocated by Lancelot Andrewes and James Buckeridge. Donne may well be hinting that "to mend" the church through contemporary efforts to beautify the visible structure is rather wide of the mark of true reform.

28. See Hos. 10:2, Ezek. 21:31, 22:21, and Jer. 34–36.

29. Here, Donne adopts the terms that conformist churchmen Joseph Hall was employing to characterize the Roman Church, hinting that the English Church (and he himself) is complicit in the same adultery and need for purification. Hall says: "A sacred place loseth not the holiness with the demolished walls, no more doth the Roman lose the claim of a true visible church by her manifold and deplorable corruptions. Her unsoundness is not less apparent than her being. If she were once the spouse of Christ, and her adulteries are known, yet the divorce is not sued out" (*The Old Religion*, 639). Donne's speaker asks for a "divorce" from Satan.

communion and a final purification, making her inviolable. In the time "between," she remains in this world and, as Donne suggests in Sonnet 18, open to all. Donne thus articulates his own response to the question over which many theologians of his time were in disagreement, one concerning the evident corruption of the visible church, and her frequently impure membership. Donne puts his answer in the words of the church and so makes her chastity the final, liberating act of God himself.

5

Body Language
The Political Design of Herbert's Temple

After whose sacrifice offered on the Crosse, which was the conclusion and
consummation of all sacrifices: the whole Ceremoniall Law, Mosaicall Sacrifices,
and Priesthood, were to end, with the beautifull Temple, and Altar therein.
— Peter Smart, *The Vanitie and Downe-fall of*
Superstitious Popish Ceremonies

A T THE very moment that God quits Solomon's beautiful and mystical
temple to "meet with sinne" in the human heart, Herbert's "Sion"
offers a cryptic, even riddling explanation: "Something there was, that
sow'd debate."[1] The "debate" that Herbert acknowledges and suppresses
here and the "something" that causes it point beyond the confrontation
between Christ and the Jews over the meaning of the temple in the New
Testament to a contemporary seventeenth-century controversy. An increasingly charged term, the "temple" was figuring prominently in the disputes
between Roman Catholics, Puritans, and conformists over the origin of the
true church.[2] Turning back to the "temple" in Saint John's Apocalypse, each
group analyzed this text with the specific intention of finding the prophetic

1. I quote Herbert's poem "Sion" in *Works of Herbert,* 106.9. Future references with page
and line numbers will be cited parenthetically within the text. The debate that is "sown"
highlights the dialogue that occurs when the tares are sown along with the wheat in Matt.
13:24–30, a passage often quoted to indicate the difficulty of sorting out the true church
from the false (see Richard Hooker, *Laws of Polity,* 1:288–89, 3.1.8–9; and Laud, *Works of
Laud,* 2:148). In essence, the "temple" became a site of heterodoxy as each group located
their church within the temple in Revelation. Although Amy M. Charles does not think *The
Temple* is Herbert's chosen title, few others have concurred. The title can, in fact, be read as a
response to the controversy over the true church taking place during the seventeenth century.
2. For a thorough historical analysis of the controversy over the temple, see Anthony Milton,
both *Reformed and Catholic* and "The Church of England, Rome, and the True Church: The
Demise of a Jacobean Consensus." Interpretations of the "temple" became even more specific
in the ecclesiastical debates taking place between "Puritans" and Laudians. Quoting Thomas
Cartwright, Richard Bancroft characterized what he considers a particularly "puritan" way of

and ecclesiastical design of their church in early Christian history. Out of these debates, I believe, the political design of Herbert's tripartite structure emerges.[3]

The Roman Catholic position in this controversy was that only their church could be traced to the apostles. On this basis, they attempted to force English Churchmen into admitting their "newfangledness" and thus their departure from the true church. To this John Foxe responded by turning to the very passage that Herbert hints at in "Sion," the debate over the temple: "Of this church meant Christ, speaking of the temple which he would raise again the third day; and yet after that the Lord was risen, he showed not himself to the world, but only to his elect, which were but few."[4] Citing the tendency of "worldly Jews" to equate the physical structure of the temple with the true church, Foxe argued that Christ's manifestation of himself as "temple" was evident only to the elect. The Jewish question about the "temple" could thus be seen to foreshadow the Roman question about "the Church before Luther," implicating this later group in the same blindness and persecution carried out by their precursors.

---

reading: "Maister Cartwright affirmeth, that if the now Lord Arch-bishop of Canterbury had read the ecclesiasticall stories, hee shoulde have founde easily the [Presbyterian] Eldership most flourishing in Constantine's time" (*A Survay of the Pretended Holy Discipline*, 383). And Laudians made the same move. According to Peter Lake, "Authors cited scriptural texts on the temple and tabernacle under the Old Testament as well as passages from Revelations and the Apocalypse on the practices of the Church triumphant in order to justify both general Laudian positions on the church as the house of God and the beauty of holiness as well as more specific Laudian and conformist practices like kneeling" ("The Laudian Style: Order, Uniformity, and the Pursuit of the Beauty of Holiness in the 1630s," 183).

3. Until quite recently, most critics followed Leah S. Marcus in believing that "in *The Temple* doctrinal disputation has no place" (*Childhood and Cultural Despair*, 100). Now, however, critics have begun to recognize the extent to which Herbert responds to the social and political realities of his time. See, for examples, the work of Claude J. Summers, Ted-Larry Pebworth, Sidney Gottlieb, John N. Wall, Debora Shuger, Michael C. Schoenfeldt, and Christopher Hodgkins. The enigmatic structure of *The Temple* has been discussed in terms of meditation, Protestant theology, catechizing, architecture, manuscript editions, music, and most recently, in terms of its disunity. Not until now have we viewed it in terms of an ecclesiastical controversy occurring during the seventeenth century (John David Walker, "The Architectonics of George Herbert's *The Temple*"; Annabel Endicott Patterson, "The Structure of George Herbert's *Temple*: A Reconsideration"; Valerie Carnes, "The Unity of George Herbert's *The Temple*: A Reconsideration"; Kathleen Lynch, "*The Temple*: 'Three Parts Vied and Multiplied'"; and Shuger, "The Structure of *The Temple*," in *Habits of Thought*, 91–119).

4. For an excellent analysis of Foxe's position, see Facey, "Foxe and the Church." Quote is from Foxe, *Acts and Monuments of Foxe*, 1:xix-xx. Future references will be designated *A&M* and cited parenthetically within the text.

Nevertheless, Foxe answered the Roman question by making the "church before Luther" visible to contemporary eyes, arguing in fact that the true church had never been entirely hidden. Identifying himself with the early Christian historian Eusebius, Foxe follows his predecessor in bringing the truth out into the light. His account parallels Eusebius's chronicle as he outlines the liberation from persecution provided by his own Constantine, Elizabeth.[5] Tracing "the descent of the right church . . . from the apostle's time: which hitherto, in most part of histories hath been lacking" (1:xix), he uncovers the line of succession leading from the martyrs of the persecuted church to the visible "temple" of Elizabeth.[6] Nevertheless, Foxe warns, the church must not lose "that which they have obtained, but . . . proceed in all faithfulness, to build and keep up the house and temple of the Lord, to the advancing of his glory, and our everlasting comfort in him" (*A&M*, 7:466). In rebuilding the temple, true believers must remember that they remain in open conflict with the false church of Rome, a corrupt institution that will, in the apocalypse, be destroyed.

The paradox at the center of Foxe's history—that the marginalized, previously hidden church of martyrs had become the visible and reformed Church of England—was a point upon which the Presbyterians quickly focused as they too attempted to recover the true church from Christian antiquity.[7] Rereading Eusebius through the filter of the true church in Revelation, Thomas Brightman argued that this church was not coterminous with the Caesaro-papal structure visible during the reign of Constantine, but with

5. In his first edition, John Foxe makes this series of connections between Eusebius and himself (see "Dedication to Queen Elizabeth," in *Actes and Monuments of these dayes*, n.p.) Because Constantine's mother was traditionally believed to be British, Constantine's lineage became a favorite genealogical resource for Renaissance historians. Elizabethan and Jacobean scholars refer to Constantine repeatedly, linking the emperor first with Elizabeth and then with James. As Patrick Collinson indicates, this "almost mythical Constantine" supplied "all that was needed from antiquity to bolster a polity which attributed so much to the benevolent initiative of the godly prince" ("If Constantine, Then Also Theodosius: St. Ambrose and the Integrity of the Elizabethan *Ecclesia Anglicana*" esp. 208).

6. See Foxe, *Actes and Monuments of these dayes*, fol. Bijv.

7. As Peter Lake argues, the Presbyterians and the conformists were agreed on the importance of early church history, but their interpretations were remarkably different: "The *iure divino* apologists for episcopacy made rather greater play with arguments drawn from the Fathers and church history than did the Presbyterians, but that was because both the Fathers and the history of the church seemed to support their claims that the church had not been governed other than by bishops from the time of the apostles until the reformation. Such a claim was scarcely open to Presbyterians, for whom the dominance of the early church by episcopacy provided sure evidence of the presence and gradual rise of Antichrist" ("Presbyterianism," 208–9).

the Presbyterian believers hidden inside of it: "The Temple then that is onely measured, doth declare that the Church was to be brought into great straits, to be limited with small bounds, and to be altogether remooved from the eyes of men" (*Rev*, 351). The small group of believers hidden within the temple was obscured by the vast majority of those who worshiped in the visible and corrupt outer court. What drove this group into hiding was the sin apparent in the temple's visible structure, a sin recorded, according to Thomas Brightman, in Eusebius's *Ecclesiastical History:*

> And indeed the Holy Ghost most wisely providing to meete with your crafty conveniences so guided the hands and pennes of those that wrote about that time, when Antichrist should peere & peepe out, that they should give the name of a Temple, even to the holy places of the Christian assemblies, that so it might be made every way evident, that [the Antichrist] sitteth in the Temple of God.[8]

According to Brightman's evaluation, the Antichrist sitting in Constantine's temple even now was infiltrating the English Church through its visible episcopal hierarchy, false doctrine, Romish ceremonies, and idolatrous ornamentation.[9] As Milton would later, Brightman challenged the men of the English Church to discard the Romish regiment of episcopacy, taking for themselves the apostolic "discipline" found in the Presbyterian churches on the Continent.[10]

Conformist churchmen responded to this attack in a number of ways. Some of them reinforced Foxe's perspective regarding the "relative invisibility" of the true church by arguing that the Presbyterians were, like the Jews

8. In *Against Bellarmine, the Confuting of that Counterfaite AntiChrist*, Thomas Brightman argues that the church goes "within" at the very moment that the papal "AntiChrist" takes up residence in the visible church, a moment Eusebius manages to prophetically record (737). That Eusebius bears witness to this remarkable division between the corrupt church and the true church, the corrupt "outer court" and the true "inner temple," appears elsewhere in puritan polemic (Peter Lake, *Moderate Puritans and the Elizabethan Church*, 250–51). Quote is from Brightman, *Against Bellarmine*, 739.

9. Brightman traces the corruption in a series of ways: "The doctrine was shamefully defiled in many heads of it, reliques began to be in account, the Temples to be oversumptuously decked, all kinds of superstition began to grow . . . Church dignities were augmented, all thinges being diligently sought for, that might rather serve for pompe, then for truth" (*Rev*, 47).

10. By the 1640s this interpretation had gained parliamentarian support. According to John Morril, "The threat to the protestant foundations of the Church of England was so great, and the penetration so deep, that remedial action was insufficient. Only the total demolition of the existing edifice, only the sterilization of the site and the erection of a new Temple could protect the nation from Antichrist" ("The Attack on the Church of England in the Long Parliament, 1640–1644," 108).

before them, confusing the visible church that they wished to establish with the invisible true church of the elect.[11] Because the true church was made up of all of God's elect throughout history, its membership was impossible to tally. And because no one could see into the hearts and souls of its membership, those who were truly "elect" could not be discerned by the human eye. Both as a group and as individuals, then, the elect could not be singled out, making the notion of an elect, visible church a contradiction in terms.[12]

Bishop James Ussher was one of the many voices articulating this position. Focusing on Foxe's paradigm of the temple once again, he attempted to unpack the meaning of "relative invisibility": "If you demand then, where was God's Temple all this while? the answer is at hand. There where antichrist sate. Where was Christ's people? even under Antichrist's priests."[13] Acknowledging with Brightman that "God's Temple" was found in close proximity to the place "where antichrist sate," Ussher refused to separate it by locating it in a hidden inner realm. Even at this early point in time, he argued, the true church might be considered visible or invisible, depending on who was doing the observing: "The Christian Church was brought unto a lower ebbe, than was the Jewish Synagogue in the dayes of our saviour Christ. . . . And yet a man at that time might have seene the true servants of God standing together in the self-same Temple: which might well be accounted as the House of the Saints in regard of the one, so a Denne of Theeves in respect of the other." By noting that the "true servants of God" were visible in the temple, Ussher undercut Brightman's reading of a "hidden" Presbyterian church. True believers could be found in the church at all times, he argued, for the doctrinal foundation of the church had never changed: "There we doubt not but our Lord had his subjects, and we our fellow servants. For we bring in no new Faith, nor no new Church. That which in the time of the ancient Fathers was accounted to be truely and properly Catholick in the succeeding ages hath evermore been preserved."[14] As Ussher saw it, the patristic writings

11. In Peter Lake's words, "The claim that the Presbyterians confused Christ's spiritual government of the invisible church with their own government of the visible church" was at the core of conformist polemic. However, the Laudians, like the Presbyterians, began to argue for their own visible episcopalian church as they attempted to validate the *iure divino* case of the bishops; both had inflexible, diametrically opposed positions regarding church structure (Lake, "Presbyterianism," 215). A. Milton discusses this issue in even more detail in *Catholic and Reformed* (278–321).

12. See A. Milton, "Church of England," 189.

13. Ussher, *A Briefe Declaration of the Universalitie of the Church of Christ*, 29.

14. The terms *invisible* and *visible* are paradoxically employed since the Presbyterian reformers use the invisible group in the temple to sanction a visible Presbyterian discipline in the

of the Christian church revealed the presence of pure Protestant doctrine persisting despite Romish corruption.[15] The English Church and the Church of Rome could therefore be traced to the same foundation, but because the Church of Rome had departed from this originary purity, both it and the papal Antichrist sitting within it would eventually be destroyed.[16] In taking this position, Ussher opposed Laud and the increasingly pacifistic attitude toward Rome prevailing in the Stuart church.

As early as 1603, Laud had turned away from Foxe's understanding of the "relative invisibility" of the true church as well as his apocalyptic interpretation of history. That year, Laud and Abbot, both future archbishops of the English Church, had disagreed over the "hidden" proto-protestant line of descent that Abbot then identified as one of the church's possible origins. Out of fear that this potentially subversive "line" would threaten episcopal succession, Laud flatly rejected it. And later, when Abbot returned to this proto-protestant line of descent in his *Treatise of the Perpetuall Visibilitie,* Laud characterized it as dangerous to the church. He determined to replace Foxe's notion of "relative invisibility" with the visible episcopal succession of the orthodox national church.[17]

Consequently, the ideal model for the English Church became the visible temple of Constantine. As we have seen in Chapter 2, it was to this model that Lancelot Andrewes directed his own listening audience. In highlighting the Church of England's visible episcopal succession and history, however, Andrewes blurred the clearly drawn boundaries between the English Church

---

seventeenth-century church while the Laudians and conformists use the visible episcopalian temple as a means of including the invisible elect throughout history. Quotes are from ibid., 29, 27.

15. Moreover, outside of the temple of the Apocalypse, the true church could be discerned in the Egyptian and Ethiopian Christians in the South as well as the Greek Christians in the East. A wide variety of Protestant churches could be located before Luther's time that had no connection with Rome (Ussher, *The Whole Works of . . . James Ussher,* 2:494–5.

16. A. Milton, *Catholic and Reformed,* 302–10. Milton notes that Ussher's argument is in keeping with that of John Prideaux and Archbishop Abbot who similarly argued that the true church was visible in the Greek churches and would have continued in time if neither the Protestants nor the Church of Rome had ever come into being.

17. Apparently, Laud read Abbot's *Treatise of the Perpetuall Visibilitie and Succession of the true Church* (1624) and showed it to Buckingham, with a warning of "what was like to ensue upon it." He had a conference with King James the very next day in which it became clear that he saw it as a "dangerous tract" (*Works of Laud,* 3:145). A. Milton argues that Laud misrepresented Abbot's position since Abbot argued for the visibility of the true church within Rome and other churches of the East and South, making the proto-protestant line of descent one of a number of possibilities (*Catholic and Reformed,* 302–3). Nicholas Tyacke comments on this confrontation as well in "Archbishop Laud" (57).

and the Church of Rome, a position that Ussher and other conformists found impossible to accept.

Nevertheless, by the 1620s and 1630s, Foxe's notion of the "relative invisibility" of the elect within the temple was losing ground, particularly as Laud gained political power.[18] By 1629, Laud was beginning to suppress Calvinist sermons, to regulate religious lecturers, to turn afternoon sermons into catechisms, and in certain cases, to alter the altar—the placement of the communion table within churches. In this political climate and, I will argue, in response to this political climate, Herbert constructed *The Temple*.[19]

Like Foxe, Brightman, Ussher, and Andrewes, Herbert turned back to Saint John's Apocalypse and Eusebius's *Auncient Ecclesiasticall Histories* for his own ecclesiastical model. But while Foxe had identified Eusebius as the historian of ecclesiastical persecution, Brightman as the recorder of ecclesiastical corruption, and Andrewes as the affirmer of ecclesiastical succession, Herbert saw Eusebius as the architect of the first Christian temple in antiquity.[20] In Book 10 of *The Auncient Ecclesiasticall Histories,* Herbert found a model for the church of his time, a model that would enable him to respond to the growing controversy over the invisible or visible nature of the temple itself. By observing Herbert's revision of Eusebius's temple, we are able to identify a series of intertextual transformations. Moreover, as Thomas Green indicates, intertexts are particularly resonant in encoding historical processes: "When an allusion is organic rather than ornamental, when it is structurally necessary, then it begins to sketch a miniature myth about its own past, or rather about its emergence from that past. When in other words intertextuality becomes self-conscious, it tends to become etiological, and we are able to analyze the function of the subtext in terms of a specific retrospective vision." In this particular instance, Eusebius's temple enables Herbert to sketch "a miniature myth about the past" of the English

18. Laud began his presidency of St. John's College, Oxford, in 1611 and was eventually elected vice chancellor of Oxford in 1630. He was appointed bishop of St. David's in 1621, bishop of London in 1628, and promised the archbishop of Canterbury in 1626 when Abbot still had seven years to live (Tyacke, "Archbishop Laud," 65, 67). Kenneth Fincham notes many of the same policies in *Prelate as Pastor: The Episcopate of James I* (239–40), but Kevin Sharpe's view of Laud is that he did not rigidly enforce either the altar policy or others attributed to him (*The Personal Rule of Charles I,* 333).

19. In her essay " 'By this Book': Parishioners, the Prayer Book, and the Established Church," Judith Maltby locates George Herbert within the conformist wing of the church, describing his advocacy of auricular confession, good works, and administering the sacrament to the ill (122–24).

20. Translator Kirsopp Lake notes this fact in Eusebius, *The Ecclesiastical History* (2:185–86 n).

Church by providing him with a historical model for the English Church itself. At the same time, this ancient structure allows Herbert to mark the English Church's "emergence from that past" and so to acknowledge the various debates confronting the present church. Consequently, by creating *The Temple* in the temporal gap between a lost ideal and the present church, Herbert reveals more than his nostalgia for the past; he speaks eloquently as a prophet and a peacemaker to the issues dividing his own seventeenth-century audience.[21]

What we find in Book 10 of Eusebius's *Auncient Ecclesiasticall Histories* then, is a miniature outline of *The Temple,* complete with dedication, church porch, temple design, and temple furniture.[22] The marginal glosses of Hanmer's 1585 English translation neatly signpost these divisions, not only identifying "the church" and "the porch," but also noting the rather lengthy "space betwene the Sanctuary & the porche." Described here are the temple's most salient architectural features: its baptismal "Welspringes cockes or cunditts," "gates," "Porches," "Windowes," and even its "floore or pavement."

The relationship between the various parts of Eusebius's temple is more than architectural, however. The different parts of this edifice actually engage in edification—in building up one another:

> Some he hath firmly set about the inner court with chiefe pillars, after the manner of a quadrangle and to the chiefe Bulwarks he hath referred the scripture of the four Evangelists. Again some he hath coupled with fortresses on either side about the princely palace, which are yet as novices in the faith. They both increase and prosper, yet set farther off from the inward contemplation of the faithful. Of these he hath taken the incorrupt soules, purified with the divine fountain after the manner of gold, and others hath he set up with pillars, far mightier than those outward, out of the inner writings of mystical Scripture and sett them forth lively and to minister light. The whole Temple he adorneth with

21. Thomas Greene, *The Light in Troy: Imitation and Discovery in Renaissance Poetry,* 17–18. Like Christopher Hodgkins, I believe that Herbert is engaged in "regenerative nostalgia" (*Authority, Church, and Society,* 1). I argue, however, that Herbert returns to the patristics or "Antiquity" to clarify his ecclesiastical choices rather than to the Elizabethan Settlement of 1560. Because Puritans and Laudians were both employing patristic writers to buttress their positions during the Caroline reign, the particular way that Herbert's reconstructs Eusebius's temple pinpoints his politics.

22. Although Herbert knew *The Auncient Ecclesiasticall Histories* in Greek, the work was available to a readership in English, having been published repeatedly: in 1577, 1585, 1607, 1619, and 1636. Throughout this chapter I will be citing Book 10 of *The Auncient Ecclesiasticall Histories,* 189–202; future references will be designated *AEH* and cited parenthetically within the text.

a single, mighty gateway, even the praise of the one and only God, the universal King. (*AEH*, 202)

In Eusebius's temple, the spiritual aptitude of each individual coincides with a clearly defined architectural space. Each, then, is "coupled" to all of the others yet remains individually distinct, offering both communal and individual spiritual insight.

In *The Temple*, Herbert follows this same architectural pattern by creating a wide range of personae who speak not only as individuals but also in response to a larger Christian community. Consequently, the speaker of "The Church-porch" catechizes "novices" who lack wisdom and remain "farther off," while those within "The Church" have fuller musical range and contribute new architectural dimensions to *The Temple* itself. Some, like the speakers of "The Sacrifice," "Christmas," "Lent," and "Easter Wings," are just as Eusebius describes them, "chiefe Bulwarks," reviewing central aspects of Gospel narrative and important "holy-days" in the church calendar. Others are slowly baptized into fuller knowledge, such as the speakers of "Redemption," "Jordan I and II," "Affliction," and "The Collar." Still others "minister light" (as Eusebius hints) by exploring the demands of sacred office in "Aaron," "The Priesthood," and "The Windows." Although all are not priests in Herbert's *Temple*, all are certainly teachers, and so all are engaged in the process of edification.

While the structural parallels that Herbert draws between the Eusebian temple and his own allow him to reinforce the importance of a visible, patristic pattern for the present church, Herbert does not stop there; he subtly remodels this ancient structure to respond to contemporary controversies occurring in the wake of Laud: controversies over temple dedications, kneeling, preaching, holy days, altar placement, and divine service.[23] In essence, Herbert reacts against the escalating anger of the moment, an anger articulated in 1628 when Peter Smart attacked the priests of the English Church for turning the church into a temple, preaching into a liturgical performance,

---

23. Davies discusses the extent to which reformation scholars as well as Laudians turned back to the patristics, employing these writers to stress the inherent holiness of place and object. Herbert is doubtless closer to the reformation scholars than to the Laudians (*Caroline Captivity*, 51–52). Davies goes on to discuss the extent to which patristic saturation within the universities caused "a more pronounced emphasis upon the visibility and catholicity of the historical Church, upon the liturgy, and a deeper sacramental theology, all salient features of the Laudian renaissance" (53). As I argue here, however, patristic texts allowed Herbert to pursue a reformation agenda, and, at the same time, to maintain his conformist stance and sacramental vision.

and the communion table into an altar: "Whereupon I conclude that where no congregation useth to meete to heare Sermons, that place is no Church; and consequently the Font being set in no place of assembly, it is not in the Church: I confesse it is, *in Templo*, in part of this vast fabrike, but there it is where the people never meet to hear Gods word preached no more then they doe in the steeple where the bells bang."[24] In an attempt to mediate against the rising anger over specific Romish innovations in the visible church—innovations that included the removal of the baptismal "font" to the entrance of the church, the privileging of the liturgy over the sermon, and the relocation of the altar—Herbert demonstrates that the ancient visible church, through these outward forms, prepared its membership to enter into the "relatively invisible" body of believers who have edified the church throughout the ages.

The tripartite structure of Herbert's *Temple* thus manifests three different but related responses to the debates of the seventeenth-century church: In "The Church-porch," Herbert opens the temple to everyone, his initial speaker introducing those who enter to the rules of the visible church; in "The Church," he reveals the means by which the visible church engages in the far more mystical, invisible activity of a membership building up one another; and in "The Church Militant," he traces the apocalyptic nature of redemptive history. In each case, Herbert adopts an inclusive, conformist stance that seeks to heal the widening breaches in the English Church by subtly calling the exclusionary attitudes of both Laudians and Puritans into question.

Consequently, something of the disjunction between the past Eusebian ideal and the present English Church emerges in the opening lines of Herbert's "Dedication":

> Lord, my first fruits present themselves to thee;
> Yet not mine neither: for from thee they came,
> And must return. Accept of them and me,
> And make us strive, who shall sing best thy name.
> > Turn their eyes hither, who shall make a gain:
> > Theirs, who shall hurt themselves or me, refrain.
> > > (5.1–6)

While in the ancient work, a second "Zorobabel" dedicates a temple with joyful abandon, his audience responding with heartfelt "consent" (*AEH*,

---

24. Peter Smart, *The Vanitie and Downe-fall of Superstitious Popish Ceremonies*, 17.

189), Herbert's "Dedication" acknowledges an audience that is far more resistant. In this group capable of hurting "themselves or me," Herbert may hint, however briefly, at Puritan fury over the dedication of church buildings and other seemingly "idolatrous" activities.[25] To this he responds by invoking divine supervision. God himself must "turn their eyes" toward this structure or away from it, not only directing the gaze but also sanctioning the object of the gaze, poetic and ecclesiastical "dedications" alike.

A similar alteration is apparent in Herbert's revision of Eusebius's "church-porch." Clearly rejecting Brightman's puritanical vision in which the faithful have no dealings with the corrupt members in the "outer court," Herbert makes the "porch" a place of gradual transformation. He thus acknowledges the pacifistic and purifying properties of the "porch" as clarified by Eusebius: "Salomon an earnest maintainer of Peace, and builder of this Temple hath brought [this] to passe, for such as yet want ye sacrifice and sprinklings done by water and the holy ghost" (*AEH*, 190). Having yet to undergo baptism, those who enter here lack a crucial sacrament of the spiritual life, that "sprinkling done by water and the holy ghost" that establishes peace with God. Herbert, however, makes the task of "maintaining Peace" still more inclusive as he attempts to mediate not only between Man and God but also between Laudians and Puritans.[26] Directing his audience toward the "sprinklings" occurring in the first Christian cathedral, he makes "Perirrhanterium" the subtitle of his lengthy opening poem. This Greek term has troubled modern critics, since, in Stanley Stewart's words, "Sprinkling holy water at the church door, or anywhere else, would have been neither common nor legal, because the use of holy water went out with the Reformation." But "Perirrhanterium" exemplifies what Michael Riffaterre calls a "connective": a word that calls attention to a text's intertext.[27] The Greek term underscores its origin in Eusebius's *Auncient Ecclesiasticall Histories* and illuminates the "sprinklings" occurring in the first Christian temple. By this means, Herbert questions recent Puritan attempts to identify the recent removal of the "Font" to the church entrance as an indication of Romish practice and a devaluation of

25. See Hooker, "The Dedication of Churches," in *Laws of Polity,* 2:39–44, 5.12.1–6.

26. For these two positions, see Thomas Cartwright, *A Christian Letter of Certaine English Protestants,* 3–49; and William Laud, *A Speech Concerning Innovations in the Church,* 1–77. For excellent analyses of Laudianism, see Peter Lake, both "The Laudians and the Argument from Authority" and "Laudian Style."

27. Stewart, *George Herbert,* 85. Riffaterre argues that obscure or incomplete utterances "are both the problem, when seen from the text, and the solution to that problem when their other, intertextual side is revealed" ("Compulsory Reader Response: The Intertextual Drive," 58).

purity; he highlights instead the antiquity of the purification rites occurring on the porch.

Just as Eusebius's "sprinklings" enable Herbert to emphasize the unfallen Protestant origins of purification, the rather lengthy porch that Eusebius describes enables Herbert to reveal in full detail the rules and demands of the spiritual life:

> Them also who already are entred within the gates he suffreth not with foule and unwashed feete to drawe nighe unto the inner partes of the most holie places. For making a separation with greate distance betwene the Temple itselfe & the first entrance he hath beautified this place on everyside. The first exercise for such as enter yieldeth unto everyone beauty & brightnes to witt the washing of their hands and clensing of their body, but unto them that desire the knowledg of the first principles of our religion a fitt mansion place to continewe. (*AEH*, 190)

Again following this design, Herbert provides a structure "separat[ed] with greate distance" from "The Church," as well as "a fitt mansion" where entering readers might be instructed in "the first principles." But his speaker also seeks to correct particular seventeenth-century errors by asserting a conformist position on a number of hotly contested ecclesiastical points.[28] Initially, he appears to follow the Laudians in defining the church rather than the home or conventicle as sacred space:

> Though private prayer be a brave designe,
> Yet publick hath more promises, more love:
> And love's a weight to hearts, to eies a signe.
> We all are but cold suitours; let us move
> Where it is warmest. Leave thy six and seven;
> Pray with the most: for where most pray, is heaven.
>
> (22.397–402)

But in privileging "public" over "private" prayer, he refuses to describe the private meeting of "six and seven" as a hidden and potentially subversive activity as some of the Laudians were doing. As we have seen in Chapter 4, Herbert's family friend John Donne also addressed this issue rather pointedly:

---

28. See "The Church-porch," pp. 22–24, stanzas 68–74, ll. 403–44, and Hooker's argument with the puritans regarding kneeling, preaching, and lengthy praying (*Laws of Polity*, 2:104–60, 5.23.1–5.41.4).

So when these men pray in their Conventicles, for the confusion, and rooting out of Idolatry and Antichrist, they intend by their Idolatry, a Cross in Baptism; and by their Antichrist, a man in a Surpless; and not onely the persons, but the Authority that admits this Idolatry, and this Antichristianism. As vapors and winds shut up in Vaults, engender Earth-quakes; so these particular spirits in their Vault-Prayers, and Cellar-Service, shake the Pillars of State and Church.[29]

Herbert, however, highlights the benefits of public prayer rather than the dangers of private, arguing that its very visibility provides an evangelical "sign" to others of the heaven to be found here. By making the visible act sacramental—a means of transforming and redeeming those who participate in it—Herbert fills public prayer with the light and heat of reformation values. And he continues to readjust both Laudian and Puritan perspectives in the next stanza:

When once thy foot enters the church, be bare.
God is more there, then thou: for thou art there
Onely by his permission. Then beware,
And make thy self all reverence and fear.
Kneeling ne're spoil'd silk stocking: quit thy state
All equall are within the churches gate.

(22.403–8)

Realizing that some Puritans were entering church with their hats on and their heads covered, the speaker seeks to correct this behavior by reminding his readers that God fills the entire fabric of the temple, causing the divine presence to be "more there," more in the sacred, public space of the gathered Christian community than in the private space of the individual. Before this divine majesty, he asserts, one must kneel in reverence. Thus, the speaker clearly aligns himself not with the Puritans who considered kneeling Romish, but with proto-Laudians such as Andrewes who traced kneeling back to the primitive church. As Andrewes put it, "They in Scripture, they in the Primitive Church did so, did 'bow.' And verily, He will not have us worship Him like elephants, as if we had no joints in our knees; He will have more honour of men, than pillars in the Church. He will have us 'bow the knee;' and let us bow then in God's Name."[30] Following Andrewes, the speaker emphasizes the importance of universal reverence before God, but he also

29. Donne, *Sermons of John Donne*, 5:219.
30. Andrewes, *Works of Andrewes*, 2:334.

subtly critiques the tendency of some Laudians to establish a stratified social structure within the church, a tendency all too visible in the work of Giles Widdowes: "Church order gives every one his convenient place, to superiors, superior places; to equalls, equal places; to inferiors, inferior places; to every church-necessary, a necessary place."[31] In contrast to this perspective, Herbert's speaker reinforces the leveling effect of kneeling, noting that it places the silk stockings of wealth and privilege on the same ground with the woolen socks of the poor. Before the divine presence, he asserts, neither Puritan irreverence nor Laudian privilege has any place.

In the next stanza, the speaker takes up yet another contested issue: the debate over sermons and prayers. As we have already seen, the Puritans emphasized preaching while the Laudians emphasized prayers. And Lancelot Andrewes acknowledged both but clearly privileged the latter: "Yet, we see, by the frame of this text, [prayer] is the higher end; the calling on us by prophecy, is but that we should call on the Name of the Lord. All prophesying, all preaching, is but to this end."[32] Herbert's speaker follows Andrewes in asserting that prayers are the true "end" of sermons and thus of higher priority:

> Resort to sermons, but to prayers most:
> Praying's the end of preaching. O be drest;
> Stay not for th' other pin: why, thou has lost
> A joy for it worth worlds. Thus hell doth jest
> Away thy blessings, and extreamly flout thee,
> Thy clothes being fast, but thy soul loose about thee.
>
> (23.409–14)

Again, the speaker underscores the extent to which the visible order of the church contains hidden and divine operations.[33] Noting that the "outer" and ceremonial aspects of church liturgy provide "inner" clothing for those in

31. Lake identifies this tendency in the "hands of some Laudians" who used the motif of the stratified congregation "to establish an elaborately variegated vision of the social body of the church . . . These were defined in terms of their greater or lesser proximity to the altar and served both to express and enforce certain differences in status among the lay members" ("The Laudian Style," 177). Widdowes, *The Schismatical Puritan,* sig. Fv1.

32. Andrewes, *Works of Andrewes,* 3:318.

33. Proto-Laudians such as John Buckeridge and Lancelot Andrewes identified the external act as an extension of internal devotion. As Buckeridge put it, "First, internal Adoration, that is, the devotion of the heart, and inward worship; and next outward worship, that is Prostration, falling downe, or bending the body, and kneeling" (*A Discourse concerning Kneeling at the Communion,* 11).

attendance, he suggests that the final "pin" of prayer holds the well-dressed soul together. Consequently, those who stay only for the first "pin" of the sermon—arriving late and leaving early as the Puritans sometimes did— have a "loose" and unkempt soul. In giving excessive value to preaching, they have failed to keep themselves internally ordered and are in danger of missing the joys of heaven on earth.[34]

In closing, the speaker of the porch moves beyond Laudian and Puritan arguments over sacred space, sermons, and worship to address the issue behind them. Now he asserts that refusing God because he does not take the appropriate form may be the most problematic activity of all since such judgments make Man and not God the arbiter of holiness: "The Jews refused thunder; and we, folly. / Though God do hedge us in, yet who is holy" (24.449–50). In posing the question, "Who is holy" to Laudians as well as Puritans, Herbert calls attention to the problematic nature of all such human evaluations, an attitude overwhelmingly evident in the self-righteous exclusivity of both groups. By attempting to circumscribe "holy" space, both have erred, for only God sets the ever inclusive, ever expanding boundaries on the sacred.

After establishing this insight into the problematic nature of holiness, "Superliminare" invites only those who long to be pure through the door. It is this longing that defines, for Herbert, the invisible elect in the visible church, a longing that is "relatively invisible" to the human eye. The "repast" "tasted" here is similarly "mystical," a repast in which the Word is broken and offered anew for the entire spiritual community.

Inside the door of "The Church," then, Herbert appropriates a number of smaller architectural features from Eusebius's design, the altar, "windowes," and "floore" made out of "marble stone." As in the case of "Perirrhanterium," these visible church furnishings allow Herbert to offer legitimate decodings of supposedly Romish architecture and terminology as he traces them to their unfallen origins in Christian antiquity.[35]

---

34. In one of the earliest and finest books on George Herbert, Joseph Summers establishes the importance of "order" to the poet. ("The Conception of Form," in *George Herbert: His Religion and His Art*, 83–84).

35. For a discussion of the controversy over the spatial placement of the altar, see Francis Yates, *Buildings, Faith, and Worship* (31–32), and for an excellent analysis of various contemporary contexts for "The Altar," see Thomas B. Stroup, " 'A Reasonable, Holy, and Living Sacrifice': Herbert's 'The Altar.' " Stroup argues that the altar is "best understood as a liturgy for the dedication of the Church's altar" (150), a reading that reinforces my sense of "The Altar" as a visible structure in the Eusebian cathedral. Kathleen Lynch, in "George Herbert's Holy 'Altar,' Name and Thing," traces in some detail much of the contemporary controversy surrounding the altar.

"The Altar" is a clear case in point. The fact that Herbert builds it of stones suggests his hand in one of the hottest debates of the earlier seventeenth century. At a time when the Laudians were inciting Puritan anger by turning communion tables into altars (not only by placing them "altar-wise" but also by building them out of stone), Herbert creates an altar that incorporates both perspectives. Like the Laudian Richard Montagu, he turns back to Old Testament narrative and the primitive church to locate the "stone" for the altar itself, a material, in Montagu's view, that predated Romish corruption: "These Altars were not of stone at first, untill the dayes of Constantine, that the Church came to have rest and peace; nor then frequently and in ordinarie churches, but in Cathedrall only or in great Cities. But of stone they were, it is certaine, and I prove it elsewhere, before that popery was heard in the world or in the Church of Rome itself." Herbert returns to Constantine's temple to locate the design for "The Altar" but he does not place it "in the middest" of the temple as his patristic author does, choosing rather to rear it at the door. In making this rather remarkable change, Herbert moves "The Altar" much closer to Thomas Brightman's altar in the temple of *Revelation:* "Nowe all the faithfull are said to worship in the Altar, because they place all their hope, and affiance in Christs death alone; which kind of sacrifices belonge not onely to the Tribe of Levi; but as well to very truly godly one" (*Rev,* 353). Rejecting the Laudian tendency to move the altar into the recesses of the church—away from the people and closer to the priesthood—Herbert makes his altar immediately accessible to "all the faithful." At the same time, by constructing a visible altar within the lines of the poem, Herbert undercuts the tendency of William Prynne and other Puritans to equate the physical altar with idolatry. Prynne had argued, "Christians have no other altars but Christ alone, who hath abolished all other altars, which are either heathenish, Jewish, or Popish, and not tolerable among Christians."[36] Clearly contesting this perspective, Herbert's visible poetics points repeatedly to that shining "Other" to whom he dedicates his altar, to that high priest standing just on the other side of the field of vision. In making what his audience cannot see as important as what they can, he negotiates them toward a brokenness that

---

36. As Kenneth Fincham notes, Laud's patron, Richard Neile, "permitted the conversion of the cathedral communion table into a stone altar" in Durham Cathedral (*Prelate as Pastor,* 239). This was only one of several other "conversions." Richard Montagu, *Appello Caesarem: A Just Appeale from two Unjust informers,* 286; George Herbert sat on the parliamentary committee that reviewed Montagu's work, so he was certainly familiar, though not in agreement, with Montagu's position (see Lynch, "Herbert's Holy 'Altar,'" 48). Eusebius, *Auncient Ecclesiasticall Histories,* 190; Prynne, *A Quenche-Coale or a Briefe Disquisition and Inquirie,* title page.

makes wholeness possible, one that, like "The Altar" itself, unites "parts" framed by God into a communion of saints.

In the intertextual structure of *The Temple* and in individual poems as well, Herbert carries out a subtle political critique of the Puritan and Laudian positions. Hints of this debate are encoded in "Sion," the poem with which I open this chapter. Here, Herbert appears to follow the Laudians in celebrating the external beauty of Solomon's temple. But instead of focusing on the temple's beauty and grandeur as the Laudians would do, he turns the "gold" and "embellished wood" into signs showing the hearts of the builders:

> Lord, with what glorie wast thou serv'd of old,
> When Solomons temple stood and flourished!
> Where most things were of purest gold;
> The wood was all embellished
> With flowers and carvings, mysticall and rare:
> All show'd the builders, crav'd the seers care.
>
> (106.1–6)

Herbert's awed appreciation of the "glorie" of divine service undercuts the Puritan error of devaluing the physical space of the temple, even as his shift toward the "mystical" inner realm reorients Laudian fears away from the threat of private subversion. His emphasis on the inner glory and reverence that the external beauty of the temple "shows" affirms both building and builder, incorporating Laudians as well as Puritans into his all inclusive design.

This same series of spiritual and ecclesiastical readjustments takes place in the second stanza as well: God reacts to the debate over the temple by suddenly shifting inward, but not to escape the corrupt Romish structure as the Puritans had often argued. In fact, God enters to "meete with sinne" (106.11) more directly, for he does not, as Milton later asserts, "prefer / Before all Temples the upright heart and pure." He prefers the far more problematic battleground of the sinful heart.[37]

Thus, here as elsewhere in *The Temple,* divine "Architecture meets with sinne" rather than fleeing from it as God consigns himself to this space

---

37. John Milton, *Paradise Lost,* bk. 1, ll. 17–18, in *Milton: Complete Poems,* 212. Richard Strier states the contrary opinion: "Nothing more strongly distinguishes Herbert from a thinker like Richard Hooker," who "sees no problem with Solomon's temple" (*Love Known,* 183). Debora Shuger and Christopher Hodgkins similarly identify Herbert's emphasis on inwardness in "Sion" with a movement away from ecclesiastical structures (Shuger, *Habits of Thought,* 93–106; Hodgkins, *Authority, Church, and Society,* 174–75).

to transform its boundaries, to eradicate sin rather than to escape its corruptive influence. What becomes essential, in fact, is that musical "lines" and antithetical voices "cross" one another, a cross that makes a harmony of Laudian and Puritan positions by bringing them together rather than allowing their exclusionary tendencies free reign.[38] What finally resonates out of this political and spiritual counterpoint is "musick for a King," music arising from a living liturgical structure bent on honoring both heavenly and earthly authorities.

Thus, "Sion" traces God's movement into the darkest recesses of the human heart to reclaim piece by piece and heart by heart those who sing within *The Temple.* "The Windows," in contrast, turn back to the visible structure, both raising the eyes upward in space, and foregrounding, in Eusebian terms, the preacher's ability to minister within the temple. Yet Herbert's "Windows" open outward as well on the sociopolitical moment that he composes *The Temple,* a moment in which a broken church window in Salisbury was creating a stir in Herbert's immediate spiritual community and a politically charged controversy in the country at large.[39] The public reaction to this act of iconoclasm highlights the contestatory nature of the debate taking shape between the more zealous reformers, conformists, and Laudians over the status of the temple, a debate in which we find Herbert actively engaged.

The events surrounding the broken church window in Salisbury reveal the reformers and conformists at odds with one another as well as with Laudian authority. Apparently, the vestrymen of the church were committed to spiritual reform and had repeatedly brought in Puritan ministers. They authorized the replacement of a "superstitious" window that represented God "in the Form of a little old Man in a blue and red Coat," but their decision was overturned by the conformist bishop of Salisbury, John Davenant, who declared that the stained-glass window should remain in place.[40] In response, Henry Sherfield, one of the vestrymen, purposely destroyed the window in October 1630, and Bishop Davenant, angry at this violation of

---

38. Hooker points to the temple in Book 10 of Eusebius—the same model I believe Herbert "copies"—to argue that temples "built unto God's glory" should be beautiful (*Laws of Polity,* 2:48–50, 5.15.2). Later he questions Thomas Cartwright's assessment that the singing of psalms "is not commendable" by contending that the music "interchangeably" voiced by God, Man, and angels unites all in perfect harmony (2:149, 5.39.1).

39. For details of this incident, see Paul Slack, "Religious Protest and Urban Authority: The Case of Henry Sherfield, Iconoclast, 1633"; and Sharpe, *Personal Rule of Charles I,* 345–48.

40. *Churchwardens' Accounts [of S. Edmund and S. Thomas, Sarum 1443–1702]* (Salisbury, 1896), 190.

his authority, turned Sherfield over to a Laudian ecclesiastical court. This court fined Sherfield five hundred pounds and ordered him to make public acknowledgement of his offense before the bishop, although Laud and others wished for stricter punishment. Meanwhile, the window was replaced with plain, clear glass at Sherfield's expense.[41]

From this historical distance, Davenant's attitude toward Sherfield remains hard to decipher, especially because Davenant had repeatedly come into conflict with the Laudian court for his own Calvinist beliefs. When the issue of authority was at stake, it appears, Davenant was no more willing to contest the ecclesiastical structures that legitimized him than he was willing to have his own authority overruled by alternative governing bodies within individual churches. Davenant's desire to establish a position midway between Laudian and Puritan perspectives inevitably placed him at odds with each group.

In "The Windows," Herbert negotiates far more circumspectly between Laudian and Puritan positions by appropriating Eusebius's awareness: that preachers, like windows, "minister light." In making the act of preaching the Word correlative with the act of illuminating the church, Herbert blurs the boundaries between the aural and the visible, turning each into a function of the other. Thus, his opening line directs our attention away from "The Windows" of the title as it makes preaching—not stained glass—the focus of interrogation: "Lord, how can man preach thy eternall word?" (67.1). By way of response, Herbert identifies man as a "brittle crazie glasse" (67.2). Rather like the cracked window in the nearby parish, man preaches the Word with a rigid, often iconoclastic intensity that provides neither heat nor light. Despite these all too human limitations, however, God takes an active role in refashioning the preacher into an appropriate medium:

> Yet in thy temple thou dost him afford
>   This glorious and transcendent place,
>   To be a window, through thy grace.
>   (67.3–5)

Herbert shows God in the process of readjusting (and thus reforming) human limitation by making the transcendent office of minister a revelation of

---

41. Slack, "Religious Protest," 296. Sharpe notes the reparation: "Significantly, Charles I ordered the window be repaired (at Sherfield's expense) with plain glass—even though the original glass was reparable" (*Personal Rule of Charles I*, 347). Coke MS 44: letter to Davenant, 15 Feb. 1633.

"grace." Replacing himself what is brittle and cracked, God turns the window into a pulpit, forever blurring the visual and aural boundaries between "doctrine and life, / Colors and light" (68.11). Now the "light" of the Word and the multifaceted life of Christ reflect though the prismlike life of the preacher. By this means Herbert subtly critiques the spare Puritan position that had identified the "naked" Word as the only means of revealing God. "Speech alone," he asserts, is "watrish, bleak, & thin" (67.10), very like the plain-glass window installed in the nearby church. Vanishing "like a flaring thing," it leaves no imprint on the memory. But, Herbert hints, the Laudian emphasis on the "beauty of holiness" is just as limiting, for the material "colors" of the window convey nothing if the story of Christ is missing. Thus, Herbert advocates neither breaking with the past by breaking church windows nor creating beautiful visual icons that displace the human representation of the Word. Instead, he advocates the process of incarnation, the complete integration of the Word into the visible life and language of the minister. Only then will the audience experience "awe," as, freed from the limitations of a single perspective, they are transfigured by the memory of Presence.

Even the concluding poem of this middle section, "Love III," engages in the controversies of the 1620s and 1630s. As the last poem in "The Church," this lyric negotiates the ultimate boundary between the visible church—in the act of communion on earth—and the invisible church of the elect. Consequently, the lines dramatize the loving encounter between man and God, between guest and host, between the visible church and the invisible bride. "Love" in this allegory is both male and female, both Christ, the "Head," and the woman of the Apocalypse who is his elect body. Like faithful Una and Donne's "true spouse," she has been awaiting the speaker across earthly time, the all too dusty and error-prone figure of the visible church.

She must, of course, again overcome the speaker's perceptual limits as, like the Puritans, he finds purity so important that he must finally exclude himself and, like the Laudians, he desires so much to "serve" that he forgets what divine union is really about. Speaking the language of the Body, she manages to turn the communion of the elect into a demonstration of it, for in the intercourse that her Word makes possible, she overcomes every one of the speaker's limitations: his sexual impotency, ashamed withdrawal, verbal acknowledgment of failure, and belated attempt to serve.[42] Getting the last word, she explains that this is not finally about *his* body but about *hers:* "You

42. Michael Schoenfeldt, in " 'That Ancient Heat': Sexuality and Spirituality in *The Temple*," offers an extraordinarily subtle reading of the sexual dimension of "Love III." In Herbert's

must sit down, sayes Love, and taste *my* meat" (189.17; emphasis added). His response enacts communion and consummation both: "So I did sit and eat" (189.18).

That the speaker has not been sitting throughout this narrative, but first backing away in hasty flight, and then kneeling in humble service, suggests the way in which Herbert negotiates yet another controversy of the time, this one about one's posture in receiving the Eucharist. In his prose work *A Priest to the Temple,* Herbert articulates his reaction to this debate in specific terms:

> For the manner of receiving, as the Parson useth all reverence himself, so he administers to none but to the reverent. The Feast indeed requires sitting, because it is a Feast; but man's unpreparednesse asks kneeling. Hee that comes to the Sacrament, hath the confidence of a Guest, and hee that kneels, confesseth himself an unworthy one, and therefore differs from other Feasters: but hee that sits, or lies, puts up to an Apostle: Contentiousnesse in a feast of Charity is more scandall then any posture.[43]

In "Love III," the speaker enters with perhaps too much reverence, his "unpreparednesse" clearly showing in all that he says and does. That he longs to be worthy of being a "Guest" is his first stated desire, followed quickly of course by his acknowledgement of guilt, and then his desire to "serve" since he does not really belong at this feast in any other capacity. It is Love who decides that he must sit, must feast, must act as an apostle, and it is Love that makes him one. Through the most delicate of movements, Herbert accommodates both "kneeling" and "sitting" into his version of "Love III," making each—informed by Love's directive—altogether appropriate.

An architectural model of "Love III," Eusebius's ancient structure repeatedly blurs the boundaries between the church on earth—in its social and political milieu—and the church in heaven: "The chiefe tips and foreshewes spiritual of these do exceed al marvelous & miraculous things, the intellectual and theological patterns, to wit, the renewing & repairing of the devine and reasonable building in the souls" (*AEH,* 201). For Eusebius, the material temple is a "theological pattern" of the temple that cannot be seen, its outward renewal and repair a record of internal transformation. Thus, though he begins his description in Book 10 by assigning the building of the

---

stunning version of "Body Language," Love presents herself as bride and is, in the end, re-presented to us by the narrator.

43. Herbert, *Works of Herbert,* 259.

temple to a particular historical moment, he closes by articulating the fact that the structure is also prophetic, pointing beyond itself to the hidden and eternal church triumphant.

Not surprisingly, critics have long identified the third division of *The Temple* with the church triumphant, but it is actually in the context of the political and historical debate over the temple that the poem gains its fullest meaning. In "The Church Militant," Herbert establishes the intertextual connection between his own structure and the "temples" described by Eusebius, Foxe, Ussher, and Brightman in their own interpretations of history.[44] Following the example of these prophet-historians, Herbert concludes his work by seeking to complete Eusebius's design.[45] He thus extends his vision beyond the temple itself to the overarching apocalyptic and historical contexts in which the structure was originally located.

The speaker of "The Church Militant" accordingly jumps the 1260-year gap in time between Constantine's temple and the emergence of the English Church in the sixteenth century by hinting that the first prophetically records the advent of the second. This "mysterie," the speaker suggests, can be read in a "paper" torn out of "times great Chronicle":

> Constantines British Line meant this of old,
> And did this mysterie wrap up and fold
> Within a sheet of paper, which was rent
> From times great Chronicle, and hither sent.
> (192.93–96)

Through "Constantines British Line," Herbert's speaker manages to answer the question of the church's status "before Luther." Like Ussher, he finds the true church and its redemptive presence in various works of the past, including those of patristic antiquity: "Holy *Macarius* and great *Anthonie* / Made *Pharoah Moses,* changing th'historie" (191.42–43). With Ussher and

---

44. Most critics have interpreted "The Church Militant" in order to identify its relationship to *The Temple.* Two have focused expressly on "The Church Militant" as prophetic history, however (Raymond Anselment, "'The Church Militant': George Herbert and the Metamorphoses of Christian History"; Kenneth Alan Hovey, "'Wheel'd about . . . into Amen': 'The Church Militant' on Its Own Terms").

45. Herbert doubtless draws on a number of church histories, past and present, in writing this poem. He considers Eusebius's *Auncient Ecclesiasticall Histories,* and Foxe's *Acts and Monuments* to name a few. But he also may draw on Luther's interpretation of prophecy, which, according to Firth, "allowed historical significance to the prophecies in only two limited periods: the early Church before Constantine and [Luther's] present age" (*Apocalyptic Tradition,* 11–12).

other conformist churchmen, this speaker carefully follows the movement of the church through the Egyptian, Ethiopian, and Greek churches up to and including the Roman Church of Constantine's reign. But he also traces Rome's gradual corruption of the church's religious, political, and artistic life. Realizing that the pope continues to "sit in the temple" as a corrupt inversion of this ideal, the speaker suddenly loses the distance and objectivity that has informed his writing throughout. He reacts to the Romish threat in an immediate, almost visceral way, introducing himself, for the first and only time, into the action of his poem:

> Sinne being not able to extirpate quite
> The Churches here, bravely resolv'd one night
> To be a Church-man too, and wear a Mitre:
> The old debauched ruffian would turn writer.
> I saw him in his studie, where he sate
> Busie in controversies sprung of late.
>
> (194.161–66)

It is as a "writer," of course, that Herbert's speaker confronts his Romish opponent, a confrontation that opens a window on Herbert himself and the "controversies sprung of late" in which he also participates. As Herbert was clearly aware, "anti-papal" prophecies were being suppressed during the seventeenth century as the king sought to contain antipapal sentiment and to move toward greater conciliation with the Roman Church.[46] Yet Herbert's speaker does not mince words: "As new and old Rome did one Empire twist; / So both together are one Antichrist" (196.205–6). This candid evaluation may be the real reason that *The Temple* was almost denied publication in 1633.[47] Certainly, Herbert's refusal to sanction the ecclesiastical and royal interests of the moment might well have created as much of a stir as his prophetic passage about America.[48]

---

46. According to Christianson, "Authorities refused to license any works censorious of the aims or practices of the Arminian programme" (*Reformers and Babylon*, 136).

47. See Walton, "The Life of Mr. George Herbert," in *The Lives*, 315.

48. David Norbrook summarizes the nature of this suppression: "After the dissolution of Parliament in 1629, orthodox channels of political debate were still more strictly controlled; through the 1630s, ecclesiastical censorship was tightened. The period of 'the king's peace' can be seen as the most determined attempt in English history to 'aestheticize politics,' to suppress articulate discussion and to try to force the realm into a form of ritualized submission" ("The Politics of Milton's Early Poetry," 48). Herbert too "aestheticizes politics" throughout *The Temple*, but there are a series of moments when he shows his hand.

Despite this critique of Roman (and potentially Laudian) excess, Herbert's speaker declines to engage in the militant Puritan zeal of his contemporaries. Looking back rather than forward, he adopts a stance similar to the Laudians as he locates the "first" temple during "ancient times and purer years":

> So though Sinne made his latter seat the better,
> The latter Church is to the first a debtor.
> The second Temple could not reach the first:
> And the later reformation never durst
> Compare with ancient times and purer years;
> But in the Jews and us deserveth tears.
>
> (196.223–28)

Echoing Ezra 3:12, Herbert's speaker tearfully reminds his audience of the temple that has been lost to sight as he confronts the increasing darkness and division of his time.[49] The end, he warns, is yet to come. The darkness will only deepen before the dawning sun/son of divine judgment appears to make all things new.

Repeatedly, then, *The Temple* reflects in its tripartite structure and in its individual poems the contemporary debate over Antichrist's presence in the temple, but with a peculiarly Herbertean twist. Because the temple always contains within it not only Christ but also "Antichrist," not only the "true church" but also those pretenders who would displace it, "Sinne" can be found in a range of corrupt imitations that extend far beyond Rome itself. "Sinne" is paradoxically present in the Laudian desire to create sacred space as well as in the Puritan desire to "fix" internal purity. Thus, God enters site after site within *The Temple,* not because these places are "holy," but because they are not: in "The H. Communion," he conveys himself into the elements to meet "sinnes force and art"; in "Decay," he enters the darkest "closets" of the human psyche to restore purity; in "The Starre," he willingly dies to part sin and the human heart.[50] By contesting all human representations of holiness, Herbert's God overcomes the very divisiveness that isolates and corrupts, to make the life-giving movement "between" the site of divine presence.

---

49. Hutchinson explains these lines by noting that "*the late reformation* fell as far short of the primitive church as *The second Temple* did the first, and is equally a matter for tears" (*Works of Herbert,* 546). This assessment is perfectly in keeping with my reading of an Eusebian temple.

50. Herbert, "The H. Communion," in *Works of Herbert,* 52, l. 12; "Decay," in ibid., 99, l. 18; "The Starre," in ibid., 74, l. 24.

6

Contestatory Measures in "On the Morning," *Comus,* and *Paradise Lost*

Their guides are in fault, blind guides, members of ourbreak Church, rotten members I doubt, of higher degree; to whom all men and women are rank puritans and schismaticks, to be thrust out and expeld, if they refuse to dance after their fantasticall pipe in every idle ceremony.

—Peter Smart, *The Vanitie and Downe-fall of Superstitious Popish Ceremonies*

As the headnote taken from Peter Smart's sermon delivered at Durham Cathedral suggests, the contestatory debate over ceremonies was reaching a fever pitch in the early years of the Caroline reign as the music of the churchmen was increasingly heard as an imposed harmony to which everyone must move. At least some truth inhered in this assessment, for in defining prophetic discourse as the ultimate harmony, Andrewes, Herbert, and Donne turned the metaphysical lyric and prose genres into an exercise in holy order, not only containing subversive movements like Smart's but also mediating against the polarizing perspectives on prophecy at the point of dividing the kingdom. When during these same years Milton adopts their metaphysical style in "On the Morning of Christ's Nativity" and *Comus,* he turns the musical and pacifistic form of the churchmen on end. Playing their harmonies off against the apocalyptic emphasis of biblical history, he offers a parodic critique of avant-garde prophetic discourse and a compelling return to apocalyptic formulations.[1] And parody is particularly suitable to this purpose since it allows Milton to be both spiritually traditional and

1. In calling attention to the apocalyptic dimension of this poem, Norbrook notes that "apocalyptic ideas were not viewed with enthusiasm by the Caroline court" (*Poetry and Politics,* 244–45).

politically subversive: on the one hand, he is able to call attention to the innovations that have begun to inform prophetic discourse and to corrupt the message of Christ; on the other, he is able to assume a subversive stance against the dominant literary and political discourse of his age.[2]

I

In a moment rare for him, Milton identifies the year he composes "On the Morning of Christ's Nativity" and so highlights the political and ecclesiastical circumstances of its writing.[3] The year 1629 was a time when peace was much discussed but not much in evidence. After years of fighting, King Charles had managed to negotiate a peace treaty with France, but he undertook this course largely because of political dissension at home; in fact, Charles's military efforts were no longer being funded; his confidante and political ally Buckingham had just been assassinated, and his interaction with Parliament had become contentious if not openly hostile.[4]

A close look at government in 1629 reveals the significant points of conflict: convening from January through March, Parliament had condemned both Charles's collection of taxes and his "reforms" in the Church of England. Moreover, even after the Speaker announced the adjournment that Charles requested, the House of Commons determined to go ahead with business. Locking the doors against the king's messenger, they voted a series of resolutions, the first of which took a firm stand against the innovations they believed were being foisted upon the Church of England. They resolved that "Whoever shall bring in innovation of religion, or by favour or countenance seek to extend or introduce popery or Arminianism or other opinion disagreeing from the true and orthodox Church, shall be reputed a capital enemy to the kingdom and Commonwealth."[5] By way of response, Charles issued a declaration in which he emphasized the "disobedience and seditious

2. Parody, according to Linda Hutcheon, can either be conservative or radical: in the first case, it is deployed to ridicule and control innovation, in the second to attack "dominant cultural, social, or political forces" (introduction to *Romantic Parodies, 1797–1831,* 7).

3. Milton, *Milton: Complete Poems,* 42. Future references will be designated *CP* with page, book, and line numbers, where appropriate, cited parenthetically within the text. Quotes from *Paradise Lost* will be cited parenthetically within the text and will include page, book, and line numbers.

4. According to Sharpe, "Parliament now viewed both King and Council as remote from their world, even opposed to their local interests and well-being" (*Personal Rule of Charles I,* 35).

5. Roger Lockyer, *The Early Stuarts,* 350–51, quoting S. R. Gardiner, ed., *The Constitutional Documents of the Puritan Revolution, 1625–1660,* 82–83.

carriage of those ill affected persons of the House of Commons." Asserting that they had "contemned . . . our Regall authoritie" in a way that "our Kingly Office cannot bear, nor any former age can parallel," he noted that it was his "full and absolute resolution to dissolve the same parliament."[6] In "Royal Instructions" that he published in December 1629, he privileged the liturgy over the pulpit and adopted a number of measures designed to uproot nonconformity in the English Church.[7] What he was doing, of course, was precisely what the Commons had warned against, his "innovations" having for many the distinct appearance of the Romish whore, semiotically conveyed in the renewed emphasis on the wearing of the surplice, the relocation of the altar, and the necessity of kneeling.[8]

Under the conditions articulated by the Commons, King Charles was well on his way to becoming a "capital enemy" to the church. None of this was lost on Milton, and in "On the Morning of Christ's Nativity," he reacts to the innovations occurring in church and state in a subtle and illuminating way. Weaving portions of Virgil's fourth Eclogue and Spenser's *Faerie Queene* into his celebration of Christ's nativity, Milton tests both against the apocalyptic emphasis of biblical history and so engages in a subtle critique of royalist ideology and ecclesiastical politics.

Milton's choice of these intertexts is itself political: in the years succeeding 1616 and the furor over the Spanish Match, James and his son Charles had begun to replace Christian apocalypticism with the prophetic music of Lancelot Andrewes and other avant-garde conformists as well as with the mythic idealism of Virgilian prophecy. Highlighting peace as an accomplished fact—an end achieved by the Stuart father and son—James and Charles conveniently eliminated the militant struggle essential to the conquest of the Babylonian whore.[9] The new myth that underwrote their

6. See Charles I, *His Maiesties Declaration to all his Loving Subjects,* and "Of Ceremonies, why some be abolished and some retained," in *The Book of Common Prayer.*

7. As Julian Davies suggests, the "Caroline attempt to reinvest the catholic apparel of the Anglican Church was bound to blur the visible boundaries between orthodoxy and popery, and this in spite of the king's resolution 'to deal with . . . the Pope, as wrestlers do with one another, take him up to fling him down.'" Laud had already begun to suspend lecturers for "seditious statements" by the middle of 1629, but he later granted them pardons (*Caroline Captivity,* 24, 27, 159).

8. On December 8, Charles discussed a final version of the Instructions with Laud; on December 9, he received approved copies from Archbishops Abbot and Harsnet, and by December 12, he sent them off to the bishops of the church for distribution (Davies, *Caroline Captivity,* 30–31).

9. Graham Parry discusses Charles's fascination with classical myth and Roman allusion in *The Golden Age Restored: The Culture of the Stuart Court, 1603–1642,* 184–229.

reign was, as Graham Parry has argued, the myth of the "golden age restored." Parry states,

> In accordance with the prophecies in Virgil, the renewed empire would bring in, like that of Augustus, a time of peace, and would usher in a new golden age. It is extraordinary how powerful and widespread was this political fantasy in sixteenth- and seventeenth-century Europe: it was sustained by many poets in many nations who considered it as a dream that might at any moment be translated into actuality.[10]

It is hardly surprising, then, that the bishop of Winton calls King James "our Augustus" in his "Preface to the Reader" issued along with James's *Workes.* The king, he asserts, had accomplished more than Augustus Caesar in whose time Christ was born, for in James's "dayes our Blessed Saviour Christ Jesus is come to a full and perfect aage."[11]

Because Virgilian prophecy had already been coopted by royalty in this way, Milton chooses not to "convert" it to Christian purposes as critics have generally argued.[12] Instead, he contests the political ideology attached to this myth and so establishes a perfect correlation between the mythic prophecy of the Stuart court and Christ's necessary silencing of the pagan oracles. By testing this myth against a biblical model, Milton discloses two errors; first, the king has adopted a pagan paradigm to sanction his "royalist" policy, and second, contemporary prophets have reconstructed a pacifistic version of Christianity that is similarly corrupt. In the course of Milton's lyric, Christ departs, point for point, from the political and prophetic choices made by King Charles and his churchmen, his activities illuminating, by way of contrast, the hypocritical spirituality at the center of the current political and ecclesiastical system.[13]

"On the Morning of Christ's Nativity" opens by echoing the metaphysical style of the English Churchmen and their courtly reinterpretations of time, nature, history, song, and ceremony. Milton's "This is the Month, and this the happy morn" (*CP,* 43.1) rings the changes on Lancelot Andrewes's

---

10. Ibid., 16.

11. James I, *Workes of James,* sig. C2v.

12. Patrick Cullen, in "Imitation and Metamorphosis: The Golden-Age Eclogue in Spenser, Milton, and Marvell," provides an extremely perceptive reading of Milton's transformations. I agree with many of these points but identify Milton's use of Virgil as far more contestatory.

13. I. S. MacLaren similarly establishes the significance of 1629 as a particularly "momentous" year ("Milton's Nativity Ode: The Function of Poetry and Structures of Response in 1629," esp. 192–93). Helpful too are Gregory F. Goekjian, "Deference and Silence: Milton's Nativity Ode"; and Howard Dobin, "Milton's Nativity Ode: 'O What a Mask Was There.' "

celebration of divine transcendence in his nativity sermons. Andrewes had written, "Christ was born, is true any day; but this day Christ was born, never but to-day only. For of no day in the year can it be said *hodie natus* but of this." Because, for Andrewes, Christ "returns" throughout the ecclesiastical calendar, time is both mythical and mystical, the divine return coinciding perfectly with the harmonies of the seasons and Virgil's "great Sequence of the ages": in essence, the present moment is, for Andrewes, the moment of epiphany. By the end of the opening stanza, however, Milton begins to contest this mythic and seasonal evaluation, his "Son of Heav'n" (*CP*, 43.2) plummeting downward through space and time to put an end to cycles by assigning "peace" to a future, yet to be realized moment:

> For so the holy sages once did sing
>> That he our deadly forfeit should release,
> And with his Father work us a perpetual peace.
>> (*CP*, 43.5–7)[14]

Unlike the temporary "peace" offered by Augustus Caesar, Milton's "Father and Son" establish "perpetual peace" and eradicate the open-endedness of the classical paradigm so conducive to Stuart policy. Only when mythology succumbs to divine history, Milton suggests, does time become ultimately meaningful.

To highlight this historical perspective, Milton encodes a text that was becomingly increasingly controversial in 1629—the Apocalypse of Saint John. Drawing upon the nativity narrative in Rev. 12, Milton links the birth of Christ to the woman clothed with the sun/son.[15] As we have seen in the earlier chapters of this book, this woman and son had accumulated a range of political and ecclesiastical interpretation by 1629: in Napier, Forbes, and Bernard's commentaries, she was visible in the "labour" of the true church, and the politics of Constantine; in Foxe and Spenser, she was visible in Una's "sunshiny face" and the politics of Elizabeth. Milton, however, purges away these ideological accretions, offering an interpretation of the woman of the Apocalypse far closer to that of Puritan minister George Gyffard at the end of the sixteenth century.[16] Gyffard then identified the son/sun delivered

---

14. Andrewes, *Works of Andrewes*, 1:64; Virgil, *The Pastoral Poems*, Eclogue 4:5. Achsah Guibbory analyzes Milton's progressive and linear understanding of history in *The Map of Time*, 169–212.

15. Donald Swanson and John Mulryan establish this connection in "Milton's *On the Morning of Christ's Nativity:* The Virgilian and Biblical Matrices."

16. Milton thus sheds the political ideology of his poetic "original," even as he recovers his protestant apocalypticism.

by the woman as "Christ Iesus the blessed seed of the woman, who was promised as the saviour that should breake the serpents head. For there is sayd of him, that he should rule all nations with a rod of Iron."[17] Neither Constantine nor Elizabeth nor James nor Charles, this was the divine son of the *protoevangelium* who would conquer Satan and reign over the nations.

Purging "royalist" policy from his biblical poetics, Milton goes on to register Christ's difference from the representation of royalty found in Virgil; his Christ departs from the "Courts of everlasting Day" (*CP*, 43.13) to signal his rejection of secular power. Refusing to wrap himself in the clothing of majesty—"the soft glow of a purple dye" in Virgil's eclogue[18]—Christ is "meanly wrapt" instead, assuming his place "with us" in the "darksome House" of the poor:

> That glorious Form, that Light unsufferable,
> And that far-beaming blaze of Majesty,
> Wherewith he wont at Heav'n's high Council-Table,
> To sit the midst of Trinal Unity,
> He laid aside; and here with us to be,
> Forsook the Courts of everlasting Day
> And chose with us a darksome House of mortal Clay.
>
> (*CP*, 43.8–14)

Milton's language here is politically charged: Christ "lays aside" his status and chooses to overcome the distance between himself and his subjects by becoming subject himself, presenting a sharp contrast to King Charles who had wrapped himself in the mantle of "Kingly office" that year by choosing to meet only with his "high Counsel-Table"—the contemporary name for the privy counsel.

In the final two stanzas of the opening proem, Milton moves from the striking Otherness of his royal subject to the prophetic choices he makes in revealing him. Now distinguishing between the prophecy of court (with its classical and political referents), and the prophetic music of the angels, Milton establishes a contestatory dialogue between two kinds of musical

---

17. Gyffard, *Sermons upon the whole booke of the Revelation*, 197. Gyffard openly contests the way in which wealth and power corrupt the church: "If we therefore will approve ourselves to be the Lords faithfull witnesses, wee must not seeke the pompe, the riches, the pleasures, the ease, and the delicacie of this worlde: let those things alone for the ministers of Antichrist, whose bellie is their God, which mind earthly things: but wee must painefully labour to advance the trueth, to pull downe errours and wicked vices, wee must lament and mourne to see the truth so much despised, the Lord our God so highly dishonored, and men running headlong to destruction."

18. Virgil, *The Pastoral Poems*, Eclogue 4:45–46.

interchange. The words sung by the angels, he suggests, have little in common with the words chosen by the men of the episcopal hierarchy.

Milton makes this point by subtly linking these men with another group who attends on Christ besides the shepherds and angels: the "Star-led Wizards" identified in Spenser's *Faerie Queene* and Lancelot Andrewes's sermons. Spenser had employed this group to celebrate not only the birth of Christ but the reign of Elizabeth as well.[19] And Andrewes had reified the status of episcopacy by linking it with the greatness of the magi: "But there is yet more grace offered to some in particular. The shepherds were a sort of poor simple men altogether unlearned. But here come a troop of men of great place, high account in their country; and withal of great learned men, their name gives them for no less."[20] On the basis of their higher education, Andrewes noted, the magi had interpreted the star of Christ by accommodating "heathen knowledge" into divine truth:

> I add of heathen knowledge, and comprehend in it this very knowledge, that they were well seen in the course of Heaven, in the stars and bodies celestial. . . . This learning of theirs made them never the farther from Christ we see, it did them no hurt in their coming to Christ. . . . They that are seen in these learnings of Egypt, of Chaldea, of the East, are not thereby barred at all. This is their star, their guide; a guide apt and proper for them that knew the stars, for them that were learned.[21]

When Milton determines to "prevent" the activities of the "Wizards" by preceding them to the Christ child with his "humble ode" (*CP*, 43.23–24), he also "prevents" the social, political, and spiritual bid for power that such exchanges—in the form of royal patronage—inscribe. Indeed, he hints, "hallow'd fire" (*CP*, 43.27) alone purifies prophetic speech of personal, political, and ecclesiastical profit.

Thus, though Milton requests a "humble ode" in his opening proem, he receives a divine "hymn," a shift in genre that signals a musical exchange in which Christian inspiration displaces the classical. Through precisely this kind of point and counterpoint, Milton allows the natural, cyclical, and ceremonial music of the English Churchmen who sing to the rhythms of

---

19. See *The Faerie Queene*, Book 5, Proem 8, ll. 1–2. Spenser represents Elizabeth as establishing "peace universall" (Proem 9, l. 6).

20. The "star" that these wise men follow is the Gentile's star, one directing the heathen to Christ. Andrewes notes that "heathens" like Rahab and Ruth occur in Christ's genealogy and that Christ makes the focus of his sermons outsiders such as the widow of Sarepta, Naaman the Syrian, and the Queen of the South (Andrewes, *Works of Andrewes*, 1:235, 241).

21. Ibid., 244–45.

the pagan past to play off against and finally to be drowned out by the supernatural, linear, and transcendent music of the angels and prophets who move to the rhythms of the divine Word.

In his opening, then, Milton personifies Nature to unmask an all too "natural" response to the presence of Christ:

> Nature in awe to him
> Had doff't her gaudy trim,
> With her great Master so to sympathize:
> It was no season then for her
> To wanton with the Sun, her lusty Paramour.
> (*CP*, 43–44.32–36)

Nature's decision to undress herself in order to adopt the appropriate seasonal clothes enables Milton to associate her not only with the "natural" cycle of the ecclesiastical calendar but also with Duessa in the *Faerie Queene* who constantly redresses herself linguistically. As Duessa tells Sans Joy,

> But since faire Sunne hath sperst that lowring clowd,
> And to my loathed life now shewes some light,
> Vnder your beames I will me safely shrowd.
> (1.4.48)

Willfully wantoning with this "Sunne" by "shrowding" herself in his beams, Duessa is a life-in-death parody of the woman clothed with the sun. Milton's Nature recalls this very activity, her remembered infidelity neatly connecting her with a Romish past as her words and behavior continue to give her away:

> Only with speeches fair
> She woos the gentle Air
> To hide her guilty front with innocent Snow,
> And on her naked shame,
> Pollute with sinful blame,
> The Saintly Veil of Maiden white to throw,
> Confounded, that her Maker's eyes
> Should look so near upon her foul deformities.
> (*CP*, 44.37–44)

Here, the "white" veil in which Nature clothes herself allows Milton to allude not only to the "snow" of December but also to the wearing of the white surplice, the very innovation that had put zealous Protestants in a fury in

1629. Because, for Milton, material concerns cover up spiritual error rather than correcting it, Nature's fallen activities illuminate how the present church continues to choose the natural traditions of men over the supernatural and redemptive purity of Christ.

Not surprisingly, Nature's mistaken attempt to attain purity by wearing the right "seasonal" clothes coincides perfectly with her reinterpretation of angelic music; unlike the shepherds who respond with "blissful rapture" (*CP*, 45.98), she begins to impose her own mythic and cyclical evaluation upon it. When she hears the divine song, we are told, she

> Now was almost won
> To think her part was done,
> And that her reign had here its last fulfilling;
> She knew such harmony alone
> Could hold all Heav'n and Earth in happier union.
>
> (*CP*, 46.104–8)

Milton entertains what she "knows" for five stanzas as Virgilian prophecy, playing in counterpoint to the "Organ" of heaven and the "Angelic symphony" (*CP*, 46.130, 132), attains its fullest musical range; "Time" runs back to "fetch the age of Gold," peace seems an inevitability, an already achieved fact, and the "Fates" that "run even thus" (*CP*, 46.135) almost finish Virgil's musical score. But Milton does not allow this to happen. With a resounding "No," he puts a strident end to this classical and mythic reassessment of history and reinforces instead the son's descent into linear, chronological time:

> But wisest Fate says no,
> This must not yet be so,
> The Babe lies yet in smiling Infancy,
> That on the bitter cross
> Must redeem our loss;
> So both himself and us to glorify:
> Yet first to those ychain'd in sleep,
> The wakeful trump of doom must thunder through the deep.
>
> (*CP*, 47.149–56)

Initiating the battle that will finally culminate in the Apocalypse, Christ engages in a militant struggle against such corruption. Abandoning the harmonies of peace for the "trump of doom," he not only silences the pagan oracles but also sends them on their way with "hollow shrieks," sighs, and dissonant moans of sorrow. Now, we are told, "No nightly trance, or breathed spell, / Inspires the pale-ey'd Priest from the prophetic cell" (*CP*, 48.179–80). In these stanzas Milton exposes the hollow and material emphasis of heathen prophecy, linking it through allusion to recent innovations in the English Church—to the present obsession with "heathen learning," tapers, altars, temples, cells, and priests. By finally shattering the pacifistic prophecies of his contemporaries with the conflict required of a militant church, Milton exposes the delusional, "heathen" harmony the present church has too willingly embraced. The heroic babe in swaddling bands will exercise full control over such operations. In returning to him in his concluding lines, Milton offers a final brilliantly orchestrated critique of contemporary ecclesiastical politics: "And all about the Courtly Stable, / Bright-harness'd Angels sit in order serviceable" (*CP*, 50.243–44). Reversing the terms of contemporary churchmen, the stable becomes a "Court" not because it has any "material" beauty, but because it contains Christ. The angels, unlike the churchmen of the moment, are "bright-harness'd," suggesting the militant, often contestatory nature of the messages they carry; and, perhaps most revelatory of all, they are "sitting" within the stable, a posture that the avant-garde conformists of the English Church never assign to them. As John Browning, an avant-garde conformist had argued, "The very saints and angels in heaven . . . fall down and worship and cast their crowns before the throne . . . Can anything by them used be idle or needless or superfluous? Nay rather is it not our prayer and should it not be our desire that we should so serve God as they do? That his will be so done by us as by them it is?"[22] In Milton's version of "order serviceable," the "angels" most assuredly do not kneel. Instead, divine communion is open to all who will be shaped not by royalist politics, but by the life of the child in the stable.

Comus is a thorough development of the position that Milton reveals in "On the Morning," the difference between opposing prophetic styles now registered in a polyphonic musical debate that gives voice to the ecclesiastical controversies of the moment. In this dramatic work performed in 1634 (some years before Milton's *Of Reformation* and *Of Prelatical Episcopacy* delineate the antiprelatical phase of his career), Milton deploys poetry and music to set the stage for what was clearly becoming a volatile, even dangerous conflict. Stephen Honeygoskey, in *Milton's House of God: The Invisible and Visible Church*, has thoroughly illuminated the extent to which Milton's reformation prose examines the dynamic relationship between the individual

22. Browning, *Concerning public prayer and the fasts of the church*, 26.

and the church, giving rise to a theology of continuing transformation and an ecclesiology of inward change.[23] Milton was, however, affirming these same values in his poetic works—in "On the Morning," "Lycidas," and, as I argue here, in *Comus.*

The mask form provides Milton with a variety of creative options not available to him in his later prose work: it allows him, as Alice Lyle-Scoufos has argued, to turn his focus back to earlier dramatic forms centering on the Apocalypse of Saint John in particular, the "Lady Wandering in the Wilderness" of the twelfth century *Ludus de Antichristo,* Thomas Kirchmayer's 1538 *Pammachius,* and John Foxe's 1556 *Christus Triumphans.* Each of these plays represents Lady Ecclesia's encounter with Antichrist, an encounter in which, Lyle-Scoufos notes, the lady "remains virtuous under harrasment." From this "vortex of propagandist art," she accordingly argues, "Comus sprang."[24] At the same time, *Comus* as "court" drama provides opportunities relevant to Milton's immediate historical situation. That Milton chooses the aristocratic genre of the mask to render this dialogue into musical form and, even more surprisingly, that he engages Egerton's own children to address and redress episcopal error through their singing is stunningly subversive, radical, and innovative.

Nevertheless, Milton's radicalism springs directly from a critical moment in biblical narrative as Christ's contestatory measures against the chief priests and scribes of the church offer Milton a musical parallel for evaluating episcopacy. In Matt. 21, Christ had silenced his opposition in the temple by forcing them to acknowledge the prophetic music of children, children who, he asserted, were fulfilling the words of David in singing his praises: "Out of the mouth of babes and sucklings thou hast perfected praise" (Matt. 21:16). Milton turns the opportunity Lawes gives him to write the singing parts of Egerton's children into contestatory measures of his own: in scripting the words to their music, he both "perfects praise" of holiness and counters what he considers to be the increasingly Romish corruption of episcopacy.

Milton's *Comus* thus embraces wider concerns than "On the Morning"'s redefinition of prophecy; he now directs his attention at the purpose behind this redefinition: the determination of contemporary churchmen to sanction the "ceremonies" of episcopacy by asserting that this renewal of ritual actually "reformed" the church by returning it to its pristine state in the early years of the church. At the same time, their emphasis on a ceremonial visibility

---

23. Honeygoskey, *Milton's House of God,* 30–61.
24. Lyle-Scoufos, "The Mysteries in Milton's Masque," 113–19, 120.

allowed them to concentrate on what could be seen rather than what could not. They argued, conversely, that any attempt to determine who the pure and visible elect actually were involved spiritual error, involved attempting to see with eyes that only God had. Visible purity was therefore not the issue, but rather ritual involvement.

This conformist acceptance of impurity, Milton recognized, could be discerned in Spenser's "Legende of the Knight of the Redcrosse, or Holinesse," both in Redcrosse's return to Una and in her willingness to overlook his corrupt past. In essence, the church's ambivalence about its own "adulterous" history destabilized the very notion of attaining visible purity. As Bishop Williams, speaking for the conformists of the time, had argued, "How is it possible for me to know any one member of this mysticall body? and if they be not subject unto my sense, that I know not who they are, how can they be subject unto my sight, which cannot discerne of inward graces?"[25] Such questions, focusing on the inability of human beings to discern true spirituality, facilitated a universal embrace, an "open" ecclesiastical communion in which visible purity was not essential.

To correct this turn of events—in Milton's view, a complete misreading of divine grace—he returns in *Comus* to Spenser's "Legende of the Knight of the Redcrosse, or Holinesse" and, in Georgia Christopher's words, "turns the plot of *The Faerie Queene*, Book 1, on its head" by taking surprising liberties with the story line: "Instead of an unfaithful knight who is seduced by a witch, [Milton] presents a faithful lady who is *not* seduced by a sorcerer, though she will also need to be rescued."[26] Milton's changes are at once "reformed," as Christopher argues, and deeply political: he reevaluates the relationship between the invisible and visible church represented in Spenser's "historicall fiction," since it was this relationship, during the 1630s, that was at the core of ecclesiastical debate. Consequently, when Milton goes back to Spenser's apocalyptic framework, he recovers only Una, thereby purging the narrative of the problematic union that Spenser makes central.

The fact that the "Lady" is not looking for her lost beloved but her lost brothers centers the narrative on brotherly love and removes the possibility of the lady's betrayal by one supposedly committed to her. In rejecting the central thread of Spenser's narrative, the tenuous relationship between his hero and heroine, Milton rejects as well the historicist interpretation being highlighted by his contemporaries in the English Church who were willing

25. Williams, *True Church Shewed*, 11.
26. Christopher, *Milton and the Science of the Saints*, 33.

to identify with a visible church guilty of past impurity but in the process of being purged and reformed. Consequently, the heroine of Milton's *Comus* represents the visible, protestant church, and, unlike Spenser's Redcrosse, she begins chaste and remains so. This lady has not given her word as Una has, and thus she is not subject to any impure alliance. Consequently, she does not have the same problems as Una, who, while wandering in the wilderness, falls prey to the machinations of Archimago dressed in Redcrosse's clothes and the courtly words of Sans Loy. Both seek to seduce Una in alternative ways: the first by dressing like her lover, the second by speaking in appropriate love language. Neither of these "material" attempts succeeds in corrupting Una, nor indeed is either central to Spenser's narrative. Because Milton's lady does not seek her lost beloved but her lost brothers, however, she is not subjected to the male-female power structure that Una is: Spenser's heroine must, because of both her gender and her invisible status, rely on the visible actions of Redcrosse. She must even accept his past adultery and mistreatment of her with a genteel and accommodating silence.

The lady does, on the other hand, encounter problems of her own. She misinterpets Comus, but she recognizes her error almost immediately and is never taken in again; indeed, the very fact that she mistakenly assumes the rural innocence of the "shepherd" who offers directive hints at a tendency evident in the more zealous reformers of the time. They similarly saw spirituality in terms of overly simplistic dichotomies, privileging, on this basis, country innocence over court artifice, pastoral simplicity over the learning of episcopacy—when, Milton suggests, such reductive reactions needed to be interrogated as well. The truth is never so easily distinguished from falsehood. Through just such qualifying measures, Milton gives voice to a number of spiritual misunderstandings, not only exposing the all too worldly materiality of the avant-garde conformists gaining power in the Stuart court—here, brilliantly rendered in the words and music of Comus—but also uncovering the perceptual limits of the reformed position evident in the thinking of the lady and her brothers.

In this sense, Milton's decision to make *Comus* a musical debate between children provides an extraordinary instance of dialogism, one in which traditional and nontraditional views on the church could be heard in concert before a contemporary audience attuned to the underlying and subversive rhythms. These rhythms had been clearly brought out in the sermons and pamphlets of the time, rhythms documented in Peter Smart's sermon of 1628. Arguing that the piping of anthems on organs was drowning out the reflective music of the Psalms, that a "theatricall stage play" was now distracting communicants from meditating on the Eucharist, Smart underscored the sensory stimulation in which the present church was engaged: "At that very season, very unseasonably, their eares are possest with pleasant tunes, and their eyes fed with pompous spectacles, of glistering pictures, and histrionicall gestures, representing unto us *Apollo's* solemnities in his Temple at Delos." In highlighting the "heathen" impulses behind ceremonies, Smart stressed as well the material link between ceremonies and the bishops who promoted them: "For seldome shall you see a stout ceremony-monger, but the same will also be a notorious Non-resident, a very Tot-Quot; not content with one or two little ones, but foure or five great preferments and dignities."[27] Noting rather scathingly that the bishops of the time were increasing their economic profit at the expense of spiritual commitment, Smart highlighted their addiction to patronage and preferment.

When we read Milton's *Comus* in the context of contemporary sermons and pamphlets such as these, Comus's sensuousness and his accompanying materialism suggest an immediate referent as, through him, Milton parodies the "innovative" ceremonies and profiteering designs of avant-garde bishops. Unfortunately, recent literary historians have confined their analysis of *Comus* almost exclusively to one particular debate: the recreation controversy over the *Book of Sports* prompted by King Charles's sanctioning of holy-day entertainment. There is, however, a problem here that Leah S. Marcus has acknowledged: "Milton's portrayal of Comus and his rabble is, of course, unlike the holiday mirth advocated by the *Book of Sports* in its tolerance for sexual license. The king's declaration had specified that the allowable pastimes were to be 'lawful,' 'harmeless,' and 'honest.'" Comus's attempt to seduce the lady as part of his revelry is a pastime certainly not included in the *Book of Sports*. It was, however, in terms of seduction that Peter Smart and numerous other Puritan reformers analyzed the dilemma confronting the Protestant church as, they argued, her originary purity was now at stake: "So must we, love Gods law, which forbiddeth idolatry, and hate vaine inventions, and the inventours of vanities, when they would insnare and intangle us with their fraudulent impostures, to seduce, and allure us to their superstitious and idol services."[28]

27. Smart, *Vanitie and Downe-fall,* 24, 21.
28. Marcus, *The Politics of Mirth: Jonson, Herrick, Milton, Marvell, and the Defense of Old Holiday Pastimes,* 197 (other works usefully tracing the connections between *Comus* and its historical and political contexts include Maryann Cale McGuire, *Milton's Puritan Masque,* and Cedric Brown, *John Milton's Aristocratic Entertainments*); Smart, *Vanitie and Downe-fall,* 4–5.

The ceremonies that Smart sees as an attempt to "seduce and allure" an innocent church into error, are of course described by the bishops of the time as an attempt to dress the English Church in still more beautiful clothing. In Bishop Williams's words,

> The Church should use some ceremonies, that shee might be seene to be adorned with some outward decencie and glory, as well as filled with inward graces. For so the Prophet David saith, There stood the Queen in a vesture of Gold, wrought about with divers colours; to shew unto us, that although all the glory of the Church be principally within, in the Word and the Sacraments, and in the main grounds of religion, yet her cloathing and outward shew is of wrought gold, and her raiment of needle-worke, wrought about with divers colours, that is her ceremonies, orders, and constitutions, as Saint Augustine expoundeth it, are very splendid in the eyes of men, and doe as it were, allure them rather to embrace her, and the more willingly to do service unto God.[29]

Offering a positive version of Smart's evaluation, Williams argues that the "material" beauty of ceremonies makes the church still more alluring, not only calling attention to her status as "Queen" but also drawing men into the divine service of God. Similar to Andrewes, Donne, and Herbert, Williams attempts on this basis to include rather than exclude the masses from ecclesiastical communion. But he also admits that while ceremonies are things "indifferent," and therefore not matters of faith, they are appointed by an authorized episcopal body who has the right to punish those who will not honor them: "none can be excused for his disobedience, which refuseth the observance of the same."[30]

It is this kind of "disobedience" that Milton's *Comus* asks an audience to reevaluate, especially under those conditions when the church's purity is being openly violated by episcopacy. By making the lady of *Comus* the woman in the wilderness and thus a figure of the pure Protestant church, Milton gives dramatic urgency to the spiritual predicament confronting the present church. His child speakers accordingly debate one another over the very issues heard in ecclesiastical controversy: the importance of purity, the "right" response to spiritual peril, the purpose of beauty and profit, the "good" of canon law, and finally, the nature of grace. "Out of the mouths of babes" Milton manages to offer a brilliant and scathing critique of the avant-garde conforming bishops of the Caroline court.

29. Williams, *True Church Shewed*, 95.
30. Ibid., 94.

In the opening lines, the Attendant Spirit distances himself from the rhetoric of the English Churchmen by rejecting the language of open embrace, both by adopting a Neoplatonic commitment to purity and by drawing a clear line between those whom he comes to defend and guard and those who are completely "unmindful of the crown that Virtue gives" (*CP*, 90.9). The distinguishing feature, he explains, can be seen in the way they move:

> Yet some there be that by due steps aspire
> To lay their just hands on that Golden Key
> That opes the Palace of Eternity
> To such my errand is, and but for such,
> I would not soil these pure Ambrosial weeds
> With the rank vapors of this Sin-worn mold.
>   (*CP*, 90.12–17)

The Attendant Spirit is explicit about the terms of his aid, revealing both an ability to recognize true servants and a willingness to set the "just" apart from a multitude of others not worth his time or energy. He thus directs attention toward the piercing discernment and "quick command" (*CP*, 91.41) of Jove and away from the limits of human perception underscored by the avant-garde conformists, a shift upward that instills purity by eliminating the ambiguous slippage between the visible and invisible elect. God, he affirms, sees and knows.

To provide aid, the Attendant Spirit chooses, appropriately, the role of music teacher; he comes to earth dressed as a shepherd who "to the service of this house belongs" (*CP*, 92.85), a shepherd with singular musical talents:

> Who with his soft Pipe and smooth-dittied Song
> Well knows to still the wild winds when they roar,
> And hush the waving Woods, nor of less faith,
> And in this office of his Mountain watch,
> Likeliest, and nearest to the present aid
> Of this occasion.
>   (*CP*, 92.86–91)

The shepherd whom the Attendant Spirit chooses to inhabit plays music less like Orpheus's then like Christ's: the former brought nature into harmony it is true, but the latter "hushed the waves," his "faith" completely calming the "wild winds" of the storm.[31] Clearly, Thrysis, as watchman and shepherd,

---

31. See Matt. 14:22–27, Mark 6:45–52, and John 6:15–21, where Christ's ability to calm the wild winds and hush the storms is evidence of his power.

has the power of Christ, and because his clothes give bodily form to the Attendant Spirit, Thrysis makes possible a double incarnation, combining spirit, musician, and Christ in one. That the Attendant Spirit first turns his attention to the brothers rather than to the lady is rather odd unless we remember that the "brothers" can be interpreted as Reformation Protestants and thus as the active agents in Milton's allegory of the church. If the church is to be protected and eventually liberated, it is the "brothers" committed to her purity who must be instructed in the appropriate measures.

Comus, of course, reveals himself to be the antithesis of the Attendant Spirit, for he descends on the lady not to protect but to ensnare her. And, though he has an air of knowledge, he is not quite right that "Rigor now is gone to bed, / And Advice with scrupulous head" (*CP*, 92.107–8), for he will soon discover a kind of "rigor" in an innocent young woman who does not fit so neatly into his categories. Meanwhile, he gives himself away as he imitates a glitzy model of episcopacy:

> We that are of purer fire
> Imitate the Starry Choir,
> Who in their nightly watchful Spheres,
> Lead in swift round the Months and Years.
> (*CP*, 92.111–14)

As we have seen, the bishops identified themselves as the "stars" of the church, capable, as *episcopos* suggests, of "watching over" others in the night and offering spiritual directives during the daily round of the ecclesiastical calendar.[32] Though Comus is hardly of "purer fire," he appropriates their metaphor while adding to it the "rites" that he wishes to "begin" as a "vow'd Priest" of Hecate. In this way, Milton parodies the pride and increasing ceremonialism of a contemporary priesthood, disclosing at the same time their sinister rhetoric through Comus's self-revelation:

> I under fair pretense of friendly ends
> And well-plac't words of glozing courtesy,
> Baited with reasons not unplausible

32. George Downame makes precisely this connection in his own interpretation of Rev. 1:20 as he defends episcopacy by analyzing the Apocalypse. "Seeing [the Bishops] bee Starres," he says, "in Christ's right hand, they may be assured whiles they receiving their light from him, who is the Sunne of righteousness, do shine unto his people in the light of doctrine, & of a godly life" (*A Sermon defending the honourable function of Bishops*, 2). Not surprisingly, Andrewes, Donne, and Herbert identify the bishops as both "angels" and "starres."

Wind me into the easy-hearted man,
And hug him into snares.

(*CP*, 94.160–64)

Though "friendly" and seemingly "reasonable," the "well-plac't" words of
Comus are bait designed to entrap; indeed, the strategy of indirection that
he will employ against the lady reflects Henry Burton's assessment of the
bishops' "plot" against the present church: "Their way is not to doe it forth-
right, but by many insinuations, and winding wayes . . . to suffer none to
come to any place of eminencie in the Church, but through Simony-gate, or
Ambition, and such by-wayes, to make sure if possible [of] a corrupt Clergie;
if any be sincere and bold in lashing of Sinne, especially raigning sinnes, to
snap him up, and muzzle him for barking" (sig. D2). Setting the language
of "profit" against prophetic language, Burton distinguishes between the
"insinuations" of a priesthood engaged in promoting corruption and the
"barking" of a ministry that seeks to expose "raigning sinnes."

It is, of course, "reigning" that is on Comus's mind as, in meeting the lady,
he determines not to "reign" alone: "I'll speak to her, / And she shall be my
Queen" (*CP*, 96.264–65). His words recall Bishop Williams's willingness to
identify the English Church as a "Queen" whose material beauty brings
others into her "service," words emphasizing the courtly origins of the
English Church and her power over her subjects. The lady, however, chooses
a different definition of spiritual power, and it is from this power that she
draws her strength:

O welcome pure-ey'd Faith, white-handed Hope,
Thou hov'ring Angel girt with golden wings,
And thou unblemish't form of Chastity,
I see ye visibly, and now believe
That he, the Supreme good, t' whom all things ill
Are but as slavish officers of vengeance,
Would send a glist'ring Guardian, if need were,
To keep my life and honor unassail'd.

(*CP*, 95.213–20)

The lady's verbal attention to the visibility of faith, hope, and chastity
indicates in definitive terms the necessity of a visibly pure church, as,
in shifting from "Charity" to "Chastity," she calls attention to her own
unadulterated purity. Georgia Christopher argues that Milton here alters
Scripture to make "a key doctrinal distinction" about the purity of faith,

and so revises a "favorite proof-text for the Catholic position." He revises a favorite proof text for the Church of England's bishops as well, one privileged, during the increasing dissension of the 1620s and '30s, above all else. In Bishop Williams's words, "The Church hath need of nothing more than Charitie; yet now enmitie reigneth where there should be unitie." This assessment follows quickly upon Williams's evaluation of the present church, which, he acknowledges, is not pure, for purity is an impossibly high standard:

> Seeing that no Church ever breathed in so pure an aire, as that she might not justly complaine of some thick & unwholesome vapours: and that indeed there can be no place on earth, that can priviledge us from Sinne, when Paradise, a type of heaven, nay heaven it selfe, was not free from it; this should teach us, not to thinke we shall be able to finde perfection here, which doth only dwell with God, that dwells in a light inaccessible to any mortall eye.[33]

In contrast to Williams's assertion that sin is a function of life in heaven and on earth, the lady draws a sharp line between purity and impurity in order to sustain her faith and to demarcate clear boundaries between good and evil. God, she believes, will provide a "Guardian" to keep her "honor unassail'd," should the necessity arise. Meanwhile, her spirits lifted, she chooses music as the medium that can be "heard farthest" (*CP*, 95.227), and so sends her voice echoing through the woods.

Comus is stunned and enraptured by her music, turning his praise back—in awed and adoring terms—on the lady herself. Both responses cause her to reject him, for in failing to comprehend the meaning of her music, he has missed the state of loss that her words signify and misinterpreted her as well. Though he has little concern for her predicament, Comus does not take long to realize that offering to reunite her with her lost brothers will place her within his power. Never short on imagination, he weaves an encounter with them into the events of his day:

> Their port was more than human, as they stood . . .
> . . . .
> And as I past, I worshipt; if those you seek,
> It were a journey like the path to Heav'n
> To help you find them.
>
> (*CP*, 97.297, 301–3)

---

33. Christopher, *Milton and Science*, 38; Williams, *True Church Shewed*, 101, 100.

Though Comus's tendencies are clear in this brief recital and should perhaps tip the lady off, she is paying too much attention to the possibility of rediscovering her lost brothers to hear the idolatry in his representation. In what now ensues, Comus gains power over her both by emphasizing his greater skill in the woods through a series of "I know" 's and by promising her the joy of reunion. Such strategies hint at the appeal of contemporary bishops who called attention to their knowledge and their ability to unite the church into one body. The body that Comus actually seeks is, of course, the lady's own.

The next scene between the two reveals the lady already "set in an enchanted Chair" as Milton coopts a scene from Spenser's "Legende of Chastity" in a further revision of Spenser's "Legende of the Knight of the Redcrosse, or Holinesse." Because, in Milton's view, holiness and chastity are one, his lady combines the spirituality of Una with the militancy of Britomart, the knight of chastity. Thus, while she is briefly subject, like Una, to the attack of evil men and "bounden fast" like Amoret to a wicked magician, she cuts through Comus's rhetoric with the force of Britomart, her power, of course, springing from the Word of God. Here, too, Milton turns his Spenserian original in a new direction, revising the description of Amoret's bondage for political purposes. Consequently, while the earlier heroine is "girt round with yron bands, / Vnto a brasen pillour, by the which she stands" (*Faerie Queene*, 3.12.30), Milton's lady (as Protestant church) is confined to the "chair" of episcopacy, a position into which she has been forced against her will.[34] As Comus gloats over his power to immobilize her altogether, the lady blazes back at him to define his limits:

> Thou canst not touch the freedom of my mind
> With all thy charms, although this corporal rind
> Thou hast immanacl'd, while Heav'n sees good.
> (*CP*, 105.663–65)

34. The churchmen of the time supported episcopacy as the order prescribed by God and evident since the apostles' times. Its hierarchical structure rather than the "parity" of Presbyterianism was apparent in the "thrones, benches, and seats" of the earliest Christian temple on record in Eusebius's *Ecclesiastical History* (2:427). Joseph Mede returns to Eusebius's temple to highlight the ancient nature of episcopacy in his work, *The Name Altar:* "Eusebius hath left us a copy of a panegyrick Oration made at the dedication of a sumptuous and magnificent Church at Tyre: the structure & garnishing whereof the Panegyrist describing at large, and amongst the rest, the Seats erected in the sacrarium or Quire, for the honour (as he speaks) of the Prelacy, and priestly order" (9–10). Because Thronos, or "throne" is Greek for chair, it links the "throne" in the Kingdom with the "throne" in the church. In *Comus*, of course, the "chair" links Comus's "royal" authority to his coercive episcopal strategies.

Despite Comus's attempt to frighten her into submission, she again defines the boundaries, claiming a free space that his power cannot touch. Though she is bound to this chair and bound to the ceremonies that Comus seeks to institute, she has a free conscience. On this basis—the internal freedom of the externally bound—conformist Robert Sanderson had justified his position regarding the institution of ceremonial laws: "But it is no wrong to the Liberty of a Christian man's Conscience, to bind him to outward Observance for Orders sake, and to impose on him a Necessitie for Obedience."[35] But Sanderson goes still further. Identifying nonconformity as a kind of anarchy, an attempt to "overthrow all bond of subjection and obedience to lawful Authoritie," he refuses to declare the rejection of ceremonies "meerely indifferent." In his view, nonconformity signifies a larger problem, the disobedience of the subject. Milton allows his lady to fit this characterization. She actively resists her bonds, her words recalling her faith in divine providence. God will, at the right time, she asserts, provide a means of liberation.

Comus, however, merely steps up the temptation by arguing that the lady is actually rejecting natural benefits given by a good God. As Leah Marcus has noted, Comus makes this claim by interpreting the text from *The Book of Common Prayer* that had been read that day for Michaelmas: "The principal things for the whole use of man's life are water, fire, iron, and salt, flour of wheat, honey, milk, and the blood of the grape, and oil and clothing. All these things are for good to the godly: so to the sinners they are turned into evil. . . . All the works of the Lord are good."[36] In developing his "gloze" on this text, Comus accuses her of rejecting not only natural abundance but also the very "good" of God himself who, because he brings "good" to the godly, and "evil" to the wicked, offers her an untainted "good." She is, then, an "ill-borrower" similar to the steward who buried his "talent," since, like him, she refuses to invest her principle/principal in what can only profit her:

> But you invert the cov'nants of her trust,
> And harshly deal like an ill borrower
> With that which you reciev'd on other terms,
> Scorning the unexempt condition
> By which all mortal frailty must subsist,
> Refreshment after toil, ease after pain,

---

35. Sanderson, *Ten Sermons*, 29.

36. Marcus quotes this reading for Michaelmas, found in the 1632, 1633, and 1634 editions of *The Book of Common Prayer* (*Politics of Mirth*, 201–2).

That have been tir'd all day without repast,
And timely rest have wanted; but, fair Virgin,
This will restore all soon.

(*CP*, 106.682–90)

Comus revises the parable on stewardship in order to replace active commitment with "refreshment," "ease," and "rest"—a rhetorical move that completely undermines the life of faithful service that the parable inculcates. He argues, moreover, that in "scorning" this opportunity, the lady has inverted God's "cov'nant," effectively overturning the law of nature. In faulting her for her repeated rejection of the gifts at hand, Comus echoes the arguments in Cosin's *Private Devotions,* a treatise not only encouraging members of the church to add to the "exercises of the Soul" the "necessary recreation of the body," but also taking aim at "offenders of the fourth Commandment": "They that under a pretence of serving God more strictly than others (especially for hearing and meditating of sermons), do by their fasts, and certain judaizing observations, condemn the joyful festivity of this high and holy day, which the Church allows, as well for the necessary recreation of the body in due time, as for spiritual exercises of the Soul."[37]

Undaunted by this attack, the lady flatly dismisses the "necessary recreation of the body." She also rejects the "cup" that will "restore all soon," for within these words she hears the claim to "restore" her to the communion of Rome.[38] As Peter Smart had put this, "But the whore of *Babylons* bastardly brood, doting upon their Mothers beauty, that painted Harlot the Church of *Rome,* have laboured to restore her all her robes and jewells againe."[39] In turning away from the food, clothing, and jewels that Comus offers her, she provides an alternative reading of the Word that undoes Comus's exposition; her words are unrelentingly clear:

I would not taste thy treasonous offer; none
But such as are good men can give good things,
And that which is not good, is not delicious
To a well-govern'd and wise appetite.

(*CP*, 106.702–5)

37. John Cosin, *A Collection of Private Devotions,* in *The Works of the Right Reverend Father in God, John Cosin,* 2:116.

38. His words appear to make possible what can be won only by Britomart's militancy and a reverse incantation in the earlier text, but he is, of course, lying.

39. Smart, *Vanitie and Downe-fall,* 11.

Contesting Comus's gloss, she notes that he has repeatedly interposed himself between nature and God in attaining the gifts he offers. Because he is not good but evil, all that passes through his hands will result in evil, and, in drawing her into the exchange, will only corrupt her. This rereading of the passage from the prayer book leads the lady to call into question yet another authority, this time Canon 26 from the Church of England's *Thirty-Nine Articles of Religion*. It reads:

> Of the unworthinesse of the Ministers which hinder not the effect of the Sacraments. Although in the visible church the evil be mingled with the good, and sometime the evil have chief authority in the ministration of the Word and Sacrament: yet forasmuch as they do not the same in their own name, but in Christs, and do minister by his commission & authority, we may use their ministry both in hearing the word of God, and in the receiving of the Sacraments. Neither is the effect of Christs ordinance taken away by their wickednesse, nor the grace of Gods gifts diminished from such, as by faith, and rightly do receive the Sacraments ministred unto them, which be effectuall, because of Christs institution and promise, though they be ministred by evil men. Neverthelesse, it appertaineth to the discipline of the Church, that enquiry be made of evil Ministers, and they they be accused by those that have knowledge of their offences: and finally being found guilty, by just judgement be deposed.[40]

This canon, at least in part, lets Comus off the hook; it declares that if a corrupt churchman offers sacraments in the name of God, only "good" will come to those who receive them. The lady, however, rejects this evaluation, asserting instead that the "grace of Gods gifts" is indeed diminished when it is offered by an evil man. She will, on this basis, have nothing to do with it.

Recognizing that the lady has completely undermined his authority—both his interpretation of texts and his administration of the "cup"—Comus chooses to sidestep her main argument, her rejection of "evil men." He focuses instead on her final phrase, that his food is "not delicious." Behind his shift in tactics we hear echoes of the argument John Donne makes about the gourmet "taste" of those who eat their meals in private because they despise the public communion of the church. Her determination to fast enables Comus to go further than even John Donne, however, to turn her rejection of "natural bounty" and material benefits into a subversive act against the

40. See *Articles of Religion: Agreed upon by both Houses, and the principall Divines thorough all England and Wales, for the avoiding of diversities of Opinions. Whereunto is added His Majesties Declaration in confirming the same,* no. 26.

entire political and divine order. As the various texts already cited suggest, the rejection of canon law and ceremonies was, by 1634, perceived as an act of subversion against the secular and spiritual hierarchy.

Having come this far, Comus determines to go after what really sets the lady apart: her chastity. It is, of course, her failure to "consume," her unwillingness to enter into sexual or social commerce of any kind that has denied him all access to her:

> List Lady, be not coy, and be not cozen'd
> With that same vaunted name Virginity;
> Beauty is nature's coin, must not be hoarded,
> But must be current, and the good thereof
> Consists in mutual and partak'n bliss,
> Unsavory in th'enjoyment of itself.
> (*CP*, 107.737–42)

Intimating that the lady is on the one hand a tease, and, on the other, too thoroughly caught up in her own value, Comus informs her that the "Beauty" of holiness in the absence of an audience has no exchange rate and therefore no meaning until it is commodified, put into circulation, made "current." A stunning parody of avant-garde conformists such as Laud, Comus bases his system of values not on private integrity but on "mass" consumption:

> Beauty is nature's brag, and must be shown
> In courts, at feasts, and high solemnities
> Where most may wonder at the workmanship.
> (*CP*, 107.745–47)

With these words, Milton unmasks the Romish materialism and crass sensuality of those innovations intended to make the churches of the time more beautiful: Comus's terms accordingly slide from those of the courtier to those of the artisan: the lady must instill "wonder" in an almost titillating way, her "workmanship" both creating and frustrating desire.[41] As Comus seeks to re-cover the woman in the temple in the clothing of the whore, he invites her to engage in increasingly sensual and sexual transactions. The "good" he explains, is a product only of "mutual and partak'n bliss, / Unsavory in th'enjoyment of itself." In short, she as an ecclesiastical "body" must give

---

41. I am indebted to Kathy Pesta for pointing the artistic dimension of "workmanship" out to me.

herself up to "enjoyment"—on his terms as well as John Donne's—by being "open to most men."

This invitation proves almost too much for the lady who is shocked into speech, the only form of exchange she will allow herself. Though she is clearly disempowered—bound to Comus's "chair" and forced to listen to his injunctions—she preserves her chastity and remains in control by rejecting both feminine "silence" and feminine "obedience" in the face of his abuse: "I hate when vice can bolt her arguments, / And virtue has no tongue to check her pride" (*CP*, 108.760–61). Now speaking as a prophet, she openly condemns Comus's self-serving profiteering as she exposes the rampant corruption in the social, sexual, and ecclesiastical exchanges of the time.[42] And she does more. In offering a final interpretation of the passage from Ecclesiasticus under discussion, she discloses both the "right" use of nature's benefits and the social and ecclesiastical responsibility of those in charge of "distribution." First, she asserts, nature

> . . . good catress,
> Means her provision only to the good
> That live according to her sober laws
> And holy dictate of spare Temperance.
> > (*CP*, 108.764–67)

The good man will experience the good of nature if he listens to the "holy dictates" of moderation and allows right living to inform his life. Out of this individual model, she indicates, a public one also arises:

> If every just man that now pines with want
> Had but a moderate and beseeming share
> Of that which lewdly-pamper'd Luxury
> Now heaps upon some few with vast excess,
> Nature's full blessings would be well dispens't
> In unsuperfluous even proportion,
> And she no whit encumber'd with her store.
> > (*CP*, 108.768–74)

Within these words she conveys a double mandate with extraordinary rhetorical finesse. Beginning in hypothetical terms with "every just man," the

---

42. Norbrook illuminates Milton's inversion of the social hierarchy, noting that his lady comes "close to shattering the very basis of the masque form" by exposing its pretensions, and that she "lectures a man" (*Poetry and Politics*, 257–58).

lady immediately marginalizes him, placing him at the mercy of a corrupt hierarchy in which "lewedly-pamper'd Luxury" heaps all on a select few while leaving him pining in agony. She suggests not only that the "just" need to be empowered but also that the present system needs to be overthrown. In short, if someone is, as Comus claims to be, an intermediary between divine and natural benefits and so entrusted with secular or spiritual distribution, he must acknowledge his greater responsibility rather than perverting it. Only a "just" distribution provided by "just" men would correct the obvious inequities of the present system, eliminating the "profit" motive informing all current exchanges.[43] Unfortunately, only one means of contesting this corrupt system is available to the "just man" and the lady alike—that of the prophetic exchange itself.

Yet even this exchange, in the face of such corrupt opposition, has its limits, and the lady recognizes it:

> To him that dares
> Arm his profane tongue with contemptuous words
> Against the Sun-clad power of Chastity
> Fain would I something say, yet to what end?
> (*CP*, 108.780–83)

Unmasking Comus's invitation to peace and profit, she discloses it as a subtle strategy of containment, a rhetorically militant move against "the Sun-clad power of Chastity," the woman clothed with the sun herself. Thus, although Comus senses the quality of her music, defining its "sober certainty of waking bliss" (*CP*, 96.263) in opposition to his mother's, he cannot comprehend the meaning behind it, for "the serious doctrine of Virginity" (*CP*, 108.787) is out of his range. The Word, in fact, has no meaning for him except as it facilitates his own transactions. For this reason, the lady informs him,

---

43. Milton's idealistic vision is necessarily predicated on the right rule of the "just." Thus, Annabel Patterson's suggestion that "the category of the underprivileged is restricted to every just man" and consequently that the "redistribution of goods" applies to them alone completely misconstrues Milton's point (" 'Forc'd fingers': Milton's Early Poems and Ideological Constraint," 18). Milton's lady bases her argument on the passage from Ecclesiasticus, elaborating on the very point that she has made earlier: because "good" comes to the "good" and "evil" to the ungodly, only "good" men entrusted with power can actually distribute "benefits," Canon 26 notwithstanding. Richard Halpern reads this passage more as a critique of class structure than morality, noting that "it is hard to imagine how personal temperance could solve the maldistribution of wealth described here" ("Puritanism and Maenadism in 'A Mask,' " 100). Milton is actually wedding the two: a person who is personally temperate should be in charge of the public welfare.

he will be reduced to the limits of his own language, condemned to "enjoy [his] dear Wit and gay Rhetoric" (*CP,* 108.790) as an empty play of signifiers. Interestingly, in making this point, the lady invokes the "somewhat" to which Lancelot Andrewes and George Herbert refer in signaling that infinitely mysterious presence beyond the limits of language. Her "Fain would I something say, but to what end?" echoes George Herbert's "My heart was meaning all the day, / Somewhat it fain would say," of "A True Hymn." But Milton marks out a sharp difference in the end that his lady foresees. Unlike George Herbert who finds "somewhat more" in God's completion of his lines, the lady envisions a moment in which the "uncontrolled worth / Of this pure cause" will kindle her "sacred vehemence" into a telling conflagration, shattering Comus's "magic structures" in apocalyptic fire (*CP,* 793, 795, 798).[44]

This exchange is quite enough for Comus who stops talking to the lady and begins talking to himself in a quivering attempt to pull himself together. When he does speak again, it is to silence her:

> Come, no more,
> This is mere moral babble, and direct
> Against the canon laws of our foundation;
> I must not suffer this.
>
> (*CP,* 108–9.806–9)

Though critics have been slow to recognize the significance of Comus's accusations, he informs his immediate audience of what they already doubtless knew: that the lady has spoken against the "canon laws of our foundation," meaning the foundation of the church itself.[45] In calling her words "moral babble," however, Comus attempts to gain back his ground, this time by

---

44. Herbert, *Works of Herbert,* 168.3, 14, 20. For the emphasis on "somewhat" in George Herbert, see "A true Hymne" (ibid., 168) and "The Bag" (ibid., 151) as well as his prose work, *A Priest to the Temple,* in *Works of Herbert* (248). Here, in the "somewhat" with which the Parson supplies his parishioners, he combines economic and spiritual profit: he supplies them with money as well as with parables and so fuses the material and the transcendent in his prophetic art.

45. Leah Marcus is an exception; she notes rather tentatively that "Readers of Milton's Masque who were closer to its occasion than we are perceived these lines as a reference to the canon law of the Church." She argues that a range of reference is possible, including Catholic canon law, and that, given the ecclesiastical politics of the time, "Milton's lack of specificity suggests that there is no significant difference" (*Politics of Mirth,* 195). I agree completely. For those "closer to its occasion," Marcus directs us to *A Variorum Commentary on the Poems of John Milton,* 955. The commentary cites Warton who "took this as ridicule (by Milton) of ecclesiastical establishments and the Canon Law." This viewpoint is quickly undercut by

parroting the avant-garde conception of apocalyptic utterance. Like Lancelot Andrewes, he traces her privileging of morality to the pride of the tower of Babel, the very occasion that divided universal truth into a "babble" of opposing voices. But it is Comus who is babbling now in a futile attempt to preserve his dignity.

At this point, the lady and Comus have reached a stalemate as each rejects the other's terms: the lady will not taste and Comus will not hear. Fortunately, as the sensory and semantic gap widens between them, the brothers make their entrance. They too have been engaged in debate, not surprisingly, concerning what their responsibilities are as their sister wanders in the wilderness. The elder brother is initially convinced that they have no alternative but to hope for the best; his attempt to construct a positive version of what will happen to their sister takes a page from Reformation conformists such as Herbert and Donne who attempted to redirect attention away from ecclesiastical conflict: "Peace brother, be not over-exquisite / To cast the fashion of uncertain evils" (*CP*, 98.359–60).

Despite the elder brother's rhetorical efforts, the younger brother does not find his conception of their sister meditating in the woods very comforting. He exposes this as a delusional construct and so hints that the conformist attempt to turn the apocalyptic *Temple* into a place of private meditation is similarly unrealistic; it does not take into account the very real threat "Of Savage hunger or of Savage heat" (*CP*, 98.358), the insatiable appetite for power directed against the present church. His version of what their sister is up against is much closer to the mark: she does indeed have "Beauty" and "gold" that places her in immediate jeopardy. Unfortunately, he lacks the faith in divine power and in the church that the elder brother clearly exhibits. Through a willingness to correct one another in open debate, they arrive at Reformation measures that can be truly effective, attended, of course, by the harmony and the "haemony" of the spirit.

Once empowered in this way, the brothers attack with "Swords drawn," their behavior both militant and apocalyptic. But they are only partly successful. Though they frighten away Comus and his rabble, they do not manage to liberate the lady. Through this failed attempt, Milton hints that Comus is only part of the problem. Even if the church were purged of economic and spiritual corruption, she would still be "bound" to a corrupt ecclesiastical model and therefore restricted in her movement; she would,

---

Masson who argues that Milton "had not yet figured as a church-reformer and satirist of ecclesiastical laws."

in short, rest on secular power rather than relying on a militantly engaged, altogether active spiritual discipline.[46] The Attendant Spirit, though initially flustered, has a way around this obstacle; he remembers something that he "learnt" from *Meliboeus,* and so points back to the *Faerie Queene* once again. There we discover the hereditary origins of the goddess Sabrina who will bring about the lady's deliverance; her father, Spenser reveals, was an adulterer:

> The king returned proud of victorie
> And insolent wox through vnwonted ease,
> That shortly he forgot the ieopardie
> Which in his land he lately did appease,
> And fell to vaine voluptuous disease:
> He lou'd faire Ladie *Estrild,* lewdly lou'd,
> Whose wanton pleasures him too much did please.
>
> (2.10.17)

Sabrina comes into being as a result of this adulterous affair between a "lewd" king and a "faire Ladie," her origins perfectly coinciding with those that brought the Protestant English Church itself into existence. Milton picks up Sabrina's narrative after this rather unseemly beginning, thereby emphasizing her innocence. She is both "a Virgin pure" and a "guiltless damsel" (*CP,* 109.826, 829). But he focuses as well on the "enraged stepdam *Guendolen*" who pursued Sabrina, a woman much like "Rome" who attempts to recover this innocent girl only to destroy her. Sabrina, however, leaves behind her past, both the lewdness of her royal father and the rage of her stepmother, by entering another element, one not rooted in earthly lusts but springing from the freedom and fluidity of water. This is perfectly captured in Milton's language as her "flight" is indeed "stay'd" by a "cross-flowing course" (*CP,* 109.832). Her sacrificial descent into the flood becomes an ascent, her death a resurrection, her revival by the nymphs, a "quick immortal change" (*CP,* 110.841). Baptized into an alternative model of the church, she "visits the herds" and offers her "vial'd liquors" (*CP,* 110.844, 847) to heal the shepherds. Having been almost too verbose about

---

46. Once again, Milton draws on the "Legend of Chastity" where Britomart's initial attempt to free Amoret similarly fails. But instead of forcing the magician to undo his own charm as occurs in Book 3, Milton revises the narrative toward a perspective more in keeping with his recognition of the need for a new Presbyterian "discipline." Comus could never enact this.

Sabrina's history, the Attendant Spirit finally explains its relation to the lady's predicament:

> And, as the old Swain said, she can unlock
> The clasping charm and thaw the numbing spell,
> If she be right invok't in warbled Song,
> For maid'nhood she loves, and will be swift
> To aid a Virgin.
>
> (*CP*, 110.852–56)[47]

If we have missed the parallel between Sabrina's history and the lady's present experience, Milton establishes it again with a single phrase: "such as was herself / In hard-besetting need" (*CP*, 110.856–57). In fact, what ties the lady to the "chair" of episcopacy emerges in Sabrina's history as Sabrina's Romish stepmother brings to light the problematic origins of the English Church. Bound, on the one hand, to an impure history and, on the other, to an impure churchman, the lady must escape both royal and episcopal unions. Only Sabrina's fluid and healing arts—springing from purity and liberty—can free her.

To facilitate this liberation, the Attendant Spirit invokes Sabrina in song—a moment of concord in which, in the revised version of *Comus*, the brothers participate. They offer contestatory measures to the imposed music of the time as their voices rise in the darkness. Almost as soon, Sabrina responds to their request. Her means of releasing the lady is at once an act of purification and a rehearsal of the baptism she has undergone, one in which the "porch and inlet of each sense" (*CP*, 109.839) is altered for a heavenly calling. She therefore sprinkles the lady's "breast," "fingers," and "lips" (*CP*, 111.911, 914, 915) to signify not only the purity of the heart, but also the visible godliness of acts and words deployed in performing the work of the church. Though this is a ritualistic performance, as Leah Marcus has noted, Sabrina's actions do not reflect any ambivalence on Milton's part toward Romish ceremonies. Rather, they allow Milton to establish yet another contestatory moment. Because the placement of the altar and ceremonies such as kneeling, bowing, and crossing had become increasingly important, the sacrament of baptism had been removed from view. In Peter Smart's evaluation, this removal of

---

47. Though the Attendant Spirit attributes this moment of release to Spenser, he of course said nothing of the kind; Sabrina's underwater renewal and medicinal vials that heal disease are entirely Milton's fabrication.

the font reflected the pride and power of the present church in encouraging impurity: "The proud Altar mounting aloft, shouldered the poore Font out of the quire, and tossing it from post to pillar, thrust it almost quite out of dores."[48] Sabrina's action accordingly emphasizes the importance of baptism as she purifies the lady of all such innovations. Last of all, Sabrina applies "chaste palms" to the "marble venom'd seat," and so releases the lady from the "glutinous heat" of episcopacy (*CP*, 111.916–18), a phrase that, in combining gluttony with glue, signals the uncontrolled appetite constraining the present Protestant church.

The release, however, is attended by further instructions from the Attendant Spirit, for though the lady has been freed, Comus is still alive and well. What she now needs to do, like the woman of the Apocalypse, is flee his corruption, in this case, by returning to her father's house. *Comus* therefore concludes as the spirit invites the children and the audience to participate in "due steps" that have nothing to do with the dance of Comus and his crew. Consequently, the final musical measures to which they move occur "without duck or nod" (*CP*, 112.960), the very terms in which the innovations involving bowing, bending, and crossing were described by Puritan reformers.[49] Predicating the audience's capacity to move to divine music on the trueness of their ears, the Attendant Spirit reminds them that they must continue to listen. His final words offer one last reprise of Spenser's "Legende of Chastity," but again, with a difference. Spenser says,

> See how the heauens of voluntary grace
> And soueraine favour towards chastity,
> Doe succour send to her distressed cace:
> So much high God doth innocence embrace.
>
> (3.8.29)

Spenser here emphasizes the "voluntary grace" found in the "soueraine" act of succor, a royal emphasis that turns the subject of the lines into a passive recipient of divine favor. In contrast, Milton underlines the active role of the audience, at the same time highlighting the change that has occurred in

---

48. Marcus, *Politics of Mirth*, 200–201; Smart, *Vanitie and Downe-fall*, 17.

49. Although Merritt Hughes glosses this phrase as the "curtsy or bow in a peasants' dance" in *Milton: Complete Poems* (112), Peter Smart uses the same phrase to describe the Romish dance of the innovators. The movements involve "Altar-ducking, Cope-wearing, Organ-playing, piping, and singing. Crossing of cushions, and kissing of clouts, oft starting up, and squatting downe, nodding of heads, and whirling about, till their noses stand Eastward" (*Vanitie and Downe-fall*, 23).

the Attendant Spirit over the course of *Comus*. Though the spirit began by circumscribing the terms of his aid, he now encourages everyone who can hear to engage in the active climb upward:

> Mortals that would follow me,
> Love virtue, she alone is free,
> She can teach ye how to climb
> Higher than the Sphery chime;
> Or if Virtue feeble were,
> Heav'n itself would stoop to her.
> (*CP*, 114.1018–23)

Virtue liberates either by teaching everyone "how to climb" the scale of ultimate harmony, or if Virtue proves too weak for that, by opening the way for that divine stooping that establishes heaven on earth. Divine "Sovereinty" accordingly distinguishes itself from royal sovereignty in its willingness to "stoop," to make the virtuous subject the cite of transformation. By finally subjecting itself to the subject, divine grace eliminates all barriers between invisible and visible purity, between social classes, between heaven and earth. It places the kingdom of heaven within the transformed and transforming subject and thus within the measure of her own feet and hands.

When we hear the musical strains of "On the Morning" and *Comus* against a larger chorus of voices debating the ecclesiastical dimension of the Apocalypse, Milton's early poetics do not seem as "intelligently, instructively, confused" as some critics have argued.[50] His ideology in fact emerges in the creative space between the texts he reads and rewrites. In "On the Morning," he contests the royalist and Virgilian harmonies that have replaced biblical apocalypticism and so reveals Christ to be far Other than the contemporary policy of the king. And in *Comus,* through a subtle reevaluation of the *Faerie Queene,* Milton reworks portions of Spenser's "Legende of the Knight of the Redcrosse, or Holinesse," "Legende of Chastity," and "Legende of Temperance" to create his own version of the woman in the wilderness. Veiled in his Spenserian allegory is the most scathing critique of the episcopal hierarchy ever to emerge in his poetics. He would never again be as subtle and allusive as he is here, nor would he ever again be as hopeful or idealistic.

---

50. Both Annabel Patterson and Richard Halpern underscore the contradiction and apparent confusion present in *Comus*. But most of the contradictions that Patterson and Halpern cite disappear when the work is interpreted within the context of the ecclesiastical debates of the age (Patterson, " 'Forc'd fingers,' " 18; Halpern, "Puritanism and Maenadism").

II

Only a few years after the publication of *Comus,* Milton enters into what Michael Lieb has described as "apocalyptic exhortation" in the first of his antiprelatical tracts. A text emerging directly out of ecclesiastical controversy, Milton's *Of Reformation* attempts to loosen the English Church's stranglehold on spirituality by exposing the fallacious nature of the reformation being promoted by the churchmen of the time. Thus, in this work as in *Comus,* Truth appears as a woman bound by external and coercive force, leaving Milton with a task similar to that of the lady's brothers. He must, he tells us, "vindicate this spotlesse Truth from an ignominious bondage, whose native worth is now become of such low esteeme that she is like to finde small credit with us for what she can say, unlesse shee can bring a Ticket from Cranmer, Latimer, and Ridley, or prove herself a retainer to Constantine."[51] Truth's "low esteeme," her inability to speak or to be heard against the deafening roar of other voices, is, in Milton's view, a result of the churchmen's recent privileging of "antiquity," evident in both their love of ecclesiastical history and their celebration of Constantinian politics. These churchmen have, in short, silenced Truth by quite literally "re-covering" her, removing her "poore thred-bare" clothes that, Milton notes, signal the "plaine and homespun verity of Christs Gospell" (*OR,* 56). In place of these, they have "overlai'd" her "with wanton *tresses,* and in a flaring tire bespecckl'd her with all the gaudy allurements of a Whore" (*OR,* 56–57). Milton's tightly telescoped metaphor of a much changed woman enables him to link Brightman's apocalyptic interpretation of the woman clothed with the sun with Constantinian corruption itself by calling attention to the way one "son" has been substituted for another: the light of the Gospel has been put under wraps, veiled and made inaccessible by the profit and politics of state craft. In every way, then, the English Churchmen's attempt to "re-dress" truth has only inculcated error, has only turned the bride into a whore by seducing her into accepting monetary and political power.

At the same time as Truth has fallen prey to political ideology, Milton asserts, churchmen have exploited the poor "to cover their insatiate desires" (*OR,* 74). What has resulted is an extraordinary emphasis on materiality in the church, "in the Idolatrous erection of Temples beautified exquisitely to out-vie the Papists, the costly and deare-bought Scandals, and snares

---

51. Michael Lieb, "Milton's *Of Reformation* and the Dynamics of Controversy," 76; see *Of Reformation* in John Milton, *The Prose of John Milton,* 47. Future references will be designated *OR* and cited parenthetically within the text.

of Images, Pictures, rich Coaps, gorgeous Altar-clothes" (*OR*, 74). Milton thus attacks the renewed emphasis on antiquity, Constantinian politics, and ceremonial worship (issues evident in the conformist writings of Donne and Herbert as well as in the avant-garde conformist writings of Andrewes and Laud), arguing, in opposition, that the Gospel requires no extensive knowledge of history, antiquity, or languages. It is accessible to everyone, despite the English Churchmen's attempt to limit it to a particular class, gender, and educational background:

> If we will but purge with sovrain eyesalve that intellectual ray which *God* hath planted in us, then we would beleeve the Scriptures protesting their own plainnes, and perspicuity, calling to them to be instructed, not only the *wise* and *learned,* but the *simple,* the *poor,* the *babes,* foretelling an extraordinary effusion of *Gods* Spirit upon every age, and sexe, attributing to all men, and requiring from them the ability of searching, trying, examining all things, and by the Spirit discerning that which is good. (*OR,* 61)

Having made the text accessible and having argued for an "extraordinary effusion of *Gods* Spirit" on both genders, Milton nevertheless recognizes that alternative, corrupt interpretations of the Word will be introduced along with pure ones. All illumination must, for this reason, be guided by searching, trying, examining, and discerning, both through heightened intellectual engagement and through concerted reliance on the Spirit of God. Perhaps best understood in the free act of engaging and responding, one's individual interpretation must remain unfettered by the "forced," coercive, or binding interpretations of others, especially those interpretations that have already been fixed in place by a religious or political institution.[52] Thus, "the very foundation of Milton's theology," argues Stephen Honeygoskey, is *Kenosis,* "God's rhetorical intervention" when Christ, as Word, comes to empty "the familiar terms of their accreted, expected meanings," particularly those "presumed to secure spiritual life." In their place, Christ seeks to "raise the transfigured terms to new life and their original 'true' meaning." Not surprisingly, the term *Kenosis* itself arises out of Pauline theology "as a breaking device" in Harold Bloom's words, "a movement towards discontinuity with the precursor."[53] Milton's prose and poetry enacts *Kenosis* in both of

52. For the impact of this understanding on Milton's developing career, see Christopher Grose, *Milton and the Sense of Tradition.*
53. Honeygoskey, *Milton's House of God,* 230–31; Harold Bloom, *The Anxiety of Influence: Theory of Poetry,* 14.

these senses as he repeatedly empties words like "reformation," "spirituality," "liberty," and "prophecy" of the meanings so carefully crafted by his contemporaries, restoring them to a dynamic spiritual truth. He shatters, beyond recognition, the political and ecclesiastical formulations of his precursors, whether conformists, avant-garde conformists, or Presbyterians.

One instance of Pauline *Kenosis* in Milton's work must suffice here. As I have argued throughout this book, the parable in Matt. 13:26–31 involving the sowing of wheat and the tares in the church quickly established the dividing lines in much ecclesiastical debate, enabling Hooker and other conformists to argue that the separation of the wicked or, conversely, the purification of the holy was not to take place until the end of time.[54] All Puritan, Presbyterian, Anabaptist, and Separatist attempts to set themselves apart as a holy community were, on the basis of this passage, considered heretical, and conformity to the established church became the only acceptable response in matters of religious life. In *Treatise of Civil Power*, Milton turns this parabolic meaning on end, arguing that the passage is not about the inevitable mixture of good and evil men. Rather, it is about the freedom of interpretation itself and thus about the necessity of all individuals to follow the dictates of their own consciences over the coercive action of authorities, including "church-governors themselves." Milton argues:

> They neither can command nor use constraint, lest they run rashly on a pernicious consequence, forewarned in that parable, Matthew 13:26–31. "Lest while ye gather up the tares, ye root up also the wheat with them. Let both grow together until the harvest: and in the time of harvest I will say to the reapers, Gather ye together first the tares," &c. Whereby he declares that this work neither his own ministers nor any else can discerningly enough perform . . . and that they ought till then not to attempt it. (*CP,* 842)

What, for Milton, must remain sacred and inviolable until the end of time is the conscience of each interpreting subject.

Hooker had, of course, gone much further than this in asserting the religious conformity of all individuals and their necessary presence in the corporate life of the English Church. He had even employed the Pauline allegory of the bondwoman, Hagar, and the free woman, Sarah, to sanction the right of state officials to persecute those who went their own way: "For Agar also suffered persecution at the hands of Sarah, wherein, she which did

---

54. Hooker, *Laws of Polity,* 1:288–89, 1.3.8–9.

impose was holy, and she unrighteous which did bear the burden."[55] Hooker's primary reason for sanctioning Sarah's persecution of Hagar was to place out of the reach of any individual the claim of belonging to the "true, persecuted Church." Again, Milton turns Hooker's interpretation on end by reversing his terms for "liberty" and "persecution" and so undermining both. "Christian liberty," Milton argues, "sets us free not only from the bondage of those ceremonies, but also from the forcible imposition of those circumstances, place and time in the worship of God" (*CP,* 850). In his view, one's conscience is more powerful than the church requirement to gather at the appropriate place and time, carrying out the appropriate ceremonial gestures. Moreover, he asserts, any constraint and persecution carried out by the magistrate to accomplish this end is itself a result of bondage: "while they think they do God service, they themselves, like the sons of the bondwoman, [are] found persecuting them who are freeborn of the spirit" (*CP,* 851). Persecution is, for Milton, a sign of slavery rather than freedom, a sign of those who seek to "abolish the Gospel" rather than to give it new liberating forms. Thus, as Honeygoskey eloquently demonstrates, Milton's ecclesial theology centers on *Kenosis,* on shattering the rigidity of the "old, ceremonial Law" and envisioning an endlessly regenerative Gospel in ways wholly at odds with his contemporaries. Pauline theology accordingly maintains its presence as an energizing force throughout Milton's work, for it is, in Milton's words, the "groundwork and foundation of the whole gospel" (*CP,* 852).

But what was to be Milton's response when he encountered Cornelius Arippa's interpretation of the bondwoman and the free woman, an interpretation that foregrounded not the freedom of the conscience but the freedom of Sarah and all women after her to reveal divine truth? What was he to think when Agrippa's assessment of Pauline theology was employed both by himself and by other writers to undercut the Pauline interpretation of Genesis? As I have shown in Chapter 3, Paul's interpretation had already prompted a series of feminist, counterinterpretations in the *Querelle des Femmes,* works written in the early years of the seventeenth century. In responding to writers such as Agrippa, Milton seeks to contain these subversive responses and thus to place Paul's interpretation out of firing range. To do so, he reverses the feminist agenda promoted in the *Querelle* by elaborating on the Genesis narrative in such a way as to close the hermeneutic gaps and downplay the ambiguities brought to light by his contemporaries. His own interpretation, consequently, falls clearly within Pauline limits, leaving *Paradise Lost* to

55. Ibid., 1:105–6, 3.15.

emerge quite definitively on the opposite side in the protofeminist debate. Milton thus displaces earlier interpretations of the Fall and goes far toward eradicating the narrative minimalism and cryptic character of the Genesis narrative itself.

Both in taking up the issue of inspiration and in contesting alternative readings of Genesis promoted in the *Querelle,* Milton makes discernment central to the process of illumination. What must be tried and examined in the poem and in life alike is the nature of the "Spirit" planting the seeds of illumination. Consequently, one much search and try both the thoughts that one receives as a result of illumination and the desires and actions that those thoughts appear to be advancing.

Not surprisingly, in *Paradise Lost,* diabolical "illumination" is always linked with rhetorical coercion, with Satan's employment of knowledge, power, and mystery against the interpreting subject to completely obfuscate or pervert the clarity of the Word. In the course of this process, pride, desire, and fear become the primary tools of his trade. Satan's coercive strategies with respect to the Word first emerge in Book 5 when Satan seeks to awaken Beelzebub to an alternative interpretation of God's edict. He claims as the ground of his opening argument Beelzebub's prior allegiance to him: "Both waking we were one" (*CP,* 318, 5:678). This alliance, he hints, authorizes him to invade Beelzebub's sleep and to present an alternative interpretation of divine speech that is both constructed by him and determined to become a "Tradition." Through just such claims to solidarity and unity he will, in fact, incorporate a host of angels and humankind into his own subversive lines of authority.

Later, when Satan sits "Squat like a Toad / Close at the ear of Eve," he seeks to awaken her to the same subversive knowledge, a knowledge, the narrator informs us, involving

> discontented thoughts
> Vain hopes, vain aims, inordinate desires
> Blown up with high conceits ingend'ring pride.
> (*CP,* 297, 4:808–10)

By this means, Satan "plants" far more than the seeds of the Fall. He plants the seeds of "feminist" interpretation generally, dropping alternative readings, like so many kernels, into the fertile ground of Eve's mind. His interpretations, fabricated in the unauthorized realm of dream, suggestion, and speculation, are constructed around mysterious "gaps" in Genesis—the very gaps and alternative interpretations sponsored by the protofeminists.[56] These viewpoints, as we have seen in Chapter 3, take form in Cornelius Agrippa's *Of the Nobilitie and Excellencie of Womankynde* and Aemilia Lanyer's *Salve Deus Rex Judaeorum.* We find yet another example in William Heale's *Apology for Women.*

It is through these gaps, of course, that discontinuities arise, that ambiguities circulate, and that the clarity of the Word is confounded or stalled; it is through them, moreover, that alternative interpretations are introduced. And Agrippa is more than willing to point these out. Noting the absence of Eve in the earliest stages of Adam's creation, he argues that, because Eve "was not than created" (sig. CV1) when Adam received the command from God, the command did not apply to her. Second, he calls into question Paul's hierarchy of creation. The very notion of a hierarchical order, he points out, suggests that God keeps improving on what he has created. If this is so, then is not Eve, as God's final act, the highest creation? With these few sentences, Agrippa undermines Paul's attempt to keep Eve "subject," completely subverting the hierarchy. Eve, he observes, was "formed into this world as Quene of the same," and so "every creature worthyly loveth, reverenceth, and serveth her, and worthyly is subject" (sig. Ar). Finally, Agrippa reassesses the Pauline mandate. Underscoring Joel's prediction of women preachers, teachers, and prophets, Agrippa notes that "later Lawe-makers" suppress this truth and so break "goddes commaundemente, to stablyshe theyre own traditions" (sig. G). Proving "theyr tyranny by holy scripture" (sig. Gi4-Gii), such people quote Paul's injunction to female silence and thus reveal their carnal way of reading. In fact, Paul's doctrine of liberty encodes a far higher truth—that God has liberated women to prophesy—to bear heavenly messages.

Though William Heale does not go as far as Agrippa in removing Eve from the implications of the Fall, he nevertheless uses tradition quite literally against itself. Noting that "by tradition the woman received this commandement from the man, not by deliverie from God, he asserts that "the woman might chance more easilie to breake this lawe, then the man; since the al glorious Maiesty of God that commanded should take deeper effect in man, then the equallity of person that related could in the woman" (63). Moving on to explore yet another gap in biblical narrative, Heale suggests that when

56. Joseph A. Wittreich argues conversely, in *Feminist Milton,* that Milton is a protofeminist, basing his interpretation largely on the female reception of Milton. But James Grantham Turner, who is aware of the feminist versions of the Fall apparent in the works of Agrippa, Lanyer, and Heale, does not (*One Flesh: Paradisal Marriage and Sexual Relations in the Age of Milton,* 108–13, 285).

the temptation finally comes, only Eve contests the serpent's assertions, first responding with a "short and sharp answer," and thus exposing a "plaine falsification in his close assertion." Her verbal aptitude drives Satan to take up his "naturall trade of open lying," adding into his rhetorical sleight of hand "a vaine hope of shameful knowledge." In Heale's view, Eve's willingness to engage with Satan "in a faire combate" and "for a time to stand out at staves ends with him," contrasts sharply with Adam's response. Though Adam is pronounced "with her" in the biblical account, and though, according to Heale, he has immediate knowledge from God of the repercussions, he "never did cast anie doubt, never made question, never demurred on the matter, but streight way tasted the sweetnese thereof, whose bitter relish remaines until this day." On this basis, Heale argues, the Pauline argument that Eve was "deceived" while Adam was not is simply untrue; in point of fact, "Man was more in fault to be so suddenlie deceived, then woman who was more hardly drawne therunto." Heale accordingly concludes by reevaluating the charge against Eve so central to Christian tradition and laying the "fault" squarely on the shoulders of Adam: "And whereas al the fault of our first fall is commonly laid unto womans charge, *Evah* was but in parte the occasion thereof; *Adam* was the sole cause thereof. For had hee observed the commande of God, though shee ten thousand times had broken it, wee had not tasted of death. Wee had never for her fault been punished, for his only we were."[57]

Aemilia Lanyer adopts both Agrippa's and Heale's interpretation of Eve, but she takes Eve's absence during the divine command one step further, arguing that Eve's ignorance both contributed to her fall in that initial instance and now continues to justify the male domination of her and her sisters. Instead of rectifying their original error, in fact, men perpetuate it, witholding knowledge from women when it alone can liberate them. To correct this state of affairs, Lanyer asserts, God himself has stepped into human history, not only by giving women immediate spiritual revelation but also by taking his own body and blood from woman and offering it to the world through open rather than exclusionary communion. Female generosity has thus become central to Christianity, while male power and pride represent its antithesis, a pride all too visible in those willing to persecute and crucify the innocent in order to uphold "tradition."

Milton's own deep-seated hatred of "tradition," of interpretations passed down over time and destined to subjugate all readers and thinkers to scripted "lines" of authority, is clear in his tracts and treatises. We might infer, then,

___

57. Heale, *An Apologie for Women*, 63, 64.

that he would find much appealing in feminist argument. But Milton rejects the feminist "handwriting" of his time, attributing Eve's fall to just such overblown notions of female wisdom and superiority as his contemporaries were articulating. He is, moreover, careful to remove the gaps from biblical narrative, to have Eve hear the command both from Adam and from the heaven-sent Raphael and so to make her entirely accountable for her divine education. She does not engage directly in their discussion, it is true, but she nevertheless hears or overhears nearly everything.

And the educative gap is not all Milton fills. He establishes the creation of Eve, not as the ultimate goal of all of creation as Renaissance feminists were wont to see it, but as a direct response to Adam's socratic dialogue with God. She is, then, the "Other half" (*CP*, 289, 4:488) of man, assigned to him both as his "image" (*CP*, 289, 4:472) and as his "fit help" (*CP*, 373, 8:450) and destined to find "God in him" rather than, as Agrippa and Lanyer had claimed, to be the "similitude of Christ." Milton thus reinforces the Pauline interpretation of Genesis, not only by highlighting Eve's creation as a secondary act but also by clearly subordinating her, in the hierarchy of creation, to Adam. Following Paul still more faithfully, he goes so far as to make her a "silent" partner in all heavenly conversation; she does not "teach" nor "instruct" Raphael as Adam has the opportunity to do regarding his creation; she merely "stands and waits" on them.

But Milton's most striking additions to biblical narrative reveal an even stronger desire to "close" the hermeneutic gaps opened up by his contemporaries: he introduces a "false" dream into Eve's mind in Books 4 and 5 to highlight the connections between "feminist" thinking and the "tares" of satanic pride. And he reinforces the feminist link between this falsely inspired "dream-vision" and the later "waking" world of Book 9 as, in the end, Satan offers to "open" Eve's eyes to divine knowledge. The serpent in fact begins his temptation with Agrippa-like praise of Eve's beauty, intelligence, and grace, not only identifying her as his "sovran Mistress" and "Empress" (*CP*, 391, 9:532, 568), thereby echoing Agrippa's "Queen," but also celebrating her as the ultimate act of creation, and perhaps (if she is willing to "dare" it), a "Goddess among Gods" (*CP*, 391, 9:547). In the dialogue that ensues, Milton deftly revises Heale's combative Eve out of existence as Eve wins few of the verbal rounds, seeming increasingly confused and befuddled by Satan's rhetoric. When at last Eve does succumb to temptation and eats the fruit, she does not determine to pass it on to Adam as an act of generosity (as Lanyer certainly claims), but out of desire to make Adam share with her "in bliss or woe" (*CP*, 397, 9:831)—the emphasis, of course, falling on Adam's impending doom. Finally, as Eve moves away from the tree, she "first" in "low Reverence" (*CP,* 397, 9:835) bows to it, and so adopts an Anglican or Romish posture in the genuflecting "subjection" of her body. By making this parting ceremony a visible sign of Eve's corruption, Milton erodes the lines between the self-serving rhetoric of Renaissance feminists, the self-serving rhetoric of Satan, and the self-serving rhetoric of Anglican conformity, for all demand an "eye-service" that privileges external acts of worship over the illumination of inward truth.

Adam is not, of course, present during this temptation, for Milton carefully constructs a lengthy "separation" scene in Book 9 to close this final hermeneutic gap. Adam is thus not "with Eve" and is most certainly not "deceived" in the same way as is his wife. He chooses to sin with her with eyes wide open to the possible consequences—consequences that he understands perfectly when he sees the bough of fruit in Eve's hand. His tribute to her, even in this moment of awareness, however, suggests that he has viewed Eve much as Agrippa has, now articulated in past tense:

> O fairest of Creation, last and best
> Of all God's Works, Creature in whom excell'd
> Whatever can to sight or thought be form'd.
> (*CP,* 399, 9:896–99)

Not long before he had echoed feminist interpretation directly, telling Raphael that Eve seemed

> As one intended first, not after made
> Occasionally; and to consummate all,
> Greatness of mind.
> (*CP,* 375, 8:555–57)

Raphael's "contracted brow" (*CP,* 375, 8:565) and reprimand were then intended to remind Adam that he was "attributing overmuch to things / Less excellent" (*CP,* 375, 8:566–67) that he had quite literally forgotten himself. Now, confronted with Eve's fall, he rationalizes his action, privileging her state of loss over his own state of innocence and noting that he feels "The Link of Nature draw" him (*CP,* 399, 9:914). In choosing to be "bound" to his wife and to hear her words, he does not (as Agrippa had argued) find any liberty or grace. Instead, he becomes a corrupt and enslaved "subject," the very man Milton describes in *Of Reformation* whose "valor" is "hamstrung" as he is made "effeminate" at home (*OR,* 73–74). Milton accordingly reminds us in tract and poem alike that "Liberty consists in manly and honest labors," in resisting all acts of conformity and in choosing the "liberty of Conscience" over the bondage of a "feminized" nature or an emasculating tradition.

But Eve does not remain permanently in the dark, and, in the final books of *Paradise Lost,* we find Milton associating Eve repeatedly with the "Seed" (*CP,* 436, 11:155) of a woman and the grace of human redemption, one quite literally born out of Eve's cognizance of her own weakness and failure. Her desire to accept full responsibility for her error echoes Christ's sacrificial response in the garden and allows Adam to recall, in fuller measure, the *protoevangelium* through which both speech acts will be united in the "seed" of the faithful. Thus, while Milton rejects any authorizing of the feminine self, he nevertheless links Eve with communion, grace, and self-sacrifice, a sacrifice initiated first by Eve and only afterward by Adam. Moreover, as Wittreich has argued, Milton allows Eve to be inspired by God in a final prophetic dream and even gives her the last spoken word in the poem.[58] But this final, redemptive movement is in keeping, I believe, with Pauline, not "feminist" thought, with Paul's interpretation that women will "be saved by child-bearing" (1 Tim. 2:15). The "woman's seed" (*CP,* 466, 12:543) who bears in her body the "seed" of Christ is, for Milton, intimately linked to the woman clothed with the sun in the final pages of Revelation, the woman as true church who unites all the generations of the faithful.

Nevertheless, Milton does not end *Paradise Lost* as he does *Comus* by showing the liberation of the visible church in time. Instead, he follows the line of the true church as it travels in an increasingly inward, rather than outward, movement, a line through which spirit-directed individuals must continue to contest the religious and political authorities of the age:

> Wolves shall succeed for teachers, grievous Wolves,
> Who all the sacred mysteries of Heav'n
> To thir own vile advantages shall turn
> Of lucre and ambition, and the truth
> With superstitions and traditions taint,
> Left only in those written Records pure,
> Though not but by the Spirit understood.
> (*CP,* 465–66, 12:508–14)

Over against these "teachers," Milton sets the purity of the Word and the inspiration required for a reading of it. "Promis'd alike and giv'n / To all

---

58. Wittreich, *Feminist Milton,* 106–7.

Believers" (*CP*, 466, 12:519–20), the words of this book become fertile, contestatory ground as the sacred mysteries offered here are "understood" and unraveled by the Spirit of God. This Spirit alone roots out the tares of all corrupt, self-serving interpretations—whether encoded in the traditions of church and state or advanced by a particular gender or sect—planting in their place the seeds of a liberating, endlessly revelatory Gospel.

7

Feminist Authority in
Eleanor Davies's Prophecies

*He preferres his own superstitions before the Churches reverent Ceremonies,
and will sooner deserve a white sheete than endure a Surplesse. He prescribes
his own Lawes, and directs his faith by his own Liturgy, standing whilst others
bowe, and sitting whilst others kneele.*

—Thomas Heywood, *A True Discourse of the
Two infamous upstart Prophets*

E VEN AS the lady in Milton's *Comus* spoke, one lady was already in bonds
in 1633 for prophesying against the corrupt political and ecclesiastical
structure of the Caroline court.[1] She was Lady Eleanor Davies, a woman of
noble birth, education, and wealth. Though she had printed her prophecies
abroad and smuggled them back into the country to sidestep Archbishop
Laud's licensing procedures, she could not escape the charge of sedition.
Despite her imprisonments, however, neither she nor her prophesies could
be suppressed, and she quickly became the most prolific woman prophet of
the seventeenth century.[2]

Like Aemilia Lanyer, Davies turned to prophetic discourse to rewrite
the nature of Christian tradition, but she focused on ends rather than
beginnings, on the politics of the Apocalypse rather than that of the Fall.

1. Both Esther S. Cope and David Norbrook discuss Eleanor Davies's imprisonment
in 1633, a confinement that lasted several years (Cope, *Handmaid of the Holy Spirit*, 74;
Norbrook, *Poetry and Politics*, 258).
2. Cope carries out a thorough analysis of Davies's life and writings in *Handmaid* and
provides a brief overview in her edition of Davies's prophecies. Phyllis Mack explores "the
cage of symbols and stereotypes that conditioned the public expression of visionary women,"
noting that Davies "expressed herself in terms of a repertoire of images that formed a shared
language between herself and her audience and invited her audience to interpret" (*Visionary
Women: Ecstatic Prophecy in Seventeenth-Century England*, 18, 23). Within this chapter I
explore this shared language to reveal its feminist implications.

Encoding her agenda in a cryptic, often riddling form, she identified divine authority as feminine, thereby opening a place for the female author. But in focusing on issues of gender in her prophecies, Davies overstepped the political boundaries that might otherwise have sanctioned her, her distinctively feminist authority making her increasingly suspect to king and Commonwealth alike.

The differences between Davies's work and the apocalyptic writing of her time thus center, as Megan Matchinske argues, on authority, but Matchinske identifies this as a personal, rhetorical desire for self-validation on Davies's part, noting parenthetically that Davies "seldom addresses the fact that she is a woman." I believe, in contrast, that a gendered, feminine authority is central to Davies's writings, and that, in keeping with this agenda, Davies never conveys her "uneasy acceptance of the patriarchal strictures that make up [the state's] operations for women writer/readers," as Matchinske claims.[3] Rather, when seen in the context of other prophecies, Davies creates a new status for women that privileges female authority to male authority by deriving it from the heavenly woman of the Apocalypse. In doing so, she overturns patriarchal strictures altogether.

Davies attains this vision through her own interpretation of biblical prophecy, creating out of a pastiche of scriptural echoes a complex feminist symbolism that enables her to view her life as an authorized and prophetic text. Believing she has been called to act as the "meek Virgin" for England—to reproduce Christ during the reign of a Stuart Caesar Augustus—she delivers Christ in her prophecies in order to redeem the English Church from its impurity.[4] In *The Appearance or Presence of the Son of Man*, Davies takes an active, authoritative position in this redemption, rejecting the passive, "secretarial" role usually assumed by male and female prophets:

> *She whose throne heaven, earth her footstool from the uncreated, saying I am A. and O. first and last, both beginning and ending, by whom all things were done: Not without her anything done or made; Trinity in Unity, of Manhood the head; Who of death have the keys, and Hell: then the Queen of the South a greater, born a greater not of woman: Melea, by*

3. Megan Matchinske, "Holy Hatred: Formations of the Gendered Subject in English Apocalyptic Writing, 1625–1651," 368, 349–77. For additional analysis, see Beth Nelson, "Lady Elinor Davies: The Prophet as Publisher"; and Phyllis Mack, "Women as Prophets during the English Civil War."

4. Eleanor Davies, *The Prophetic Writings of Eleanor Davies*, 286.214; 287.35. Future references will be designated *PW* with page and line numbers cited parenthetically within the text.

interpretation, *Queen of Peace,* or She-Counsellor. And so much for this
without contradiction, she his Executor, *Made like unto the Son of God,*
the ancient of days likeness. (*PW,* 311)

Identifying her hand in her work, Davies indicates that she is more than a
bearer of divine messages, more too than an active participant in redemptive
suffering; she is, in fact, like God himself, the author of multiple texts and so
infinitely creative—*"by whom all things were done: Not without her anything
done or made."* Wielding a Word that re-forms the world, Davies is one with
the divine creator and so, she argues, her words carry absolute authority.

Deriving this authority from Christ's affirmation of the Queen of the
South in Matt. 12, Davies, unlike Aemilia Lanyer, refuses to see herself in
terms of the queen's darkness and marginality. Instead, she surpasses this
queen as Christ surpasses the prophet, John the Baptist, and so assumes
her royal position at God's right hand: "And so much for this without
contradiction, she his Executor, *made like unto the Son of God.*" Asserting
that the divine roles of creator, judge, and counselor are fulfilled in her, she
identifies herself as a "Trinity in Unity, of manhood the head." With these
words, Davies assumes a supreme position, removing man from his status as
"head of woman" and placing herself there instead. Her final triune function
is that of the Holy Spirit, making her "*Melea,* by interpretation, Queen of
Peace, or She-counsellor." Claiming her Holy Spirit is pacifistic, she seems to
embrace—at least momentarily—the dominant theme of churchmen such
as Andrewes.[5]

In this extraordinary fashion, Davies underscores her role as an originary,
apocalyptic, and prophetic writer. Actively participating in the ongoing
debate over prophetic discourse, she writes the words of her opponents
into her prophecies to highlight their distance from revealed truth and to
engage in the revolutionary politics of the civil war. Thus, even though these
prophecies are replete with abbreviated biblical allusions that render them
nearly indecipherable today, I believe they were well understood by their
immediate, far more biblically trained audience. By recovering their immediate social and literary contexts—biblical symbolism, temporal referents,
and political subtexts—I wish to demonstrate that Davies wrote to expose

---

5. Cope similarly highlights Davies's feminism, asserting that "she raised fundamental
questions about the position of women in early Stuart England" (*Handmaid,* 3). As for
Davies's politics, I believe Davies, like the conformists of Spenser's time, actually hopes for a
purified English Church—the mother church with whom she most identifies. Her prophesies
suggest that she believes the parliamentarian forces will destroy the corrupt bishops in the
church, preparing the way for the final marriage of the bride.

the limitations of her male contemporaries, both English Churchmen and Presbyterians, and to record the necessity of hearing the female voice. In her view, the English Church will be restored to purity when it sees that its own status as the bride of Christ is contingent upon its recognition that the female gender contains the ultimate prophetic truth.

Much as Milton's lady does in the *Comus*, Davies levels her prophecies at the new regulations affecting church ceremonies, Sabbatarianism, and preaching as she attempts to purify the present structure. Believing that the bishops and queen are causing division within the kingdom by influencing the king to bring Romish innovations into the church, Davies prophesies on his behalf in order to correct him.[6] In her view, the division between the king and his subjects is merely reinscribing the division that has already taken place on a heavenly level between God and the king. Charles, having turned away from divine authority and having joined himself to the "whore" of Babylon, was now actively pursuing his adultery by increasing idolatrous ceremonies and further separating the kingdom from God.[7]

The bishops responded to such accusations by noting that these prophets of doom were themselves innovators who could not tell the difference between the ceremonies of primitive Christian antiquity that churchmen were reinstating and the corruptions of Rome from which the English Church had turned away. Having misconstrued the past by failing to accurately recover it, they were equally incapable of understanding the present. It was they who were attempting to alter religion by bringing in innovations of their own. Using these arguments, Peter Heylyn attacked Henry Burton in *A Briefe Answer*, deploying a biblical passage to clarify the poisonous nature of Burton's radical discourse: "But to what purpose do I seek to *charme so deafe and Adder?*"[8] Weaving Ps. 58:3–5 into his query, Heylyn underlines Burton's moral and spiritual failure as he attempts to expose the verbal corruption that informs Burton's radical politics. Here, the Psalmist provides the organizing framework by which Heylyn reinterprets and so contains the speech of his Puritan opponent:

> The wicked are estranged from the womb:
> They go astray as soon as they be born, speaking lies.

6. The controversies of the 1620s and 1630s alternatively question or support ecclesiastical authority, and they do so by citing differing definitions of "innovation" and "antiquity."

7. This viewpoint was probably close to that of many conformists within the Church of England who longed for greater purity rather than separation from the church.

8. Heylyn, *A Briefe Answer to Henry Burton*, 49.

Their poison is like the poison of a serpent:
They are like the deaf adder that stoppeth her ear,
Which will not hearken to the voice of the charmers,
charming never so wisely.[9]

Heylyn naturally casts himself as the wise snake charmer whom Burton cannot hear, suggesting in this way that Burton's satanic and venomous prophecies remain unchecked and thus continue to infect the world.

When Davies addresses her prophecy to Parliament in 1643, she employs the metaphor of the "deaf adder" to reveal the king's deafness as well as the necessity of a hearing from Parliament. Like Heylyn, she turns the text on her opponent, in this case Parliament, the very men who would find spiritual "deafness" most objectionable:

> far be it from us to be like the deaf Adder; That because once accursed for harkning when forbidden. Therefore to forbear, charm the word of God never so strongly and sweet; like the blinde Jews under colour of shunning Idolatry and the like, that fell to be such Blasphemers of God.
>
> Preaching ye have alway, and may hear when ye please, and their large Dedicatories and Volumes may License them daily: But the little Book, The Spirit of Prophesie, Not always that. (*PW*, 111)

Including Parliament in her "far be it from us," Davies draws into her narrative of the "deaf Adder" a warning to her listeners. Having once "harkened" to the serpent "when forbidden" and experienced the curse, they must learn to distinguish the words of the serpent from the redemption she now offers as the second Eve. Reminding them that the prophetic moment, like the life of Christ, is remarkably brief, Davies echoes Christ's validation of the woman in Matt. 26:10–13. This woman was linked with Mary Magdalene and the same incident, recorded in John 12:1–8, was read on "Lady Day," March 25 in *The Book of Common Prayer.* Unlike the English Churchmen, however, Davies refuses to call attention to the woman's impurity, highlighting instead the prophetic character of Mary's act: "For ye have the poor always with you; but me ye have not always. . . . Verily I say unto you, Wheresoever this gospel shall be preached in the whole world, there shall also this, that this woman hath done, be told for a memorial of her" (Matt. 26:11–13). Identifying her "Prophesie" with the life of Christ, Davies notes that "preaching" can be heard and "licensed" every

---

9. I quote the 1611 King James edition of the Bible.

day by Parliament, while her words will not always be available. To dismiss feminine words is thus to miss both the preaching of the Gospel, where a woman is forever immortalized, and prophecy, where, according to Davies, transcendent utterance is located.

Throughout this text, Davies attempts to validate her spiritual, feminist authority by turning repeatedly to biblical precedent:

> Wherefore then not to be revealed to us, before others in such case: and as soon to his handmaids as his menservants, the Spirit of God to be poured on them: and so now, as well as then, when she had the first happy sight of him after his rising, which was sent to tell and inform them where they should meet him *first:* and what odds between *seven* Churches visited, or Sent unto. (*PW,* 107–8)

Questioning her audience's refusal to hear the prophetic "handmaids" in Joel 2:28 and Acts 2:18, Davies notes that God chooses women "now, as well as then." It was to a woman that Christ first appeared following his resurrection, and it was upon a woman that he relied "to tell and inform" others of his coming. Saint John the Divine wrote his epistle "to a Lady," and so indicated that "from another Lady" would come "the Revelations Interpretation of her writing" (*PW,* 107), an assessment pointing to her, as lady, and encoding her as the future revealer of apocalyptic vision: "For a full expression of our Lord's coming to be revealed to a woman, that secret disclosed" (*PW,* 107). But though the Apocalypse had not changed, seventeenth-century society continued to shut its ears against the radical, feminist authority through which it alone could be interpreted and understood.

By the 1640s, the kingdom was still more divided over issues of royal, ecclesiastical, and spiritual authority, and gender became a further marker of these debates. The feminine body over which so many were contending had long figured as an image of the church, leading John White in *The Way to the True Church* to identify the struggle over this ecclesiastical body with the child over which the two mothers fought in 1 Kings 3:16–28. In White's analysis, Solomon, the wise and all seeing king, was the appropriate negotiator:

> So two women laid claime both to one child, and both pretended themselves to be true mother thereunto, as the Church of Rome this day striveth with us, pleading for herselfe, that she is our holy Mother the Church, and the Child is hers: in this contention we must find out the Church by the same markes that Salomon found out the true

mother, which was by her tender compassion inclosed in her bowels and discovered by her words, that she had rather part with her child than have it cut in sunder.[10]

When Parliament analyzed this passage, however, the king's "Solomonic" position was viewed as the bloodiest of choices. It was a choice a true "mother" would never make, and that "mother" was Parliament: "The sad and unnaturall Tragedies of our times may not unfitly be compared, to the two Women striving for a child, I Kings 3 Ch. One claimeth it as her owne, the other saith Nay; but it is mine. The contention is so hot that King Solomon calleth for a sword . . . Divide." The writer concludes this narrative with a still more chilling gloss of the ecclesiastical and political repercussions of Solomon's—and Charles's—swordplay:

> Content, saith the Antichristian and malignant party: Christ, and their Arch-Bishops, Arch-Deacons, Deanes, Priests, and Deacons, and all the Ecclesiastical persons depending upon them: Christ and their devised worship, Temples, Alters, Tythes, and Offerings: Christ and the residue of their Forefathers traditions: thus let them but enjoy a divided Christ, and there will be an end to controversie. But they (Right honorable) that are holy, syncere, and faithfull . . . will have a whole Christ . . . Christ their prophet, whom they will only heare.[11]

The king, ecclesiastical hierarchy, church ceremony, and even the "Forefathers traditions" have divided Christ's whole body by failing to hear either the voice of Christ or the voice of the true mother.

When, in the same year, Davies composes a prophecy for her daughter, she takes for herself the position that Parliament was now claiming as the true mother of the kingdom. In *"Jacobs united Familie"* made up of *"his wives children and children of Hand-maids,"* she sees and recognizes the approaching "day" (*PW*, 116) of judgment. Drawing her insight from Saint John the Divine's Apocalypse, chapter 7, Davies argues that the final battle will be recognizable by "the second sexe its character." One "mother" will reveal herself in all her Romish wickedness: "*Mother not of the* Living *Child,* but of Divisions and Massacres, *where* inclusive the ador'd *sacrament* called the MASSE: Thus uttered Her voice, *Let it bee neither Thine,* nor *Mine,* but devide it: destroy it utterly" (*PW*, 118). The other will defend her child, Christ, in the midst of the conflict, but she will be subjected to tremendous

10. White, *Way to the True Church*, 123.
11. *The Vindication of the Royall Commission of King Jesus against the Antichristian faction.*

persecution as a result: "How Satan because he knows his reigne or time to be short: is ready to devoure the Woman even for the truth of the Resurrection time revealed, *as most proper to be performed by that sex, a Woman by whom death came to be the Messenger of Life*" (*PW,* 128). That Davies and the women to whom Christ appears at "the Resurrection time" are indeed "Messengers of Life" has, however, been rejected. In this sense, England has failed to heed this feminist message, has failed to hear her counsel. To register her awareness of her nation's failure and to show how her voice has been ignored, Davies re-creates the biblical passage in which Sarah prevails with Abraham to privilege the "son" of divine blessing and spiritual liberty. Sarah had said, "Cast out this bondwoman and her son: for the son of this bondwoman will not be heir with my son, even with Isaac" (Gen. 21:11). Davies, however, assumes the satiric stance of the biblical prophets as she sarcastically invites England to continue in bondage and to maintain the same deafness toward divine ends: "*O let Ismale live as it were,* prefer'd before *Isaac to be his Heire,* And *Absolom's* life before *Solomon the wise (O Absolom my sonne Absolom).* Like *Egypts* Leekes & Garlic before *Canaans* Grapes & c. And so preferred this worlds vanity & folly before everlasting Righteousnesse, and *endlesse joy, life eternall*" (*PW,* 129).[12] To ignore the liberating voice of Sarah, Davies suggests, is to live in spiritual bondage in this world and to lose the wonder and the *"endlesse joy"* that only the bride of Christ will discover.

Davies takes a still firmer hand in political events in her prophecy *Amend, Amend, God's kingdome is at hand,* which was reprinted in 1643.[13] First published in 1633, this work shows how Davies transforms a chapter from the book of Daniel into a news flash for her time. On the title page, Davies quotes as her opening "proclamation" the "handwriting on the wall" in Dan. 5, reading Daniel's analysis of Belshazzar's fall into her own historical moment. Thus, *Mene, Mene, Tekel Peres Upharsin* records the "finished" reign of King Charles who has been weighed in the balance and found

12. As Robert Alter indicates, "the archetyping force of vocative poetry in the Prophets can move in two directions beyond the primary mode of accusation, where its general effect is to fix the particular vices within an authoritative, timeless scheme of moral judgment. If the speaker sarcastically invokes the viewpoint of his human objects of reproof, conjuring up the illusory pleasures of power to which they are addicted, he produces a satirical depiction of how the evil are self-deceived" ("Prophecy and Poetry," in *The Art of Biblical Poetry,* 146).

13. Davies, *Amend, Amend, God's kingdome is at hand.* Future references will be cited parenthetically within the text. I do not use Cope's editon as the text is noticeably different from the 1648 version that Cope prints in Davies, *Prophetic Writings of Eleanor Davies* (59–68).

"weak" by his "Peres" or Parliament men; he will, like Belshazzar before him, be overthrown. But Davies is not just repeating Daniel's message; she has been "touched" (an echo of her family name, *Touchet*) by the same hand as Daniel and can provide a similarly visionary reading of seventeenth-century events.[14] Her "calling," she believes, is encoded in the letters of her name, disclosing her prophetic responsibility and new identity: "ELEANOR AVDELEY: Reveale O DANIEL." Nevertheless, Davies finds it necessary to validate her prophetic role by revising the gender markers in the biblical passage. In the process, she foregrounds the role of the woman prophet rather than that of the male interpreter.

Thus, Davies opens her lyric prophecy—sung to the tune of "Who lists a soldiers life to lead"—by echoing Ps. 137:1–9, a lyric lament of captivity that slowly shifts in tone, becoming in the end a nationalistic call to action. Davies similarly turns her "song of Sion" into a moment of political subversion by singing a song "of Babylon" instead, in this way underscoring the Babylonian captivity to which the English people have unwittingly subjected themselves. Her additions to the text of Dan. 5 thus uncover the hermeneutic gap in present readings of the passage and provide a much needed application to recent events: "Concerns *you* more: full well I wot / Then ye do thinke upon" (*Amend*, 1). Following the narrative of Belshazzar's corruption and fall fairly closely (verses 1–4), Davies pauses over the idolatry taking place in the court and spreading throughout the kingdom:

> Praysing the Gods of gold and brasse,
> of *Iron, Wood,* and *Stone*
> Which heare nor see, Not out alas
> in Court are *prays'd* alone.
>
> (*Amend*, 2)

By establishing a clear parallel between Belshazzar's and Charles's reigns, Davies indicates that it is the "idolatrous" and Romish practices of the Caroline court that implicate and finally condemn it. Because God remains attentive to royal corruption, he has chosen precisely this moment to pronounce judgment. But while the translations on which Davies relies record that the "fingers of a man's hand" (verse 5)[15] do the writing on the palace wall, Davies leaves the masculine designation out of her account. Instead, it

---

14. Cope analyzes how Davies constantly reads her name into biblical texts *Handmaid* (12, 55, 109–10).

15. Both the Geneva translation and the King James version stipulate this.

is "a *Hand*" that has to be interpreted, and it is a woman, not a man, who provides the necessary information:

> Thus now, when all at their wits end
> wise men, all those Lords too,
> A woman Loe to her they come:
> to Learne what is to doe.
>
> (*Amend*, 3)

Only in Davies's prophecy do the nobility and "wise men" turn to a woman for advice, a moment of dependency that completely revises the biblical original in which the queen enters to offer unsolicited information. Because Davies introduces this woman in stanza 5, she also establishes a numeric link between "the fingers of the female hand" that write the prophecy before us and the "hand-maid" who points to Daniel as the revealer of divine secrets. In fact, for Davies, this "handmaid" and Daniel have the same fingerprints.

Davies continues to revise the biblical passage by shortening the speech of the queen to two lines, thus eliminating from our awareness the fact that the king repeats his queen's speech word for word in his later conversation with Daniel.[16] In making this change, Davies obscures the way in which feminine insight is appropriated by the king to serve his own ends. But the bribe he offers Daniel is, of course, his own idea:

> Make known this *Thing*, then if *thou dost*
> as fayled *Thou* hast never:
> Weare *gold* and *purple* too, tis *Thine*
> choyse make of whatsoever.
>
> (*Amend*, 4)

To the king's promise of wealth and power, Daniel returns an indictment with definite seventeenth-century overtones:

> For *Courtly* phrase, returned plaine,
> Sir *Keepe your* gifts in store:
> High *offices* let others gaine,
> too much ye *have* given before.
>
> (*Amend*, 4)

---

16. Perhaps making a stylistic choice, Davies deletes the repetition that is a standard feature of biblical narrative.

Daniel speaks tersely, choosing the "plaine" language of truth as he eschews courtly excesses in language as well as behavior. Rebuking such gift-giving— "too much ye *have* given before"—Daniel refuses to play the game of mutual exchange, refuses to participate in the patronage system. Through these glosses on the text, Davies subtly condemns the way royal gifts continue to shape ecclesiastical policy by hinting that such benefits always come with a price.[17]

Clearly untainted by royal benefits, Daniel speaks an untarnished truth. In revealing his identity as a captive visionary, he notes that he has been forced to sing the Lord's song in a strange land:

> The vessels of my God are brought,
> also as *I am one*
> Of the Captivitie that mourne,
> in BABYLON so long.
>
> (*Amend*, 4)

Speaking through Daniel, Davies unravels the implications of what it means to be a "vessel" containing God by indicating that prophaning a vessel of the temple is the same as corrupting a prophet. Consequently, Daniel and she refuse to be silent about this royal abuse of power, refuse to be used and thus complicit in spiritual error.

Davies's Daniel immediately turns to recent history to make Belshazzar aware of his folly, focusing on the story of Belshazzar's grandfather Nebuchadnezzar. This story within a story takes on additional resonance in Davies's account since King Charles's grandfather Darnley had likewise experienced "a miserable fall." Darnley, of course, was murdered while Nebuchadnezzar receives a second chance:

> *Woodes* all for woe, as well as Men
> ring out, and *Echos call:*
> For mercy on this *savage King,*
> in *Holy Temples all.*
>
> (*Amend*, 7)

Through the music of the captives and the prayers of the prophets, Nebuchadnezzar obtained a moment of redemption, and it is just such a moment that Charles has been accorded through Davies's revelations. Into the text,

---

17. See Linda Levy Peck, *Court Patronage and Corruption in Early Stuart England,* 210–11.

then, she inserts her "coat of arms" to establish the significance of her prophetic calling and to highlight her message to the present kingdom:

> *Who* gave by Stare-light *for* device
> A *Harte* in silver fielde:
> An *Eagle* mounted on the *Crest,*
> graven upon his *Shield.*
>
> > (*Amend,* 8)

From this point on, Daniel's judgment of Belshazzar coalesces perfectly with Davies's indictment of Charles. Both are guilty of aligning themselves with "favourites" who are idolaters and thus increasing faction within the kingdom. Charles, however, has divided the kingdom still more completely by instituting the 1633–1634 *Book of Sports* and thereby "polluting" the "Day and Night" designated particularly for a Sabbath rest:

> Besides polluting *holy Things,*
> with *Sabaths so divine:*
> *Idolatry* and *Revels* in,
> That *Day* and *Night* made thine.
>
> > (*Amend,* 9)

For this reason, divine judgment is about to repeat itself with all the accuracy of apocalyptic foreclosure:

> Of *Mene Mene* to Thee sent
> Even twice fullfil'd to bee:
> The Hand pointing at Twenty-five,
> Heavenly *Palmistry.*
> Which yeare reveald Gods *Dreadfull day,*
> whose Hand-Mayd for a Signe:
> Our Troubles fore-told as come to passe,
> how never such a Time.
>
> > (*Amend,* 11)

Davies chooses stanza 25 in which to introduce the pointing "hand" that signals Charles's end and the "Hand-Mayd" who writes the prediction, emphasizing in this way the date of her own "extraordinary" calling. The "Heavenly *Palmistry*" encoded in a woman's "hand" and interpreted in a woman's text is further evidence of that apocalyptic moment when "upon the handmaids in those days will I pour out my Spirit" (Joel 2:29), when the woman as true church will be restored to view.

Rarely brief in utterance, Davies goes on to make further indictments specific to Charles himself. Citing Dan. 12:1 in which Michael, a great prince, stands up on behalf of his people and delivers them, she reveals Charles's disheartening departure from this spiritual ideal. Turning down the heroic role of "*Michael* who's like God," he has chosen to play the "Faithlesse *Steward*/Stuart" instead, burying his talent in the ground instead of investing it on behalf of the kingdom. Marrying "two Wifes at once" (*Amend*, 11), he has committed adultery against the "true mother" of Sion by aligning himself with the whore of Babylon. For such manifold corruption his judgment is ensured:

> Which hand as here betokn's a Blowe,
> The *Ballance* who knows not;
> Cruelty and Injustice shew,
> Sir Amend *you* know what.
> (*Amend*, 12)

While throughout this text Davies lists in some detail Charles's corrupt activities—his addiction to "favourites," his marriage to Henrietta Maria, his passage of the *Book of Sports*, and his inculcation of Romish idolatry within the kingdom—her prophetic warning leaves particular aspects of his reformation indeterminate: "Sir Amend *you* know what." It is not, however, that Davies's prophecies "disalow concerted action" as Matchinske argues, reducing everything to "belief or disbelief in her texts."[18] Numerous calls for reformation occur throughout this work. Rather, Davies leaves it to Charles's conscience—to his inner knowledge—to "amend" what he knows to be wrong, believing that it is only an appropriate response to inner illumination that will bring about a transformation of the kingdom.

In closing, Davies comes full circle, returning to her "song" of Babylon and aligning it with the "little Booke" of the Apocalypse that is bitter and sweet to the taste:

> And so goe Little Booke to bee,
> Sung as a *pleasant Song*:
> The *Times* at hand, another Note
> *Great Brittaine* sings ere Long.
> (*Amend*, 12)

Like the prophet Ezekiel who clothed his prophetic indictment in "jesting music," Davies creates the same harmonic dissonance, underscoring through

---

18. Matchinske, "Holy Hatred," 361.

this prophetic technique the generally flippant, even scornful response of those who hear.[19] Her indictments accordingly move beyond Charles and the immediate court to include all who participate in similar activities, all who drink themselves into deafness and spiritual oblivion:

> Drunkards also, Here's to You
> beware the Trumpets Call:
> For from *Pride* yours, and surfeiting,
> proceeds our Troubles all.
> Praying down with your *Twelfe tyde-Shews*,
> Stage-Playes and Foolery then,
> Lest in a Moment chang'd as He,
> Turn'd into Divels from Men.
>
> (*Amend*, 12)

Raising a glass to their destruction, Davies gives the apocalyptic "trumpet" of judgment a final part in her arrangement. If theater and other types of "Foolery" are not abandoned, if her audience does not take its reformation seriously, it is likely to undergo the same bestial metamorphosis as Nebuchadnezzar.

Davies's last words are, of course, for King Charles. Just as Nebuchadnezzar ignored Revelation and meant "to put to Death, his wise Men," Charles has taken the same pathway to his own destruction. He demonstrates in his antagonistic reaction to her words the same rejection of divine authority. His "diadem" is thus no longer fitting, his crown no longer appropriate. On this dark note, Davies provides a final message—drawn from Daniel's name— for King Charles: "DANIEL: I End ALL." In the closure that Daniel's name signifies, Davies assumes a position of absolute authority, not only over this text but also over the very writing of history.

While certainly subversive in 1633 and 1643, *Amend, Amend,* carried far more weight in 1649 when it was revised, licenced, and reissued in the days after Charles's execution. In this year, someone—perhaps Robert Ibbotson— altered Davies's text substantially, smoothing out the inverted syntax, adding marginal glosses to strengthen the relationship between the lyric and recent political events, and deleting substantial portions of the prophecy itself.[20]

---

19. As the Genevan translation phrases Ezekiel's message, it reads, "And lo, thou art unto them, as a jesting song of one that hathe a pleasant voice, and can sing wel: for thei heare thy wordes, but thei do them not. And when this commeth to passe (for lo, it will come) then shal thei knowe, that a Prophet hathe bene among them" (Ezek. 32:32–33).

20. Here, *Amend* is printed under the title "Strange and Wonderfull Prophesies by the Lady Eleanor Audeley." Cope briefly discusses this revision—the only prophecy of Davies's licensed by Parliament—in *Handmaid* (147–48) and in Davies, *Prophetic Writings* (59).

Whoever brought about these changes desired to foreground Charles's death as an act of divine judgment and to remove Davies's feminist authority from its central position. The specificity of these emendations suggests that Davies's prophecies not only were understood by those of her time but also were, in this case, rewritten to make the text advance parliamentarian interests alone.

In revising the document, the editor takes the most literal and pragmatic of approaches—something Davies never does. Writing into the margins of the prophecy a series of spatial, political, and economic details, he notes that the banquet that Belshazzar gives corresponds with the "Banquetting house" where Charles was executed, that Belshazzar's request to drink from the vessels of the temple reflects Charles's "pawning and selling of his plate," and that Belshazzar's pagan music signals the eventual "pulling down of pictures and Organs in Churches." But by commenting on Charles's economic problems and sanctioning, as divine judgment, the recent parliamentarian destruction occurring in the cathedrals, the editor manages to eliminate Davies's more subtle connection between the prophaning of the vessels of the temple and the captive prophets of God who appear to correct such abuses. Moreover, in this new and revised version, a woman is never the focus of power and insight, for the male moment of reliance on female counsel and the numerical link to stanza 5 are missing. So too is stanza 25 and the "Heavenly *Palmistry*" sanctioning female authority. Perhaps most significant, the various prophetic lyrics that echo throughout Davies's text and the inspired "handmaids" of Joel 2:29 disappear without a trace. The "Hand" revising this text has completely altered the message: "At Hand, the Hand bids it adieu, / Finish'd thy Majesties."[21] According to the editor's gloss, Davies "prophecies here that ther shal be nor more Kings in *England*," expressing, of course, a clearly parliamentarian hope that the end of monarchy was ensured. More than divine judgment, however, the "hand" that "bids adieu" in this rewriting might well be read as a sign of Davies herself, for the parting wave is the only task her "hand" is finally assigned.

Though Davies's work was, in this instance, appropriated by the parliamentarians to illustrate God's part in recent political events, her subsequent prophecies generated none of the same enthusiasm. In *The Restitution of Prophecy: That Buried Talent to Be Revived*, she returns to her role as the virgin of divine deliverance.[22] Noting that her early prophecies were "difficult

---

21. Davies, "Strange and Wonderfull Prophesies," 4.
22. See *The Restitution of Prophecy*, in Davies, *Prophetic Writings*. Future references will be cited parenthetically within the text.

to be *fathered* or *licensed*" (*PW*, 344) by monarchy or Parliament, she highlights the intimate relationship between Mary's conception of Christ (who was "unfathered" in the eyes of the world) and the unauthorized writing of the woman prophet. Her entire letter "To the Reader" follows through on these connections by demonstrating that unlicensed reproductions, for this very reason, are both feminine and divine.

Similar to the licensing laws that brought Mary and Joseph to Bethlehem, then, Davies's own text is produced under social and political constraints. Like Mary who wraps the Christ child in swaddling clothes, Davies wraps her prophecy ("This Babe") in the *"Swathe-bands"* of a "Letter to the Reader," making the "bounds of a *Preface*" the "sign" by which her readers, *"vigilent Shepherds"* (*PW*, 344–45), might find him. In "Commending" her text "unto [their] hands," Davies echoes Christ's statement from the cross ("Into thy hands I commend my Spirit"), and so offers a text in which her readers, not the Father, become the repository of the Spirit.

What she is "Messenger" of, it turns out, is "Oblivions Act" (*PW*, 344), a recovery of the erased feminine in prophecy. Consequently, she revises Isa. 40:2 that initially reads, "Cry unto her that her warfare is accomplished, that her iniquity is pardoned: for she has received of the Lord's hand double for all her sins." Davies removes "warfare" from this text and adds female "travail" instead, thereby underscoring the relationship between divine pardon and the "delivery" of women: "Tell her, That her *Travel* is at an end; Her *Offence* is pardoned, our *Jubiles deliverance:* Sirs, to be plain, as in the first place, His commission" (*PW*, 344). The fall of women and the curse resulting in the "Travel" of Eve "is pardoned," an event registered in "His commission" of Mary and, it turns out, Eleanor Davies. Thus, Davies's calling in 1625 is here doubled to become "Jubiles deliverance," a deliverance linked to the jubilee of Pentecost and the descent of the Spirit.[23] Women now receive the "tongues" to translate the divine.

Thus, even though Davies recognizes the distinctions between herself and Mary, that, for example, she does not write "in a stable" (*PW*, 344), she returns immediately to the "extremes or streits" under which both women reproduce the *logos:* "But requisit *Bridges,* and the like, the true *Narrow way* (by suffering) *that leads to life:* From him a proper *passage* or mention. Straits of the *Virgins-Womb* had passed; besides Seafaring persons

---

23. Because jubilees in the Old Testament occurred after fifty years and at Pentecost after fifty days, they signify, for Davies, her own number "doubled" and 1650—the day of the Lamb's return.

his followers in that way not unexperienced, afor arrive the *welcome haven*" (*PW*, 344). Davies here exploits the implications of the "travel"/"travail" pun by connecting the "straits of the Virgins Womb" with the "true and narrow way" that leads to life. Christ not only "traveled" this way, she suggests, but also affirmed his origin by validating the feminine in "a proper passage or mention."[24] This "passage" in human and textual terms intimately links women with the reproduction of the *logos*. But, suggests Davies, the "straits of the Virgin's Womb" have few travelers as those who take "the Broad-way" make abundantly clear. Rejecting "the Holy Spirits Presence," they are guilty of "begetting incurable blindness" and reproducing their own failure to see; they dismiss as "none-scence, not material" the "Spirit of Prophecy" (*PW*, 345) and the women who speak it. By way of warning, then, Davies closes her "Letter to the Reader" with a negative example drawn from Acts 18:17: "Galio cared for none of these matters." In Galio's willful ignorance, Davies cites without further comment a man's hell-bent refusal to take a prophet's message seriously.

Davies opens *Restitution of Prophecy* with a biblical citation, Matt. 25, and so calls attention to her mystic number, divine calling, and primary focus on the parables of the kingdom. Her subtitle, *The Great Account,* hints at the connections she establishes between her prophetic message, spiritual "profit," and the Day of Judgment, topics the three parables of Matt. 25 allow her to pursue in depth. By turning each miniature narrative into a filter for analyzing seventeenth-century political and ecclesiastical relationships, she reveals how economic interests continue to corrupt the political and spiritual accounts of her time. Such encoded indictments, she notes, are the prophet's method: "The secrets of the Gospel under Allegories covered and Parables, precious Leaven" (*PW*, 346).

In the first parable, that of the five wise and foolish virgins, Davies focuses on the moment of her prophetic calling. She accordingly glosses the "wise virgins" as "so many Handmaids, his Kingdoms epitomy at hand, or forthwith to appear Virgins, their's the priority: five perfection of numbers" (*PW*, 346). Again confirming her "handwriting," Davies makes the "hand-maids" prophesying in the latter days parallel with the watchful virgins of the kingdom that Christ highlights here. Having the "priority," they accompany the bridegroom into the marriage, leaving behind them the five whose *"Lamps are out or quencht"* due, Davies hints, to their continual "quenching"

---

24. More universally, of course, the "straits of the Virgins Womb" can be interpreted as Christian "travail": a strait through which Christ's followers always make their way.

(*PW,* 346) of the Spirit. This second group's refusal to "watch and wait" earns them the same indictment as the sleeping disciples of Christ: "*Could ye not one hour refrain:* our caveat bids *sleep on,* who allow the Spirit not transmitted beyond the Primative bounds, what real demonstration soever, as if any thing impossible with him: and thus the blinde conducting the blinde, emblems what posture Synods and Church-men found in" (*PW,* 347). Applying this passage to the English Churchmen, Davies invites them to "sleep on." She thus undermines the very meaning of episcopacy by identifying the past leaders of the church as altogether inattentive shepherds. Bound to "primative" times and tradition, they have failed to see "real demonstrations" of the Spirit and to hear Gabriel's message at the annunciation, "For with God nothing shall be impossible." Because of their refusal to acknowledge even the possibility of a feminine union with the divine, Christ will respond by knowing "their voices as much as they discern (read by them) the Prophets theirs" (*PW,* 347). In brief, their blindness to prophetic texts seals their damnation.

Those included in the marriage feast will, on the other hand, find feminine "Conception" and "supernatural anointings" confirmed. Thus, on page 5 of her printed text, Davies inscribes the date of her own "annunciation" as she notes its exact correspondence to Mary's: "Pointed to a Jubile's moiety, *Five times five.* The years prime *Anniversary Feast,* blessed throughout all Generations: her Wedding-Day, faithful Handmaid the Virgin Mary, her five and twentieth of the Moneth, as bears date 1625. Year of Grace" (*PW,* 347).

But if 1625 reveals Davies as inspired "Handmaid" and "Bride" to the Lamb, it also discloses Charles's political ascent to the throne and his marriage to the whore of Babylon who "dotes on Idol blocks" and "painted Popets" (*PW,* 348). Thus, Davies sets her prophetic voice off against the "graceless voice" of King Charles, who, like that man in another parable of the kingdom "could not come" (*PW,* 348) to the wedding supper because he had married a wife.

Reading the parable historically as well as politically, Davies identifies the transcendent marriage into which the five wise virgins enter with the unadulterated and pure faith of England, realized most fully in the reign of Elizabeth I, the virgin queen. Elizabeth's "unmatchable Reign" uniting "The Bridegroom Sun and his Virgin Spouse" (*PW,* 348) of the Apocalypse has been followed, unfortunately, by the corrupt and idolatrous "match" of Charles I, a return, Davies believes, to the "Fiery Bloody days" of Queen Mary and her persecution of the Protestant faithful.

At the core of the corrupt political and ecclesiastical alliance represented by the marriage of Charles and Henrietta Maria, Davies locates economic corruption as well, drawing on the Parable of the Talents to develop her point. Initially contrasting the master's fair evaluation of his servants' profits in Matt. 25 with the unfair trial of her brother, Mervyn Audeley, she attributes Audeley's condemnation not to any question of his guilt or innocence but rather to the jealousy of those who put him on trial and to the economic benefits that would accrue from stealing his land.[25] What happens to Audeley, she suggests, is foreseen in two other biblical accounts involving prophecy and stewardship: the story of Joseph in the Old Testament and the parable of the wicked husbandmen in the New.

In Davies's view, Joseph's visionary dreams take him first into exile and then into prison because he repeatedly affirms the position of supreme authority he will eventually have. On these grounds, an "unnatural *Jury of Brethren*" make certain he is "*scorned* and *stript* of his Garment" (*PW*, 256), first in a plot at home and later in one instigated by Potiphar's wife. Audeley, according to Davies, underwent similar imprisonment and public exposure, prompted, as in Joseph's case, by the lies, anger, and jealousy of "those of his own house" (*PW*, 256). Thus, Audeley, as Davies's version of Joseph, refuses to be silenced even when confronted with familial and sexual blackmail. Yet Joseph is "for their preservation sent thither," just as Davies offers "the word throughout all ages" (*PW*, 357) for the salvation of those who will listen.

The various plots against Audeley are, in Davies's account, instituted by corrupt stewards, and illuminated, once again, in the parable of the wicked husbandmen who "thirsted after his vineyard" (*PW*, 355). Like the wicked renters who plot against the son, the ecclesiastical and political leaders prosecuting Audeley do so to increase their financial holdings. As Davies conceives of it, their decision to execute Audeley, like their decision to murder the prophets before him, speaks volumes about their values.

These values are equally apparent in their stewardship of God's benefits, their use of divine "Talents," and their attitude toward prophecy in particular. Laud had closed his *Conference with Fisher* in 1624 by noting that he would eventually have to "go and give God and Christ an account of the 'talent'

---

25. Eleanor Davies's version of her brother's execution is a far cry from other versions. Audeley's trial was one of the most sensational of the seventeenth century; it concluded with his execution in 1631 for various sexual crimes against his wife and servants. His wife, Ann Audley, discusses his behavior in "The Trial and Condemnation of Mervin Lord Audley."

committed to my charge."[26] Davies, however, turns the parable against Laud and the entire Episcopalian priesthood by asserting that they not only have buried their talent but also have added to that evil by attempting to bury Davies herself. This brings divine judgment upon them as the death of Strafford in 1641 makes abundantly clear. According to Davies, Strafford treated her as "a second Eve; for her forwardness, ye know not what ye ask" (*PW*, 357). Davies inscribes in this quote Strafford's attempt to link her with two mothers in Scripture: the mother of human error who tempts with fallen knowledge and the mother of James and John who longs for privilege and authority; both are viewed as attempting to transcend their predefined gender roles by overreaching. Like the steward in the parable, Strafford returns Davies's prophecy without a word after keeping it three weeks, thereby increasing his sin by hiding the truth from others.

But if Strafford willfully ignores Davies's prophecies, Davies believes that King Charles commits a still greater sin by refusing to read a message "stampt" with the seal of divine authority: "Instead of *kissing hands,* stampt a *handwriting,* subscribed, Great *Britains Lamentation Mourning* and *Wo*" (*PW*, 358). In writing to Charles, Davies bypasses the fair "hand" of salutation, offering instead the "hand sent" to Ezekiel, one "written within and without" with a triple warning: "lamentations, and mourning, and woe" (Ezek. 2:10). Unfortunately, Davies hints, Charles and the Stuarts have much in common with Ezekiel's original audience: "And they, whether they will hear, or whether they will forbear, (for they *are* a rebellious house), yet shall know that there hath been a prophet among them" (Ezek. 2:5). For Davies, as for Ezekiel, it is the act of prophesying, not the receptivity of her audience, that legitimizes her voice. Those who refuse to hear and repent will one day know the prophet they have rejected.

Of those guilty of failed reception, no one in Davies's mind comes close to William Laud. His reaction to her prophecy aligns him not only with the corrupt steward in the New Testament parable, but also with Achan in the Old, who, in burying gold against divine orders, privileged his own economic advancement over the voice of God and placed the entire nation in spiritual jeopardy: "The one Talent even buried by his hand, *Achans* graceless Scholar" (*PW*, 359). Davies here sets the "scholarly" pursuits of Laud—"graceless" and without any mark of the Spirit—over against the "one Talent" (*PW*, 359) that he knows is divine but determines to hide away.

26. Laud, *Works of Laud,* 2:429.

Thus, just as Davies finds her prophetic calling concealed in her name, she decodes Laud's title (as archbishop of Canterbury) concealed in his. It signifies his desire to "bury" grace, just as his wearing of the white surplice signifies the funeral "napkins" (*PW*, 360) of the spiritually dead. A far cry from Davies herself who is "buried quick" (*PW*, 362) in seventeenth-century prisons, he is dead above ground as his interest in the externals of title, clothing, and money suggest. In concluding her prophecy, Davies continues to indict Laud as the corrupter of the English Church; he has recovered the whore, not the bride, by restoring the external, ceremonial worship of Rome. He has also instituted mass in his emphasis on the sacraments, both in his determination to "Sacrifice and Eat" and in his failure to distinguish between "Altar and Table," calling "both one, or indifferent" (*PW*, 361). He has kept the "keys" (*PW*, 363) of succession, locking all but bishops out of the ministry, and so has buried prophetic "Talent" like Davies's own. He has even decided what portions of the Bible should be read, purposely excluding "the Book of Apocalyps, and other like," by arguing that what is "least edifying, may be best spared" (*PW*, 362). His attempt to silence divine revelation is, in Davies's mind, replicated in his attempt to silence the prophets themselves: "Besides how many silenced imprisoned, other some crucified on Pillaries, whilest he and his Panders, eating and drinking with the drunken" (*PW*, 363). Nevertheless, Davies has not been thwarted by the voices of opposition raised against her, any more than she has been silenced by Laud's premature attempt to bury her. As one of the twelve apostles, she makes up a "Jury" far superior to Laud's own: "And thus proceeding, a compleat Jury, their Verdict with one consent, Prophets and Apostles; Touching our Nations story. English, Irish, Scottish and French, every one as heretofore heard in their proper Language, fulfilling nothing so secret and covered, that shall not be revealed and made manifest" (*PW*, 363). "In one accord" with that group of apostles at Pentecost, Davies discovers in their "one consent" the gift of the Spirit foretold by Zephaniah: "For then will I turn to the people a pure language, that they may all call upon the name of the Lord, to serve him with one consent" (Zeph. 3:9). The ability to translate God, to make him "heard in their proper Language," recovers the "pure language" of Eden and reverses the fragmentary and fallen discourses of Babel.

Davies follows this affirmation of linguistic renewal with an analysis of "Times reign or reckoning" as she predicts the day of judgment and the conclusion of human history. Noting that Christ did declare his ignorance of the end—the passage cited by Donne, Andrewes, and numerous others to contest predictions like Davies's—Davies argues that women actually surpass Christ in this area: "The weaker Sex preferred more proper for them, requisit for former days neither: To whose Disciples not a little earnest (answered) A thing not in his dispose, he was but the Word: but his Fathers where he pleased, a Conception; as much to say, By special Grace: Witnessed to be by them though" (*PW*, 365). According to Davies, Christ is "but the Word" and thus limited to one bodily and textual incarnation. Women, however, are offered "a Conception," the capacity to produce God anew "by special Grace" and thus to give him an infinite variety of new and revelatory incarnations. In this sense, revelation is open rather than closed, fluid rather than fixed, feminine rather than masculine, polyphonic rather than monologic. It is the *logos* liberated into a chorus of female voices.

Having taken up the issue of divine timing, Davies concludes her prophecy by analyzing the end of time—here revealed in the final parable, the separation of the sheep and the goats. Not surprisingly, it is here that Charles, the unfaithful shepherd, takes a final walk "from the fold to the scaffold" on his execution day "aforehand revealed" to Davies herself. Having imprisoned others, having not even "visited the least of those his Lambs, Hunger, starved and Cold" (*PW*, 366), he becomes the appropriate "Scape Goat," with "no Purgatory Pardon" by which to "e-scape" (*PW*, 366). On the other hand, suggests Davies, those "overcharged by their unmerciful owners," those burdened with "intolerable Tax," those bound in "insupportable Bonds" (*PW*, 367) will be freed by the return of Christ and the paradise he ushers in.

In the end, of course, Davies's indictment moves beyond the king and the churchmen that have been executed to include the blind and deaf in the present parliamentarian government: "Make *Laws* for strict keeping the *Sabbath*, notwithstanding so stupid and carnal, stop the *ear* against his *Word* and *Law, Thou shalt have no other gods*" (*PW*, 368). The Puritans, she believes, have made a "god" of their own authority by becoming consumed with legislating and lawmaking. Like the royalists before them, they too are caught up in external behavior rather than internal transformation. This tendency to privilege their "stupid and carnal" interpretations over the "Word and the Law" allows them to turn a deaf ear to the Spirit of God and the liberating truth revealed through the prophets, including Davies in particular and women in general.

Clearly, the "handwriting" that Davies draws on includes a number of texts in circulation, the "handwriting" of God encoded in biblical prophecy, the "handwriting" of the various prophets and preachers who, like herself, read the events leading up to the Apocalypse, and, of course, the fallen "handwriting" of the king, the churchmen, and Parliament. By observing Davies's "hand" among these authorized and unauthorized versions of history, we are able to decode the feminist, often revolutionary aspects of the prophecies she composes and to identify the complex shaping of a truly feminist authority.

8

Re-Covering Paul
The True Church and the Prophecies of
Mary Cary, Anna Trapnel, and Margaret Fell

*And now both Sons and Daughters of the Lord come to witness these things
fulfilled, and you Magistrates, Priests, and people do fulfill the Scriptures against
the servants of the living God, as you have done against these.*
                                                                    —*A True Testimony*

LADY ELEANOR Davies who first prophesied against Charles I and then
against the Presbyterian government that refused to license her prophecies was joined by a number of other women of the Interregnum who made
similar political and prophetic moves. Clearly diverging from Lady Eleanor
in their limited educations, middle-class status, and lucid prophecies, they
took as their biblical focus the one figure whom Eleanor Davies studiously
avoided, the apostle Paul.

These women turned to the writings of Paul because his theology was
central not only to the Reformation movement in general but to the beliefs of
the Fifth Monarchists and Quakers in particular. As they saw it, he advocated
a liberation from the ceremonial "letter" of the law visible in the corrupt
institutional hierarchies of the Stuart kings and, after that, the protectorate;
Paul found his freedom of the spirit under the reign of King Jesus. In a
passage seldom quoted in the sermons of the Stuart court but central to the
thinking of women prophets, Paul removes in his epistle to the Galatians the
hierarchical gender relations he elsewhere inscribes: "There is neither Jew nor
Greek, there is neither bond nor free, there is neither male nor female: for ye
are all one in Christ Jesus" (Gal. 3:28). When Mary Cary and Anna Trapnel
appeal to the epistles of Paul, they emphasize this erasure of national, class,
and gender markers as they attempt to foster a similar egalitarian union.
And when they do invoke the Pauline dichotomies—between female and
male, flesh and spirit, weakness and strength—they show how they break

196

down under the paradoxical pressure of divine empowerment glimpsed most fully in the life of Paul himself. Employing Pauline biography to reconceive Pauline authority, they disclose Paul's illuminating moment of insight as central to their own: "And he said unto me, My grace is sufficient for thee: for my strength is made perfect in weakness. Most gladly therefore will I rather glory in my infirmities, that the power of Christ may rest upon me. Therefore I take pleasure in infirmities, in reproaches, in necessities, in persecutions, in distresses for Christ's sake: for when I am weak, then am I strong" (2 Cor. 12:9–10). Mary Cary and Anna Trapnel interpret this passage as an affirmation of all forms of weakness including the feminine, believing with Paul in the liberation born out of limitation.

Beyond their attention to the epistolary writings of Paul and the Acts of the Apostles, these women focus, like others of the time, on the prophetic material of Daniel and the Apocalypse of Saint John. They also draw on their own inspired visions and the conventions of conversion narrative, giving increasing weight to the egalitarian nature of inspiration. This leads, as Nigel Smith has argued, to fascinating uses of language on their part: appropriations of prophetic behavior from biblical texts in the form of gesture and symbol; rhapsodic singing of divine psalms and songs; and lapses into silence and incomprehensibility, the divine taking form at the very limits of human language.[1]

The "dedicatory epistles" of the women prophets I have considered here reflect these diverging contexts and influences, for while Aemilia Lanyer appeals for patronage to a community of women at court, most of the woman prophets of the period are supported by a spiritual community. Mary Cary accordingly acknowledges the conventions of patronage in order to dismiss them altogether: "But though I publish it under your name and favour, yet doe I not thereby desire you to Patronize any thing in it (if there should be any thing) that is not truth, and for the Truth that is in it, I need desire no Patron; For great is the truth, and it will prevail."[2] Clearly rejecting the financial exchange that in her view taints textual production, Cary makes the absence of a profit motive central to the purity of her prophetic authority. Yet even this kind of spiritual support had its drawbacks, since members of the community often transcribed, edited, and revised the prophecies afterward.

---

1. Smith, *Perfection Proclaimed: Language and Literature in English Radical Religion, 1640–1660,* 18.
2. Cary, *The Resurrection of the Witnesses,* dedicatory epistle. Future references will be designated *Res* and cited parenthetically within the text.

This blurring of boundaries between the divinely authored "Word" and the prophetic transcriber(s) makes it nearly impossible for us to distinguish a prophetess's position from her spiritual community's since she was the channel by which the vision of the group was communicated to the public at large. Perhaps for this reason, feminist concerns make fewer and far subtler appearances in these texts, often emerging only in the attempt to efface such concerns altogether. As Phyllis Mack notes, the meetings of Friends censored and sometimes rejected for print numerous prophecies, including Margaret Fell's *The Daughter of Zion awakened.*[3]

Such a reliance on outside authorities—in this case, God and the spiritual community—posed something of a dilemma to Mary Cary, leading her into the vexing predicament of both revealing and concealing her hand in the authorship of her texts. In her first work, *The Resurrection of the Witnesses,* she signed her name "M. Cary," strategically eliminating her first name to circumvent the cultural attitudes toward women writers, and she continued to use this name in her next prophecy when her surname changed to "Rande."[4] The possibility of gaining name recognition, perhaps under the pretense of male authorship, is nevertheless held in check by the identification of herself as a weak instrument in the hand of God: "I am a very weak, and unworthy instrument, and have not done this work by any strength of my own, but have been often made sensible, that I could do no more herein (wherein any light, or truth could appear) of myself, than a pencil, or pen can do, when no hand guides it."[5] Like Paul who was similarly "weak and unworthy," she becomes, through the "hand" who guides her, active, verbal, and assertive, the phallic "pen or pencil" providing access to masculine authority.[6]

Cary reasserts a seemingly masculine authority on the title page of *The Resurrection* when she calls herself "a Minister or Servant of Jesus Christ, and of all his Saints." Taking the title of the apostolic writers in the first-century church—that of "servant to the saints"—she locates herself on the same ground. Moreover, in assuming the role of minister, she envisions the position much as Paul defines it in the early church when to "minister to

3. See Mack, *Visionary Women,* 368.
4. Elaine Hobby makes these astute points (*Virtue of Necessity: English Women's Writing 1649–88,* 30).
5. Cary, "To the Reader," in *The Little Horns Doom and Downfall.*
6. As Hobby argues, however, the emphasis on "a pen or pencil" actually calls attention to the hand writing the text before us in the very attempt to efface that moment of production (*Virtue of Necessity,* 30).

the saints" involves distributing the wealth equitably between rich and poor churches. Paul had written, "For I mean not that other men be eased, and ye burdened: but by an equality, that now at this time your abundance may be a supply for their want . . . that there may be equality: as it is written, 'He that had gathered much had nothing over; and he that had gathered little had no lack' " (2 Cor. 8:13–15). Cary's understanding of equality is similarly rooted in an egalitarian economics spelled out in numerous prophecies, each advocating more complete social reforms.

Nevertheless, some acknowledgment of gender occurs in Cary's *Resurrection of the Witnesses*. In this work Cary immediately takes as her example "the importunate widdow" in Scripture who prevails upon the unjust judge and eventually effects legal and social change; Cary of course interprets all of the elect as similarly engaged in "importunate praier," but the powerless and vocal woman who confronts an unjust official in a corrupt institution provides a striking analogue for her own prophetic activity. Against this kind of corruption God is acting even now, she asserts: "[God] poureth contempt upon Princes, causeth them to wander in the wilderness, where there is no way; yet he setteth the poor on high from affliction, and maketh his families like a flocke" (*Res*, "To the Reader"). In this prophetic indictment of monarchy and class structure, Cary identifies the "wandering" prince with the doomed, now captive king who has lost his way; she also calls attention to the fall of the "Babylonish" ecclesiastical hierarchy: "Now this is that which is by Saints to be observed at this time also, even how God beginneth to pour contempt upon Babylonish princes, viz. Bishops and other Babylonish followers, and to set the saints that were looked upon as poor afflicted creatures on high from affliction" (*Res*, "To the Reader"). Underlining the present moment as the time of prophetic fulfillment, she emphasizes the swiftness of divine justice. Those who are not yet "saints," but desire to be "sure of safety," she argues, should take immediate action by beginning to effect social justice in their own positions of power: "Oppose the Beast, and act for the welfare of all that wish well to Sion, and doe Justice unto all, from the highest unto the lowest, and be more forward to act for the meanest then for the highest" (*Res*, "To the Reader"). In privileging the "meanest" and thus overturning the power structure, Cary begins to suggest that her prophetic strategy is itself divine. Appropriating and transforming Christ's words, "Henceforth I call you not servants; for the servant knoweth not what his lord doeth: but I have called you friends; for all things that I have heard of my Father I have made known to unto you" (John 15:15), Cary briefly revises Christ's initial assessment: "in whom if thou be a friend to the Lord

Jesus Christ, I am thy friend to serve thee. M. Cary." Basing her friendship with the saints on their friendship with Christ, Cary acknowledges the fact that all are engaged in the same service of revelation, a service defined not by class hierarchies or power but by an open, ever expanding communion.

This egalitarian communion is, as we might expect, close to the feminist representations of Lanyer and Davies, and markedly different from the prophetic discourse of Andrewes and Donne.[7] Following the usual course of those who write prophecy, Cary turns to the Apocalypse to unravel the significance of recent historical events. Asserting in her opening letter that what she writes "is that which is not yet printed by any other," she offers her revelation to increase knowledge of the divine. Her exploration of prophetic discourse, her description of the temple, and her account of the Antichrist are a far cry from the accounts of Andrewes, Donne, and Herbert as, like Milton, she determines to open up prophetic discourse, to eliminate visible and ceremonial traditions from the true meaning of the temple, and to expose all coercive operations of power as themselves "Antichristian."

In confronting the first issue, the nature of prophecy, Cary departs temporarily from her focus on Rev. 11. She explains that she is "prest in Spirit" (*Res*, "The Preamble") to pursue this alternative course, her well-chosen phrase an exact echo of Paul's in Acts 18:5. Why, she asks rhetorically, does God choose prophets when he could speak immediately, without a mediator? Cary responds to this rhetorical question by employing a simile in which she identifies the prophets of the church as Christ's "beloved wife," a simile that returns us to the representation of the bride in the Song of Solomon and Revelation: "As a tender Husband unbosomes himself, and discovers his secrets to his beloved wife, and cannot with-hold them from her, So the Lord doth express his tender love unto his servants, in revealing his secrets to them" (*Res*, 11). In this revelatory encounter, couched in sexual as well as verbal terms, Christ removes all barriers to knowledge, both telling his wife secrets and expressing his love to her in tangible form. Because "she" is made up of so many individuals, however, Cary underscores the fact that each person necessarily reflects a different facet of Christ's love: "For if God should reveal himselfe to all alike, then would not his people have such communion one with another, as they have, to the end they may partake one of another's gifts, and therefore doth it please the Lord to make use

---

7. Her models and metaphors are similar to those of Herbert, who says that in the parson's family "all are preachers," highlighting the importance of collecting insight from others in coming to a full knowledge of divine truth (*Works of Herbert*, 240).

of instruments, whereas if it pleased him, he could have effected all things immediately" (*Res*, 15). Only in communion—in "partaking one of another's gifts"—does the revelation of Christ become complete, a communion not established by passively eating the Eucharist as occurs in the Church of England, but by intimately sharing secrets in the spiritual community. Thus, while both Donne and Cary employ the metaphor of Christ and his spouse to clarify the nature of the true church, Cary's representation focuses on Christ's openness to the spouse rather than the spouse's openness to men. Her true church comes together only to reveal Christ. Piece by piece, through a series of prophetic insights, they lovingly come together to assemble this ultimate mystery. Cary thus eliminates from view any infidelity or impurity in the true church: outsiders simply do not participate.

Cary's emphasis on the pure, even visionary communion of the saints allows her to affirm the instrumental role that the prophet plays in the process. Those who slight such instruments, she argues, "slight God himself, and do as much as in them lies, endeavor to break the communion of Saints" (*Res*, 16). Naturally, the apostle Paul must be answered as well, especially his pronouncement that a woman must not "usurp authority over the man" but "be in silence" (1 Tim. 2:11–12). Citing two prophets in Scripture who are driven to speak, Cary articulates for her readership why female silence must now be broken: "It is not possible for instruments to be silent, nor to sit still, when God hath spoken to them, and given them commission to do his work" (*Res*, 19). For Cary, the divine commission supersedes the Pauline mandate, demanding the speech and activity of women as well as men.

Beyond the enforcement of female silence, Cary also attacks the attempt to exclude the laity from prophesying, a belief crucial to the episcopalian viewpoint. Calling this belief the product of "the Babylonish darkness" and noting that it lacks "the least footing in Scripture" she argues that the gift of prophecy is "not restrained only to be done by Bishops and Deacons," but in fact is "common to be done by all" (*Res*, 121, 129). In more clearly assessing who "all" is, Cary turns all saints into prophets: "Every true Saint is a Prophet, because the Lord, in revealing his secrets to a soul, as it maketh it a Saint, so it maketh it a Prophet, and so the Lord looks upon his Saints as his witnesses and Prophets" (*Res*, 122). Here and elsewhere Cary uses the neuter form to establish the relationship between Christ and the soul, removing both masculine and feminine gender coding in the process; all saints (a category certainly including women) are now prophets, and all are engaged in divine revelation. Ironically, when Cary actually defines the prophet, she describes such a person as "a man" (*Res*, 124) who publishes the Gospel, teaches the people, and feeds the flock of Christ, activities clearly visible in the text before us. Her work, however, must speak for itself, earning acceptance for the open communion it offers rather than for any gendered authority represented in it.

Cary's emphasis on a revelatory community and an egalitarian economics leads her to unite the two in a final lyrical passage about the status of prophets: "They are precious in the eies of God and profitable to men: for they empty the golden oil they have received from the holy one into others. The Spirit is it floweth from them, sometimes [it] penetrates into those that are strangers, aliens to Jesus Christ, whereby they are brought home to the embraces of Jesus Christ" (*Res,* 150). Prophets, she suggests, increase the church by allowing the Spirit to "penetrate" even "strangers" with the divine Word and to draw them into the divine embrace. Ultimately, then, prophets are "precious" to God because they are engaged in the same activity as Christ: overcoming class, gender, and national barriers to make people one. It is through this egalitarian and divine communion, she suggests, that Christ continues to appear in the world.

When at last Cary turns from prophesying to the "measurement of the Temple" in Rev. 11, she follows Brightman and Milton in establishing clear divisions between the court and the temple, the material "outside" and the spiritual "inside," the corruption of the Gentiles and the purity of the people of God. In the Old Testament, she notes, the temple was a structure "used only for that house that Solomon built," but it has come in the New Testament to signify "the special manner" in which Christ is "present in his people" (*Res,* 35). It is, of course, in spiritual communication that he now resides. The "court" represents "outside professors, that seem to the outward eye to be near to Saints . . . yet they are not of that holy place, they are but an outside." The "Gentiles," however, are even further removed according to Cary: "the word Gentiles is here used to expresse these that were not of the church, nor of the Temple, but would have the temple ruined. Jesus gives his spirituall Temple into the hands of the mysticall Babylonians for a while" (*Res,* 40). For Cary, those who make up the episcopal hierarchy of the English Church are, of course, the "mysticall Babylonians," and it is they who turn the temple into the site of a central confrontation.

As Cary analyzes this confrontation, she removes the figure of the "Stout champion" earlier interpreted as Constantine from his position in the apocalyptic commentary of Foxe, Brightman, Napier, and Forbes by graphically revising earlier interpretations before our eyes. No longer is it possible for a king to fill this position, for this would place the Puritans and Fifth

Monarchists on the losing side in the present conflict with King Charles. Consequently, Cary's gloss clarifies a very different reading of the power structure: "Here the Psalmist speaks of executing vengeance upon the Gentiles, and punishments upon the peoples, of binding kings in chains, and nobles in fetters of iron, why? Who must doe this? Must it not be some great and mighty potentate? No, but this is to be done by the Saints, and that not only by some Saints, but as well by the weakest of Saints, as by the strongest" (*Res,* 74). Cary inverts the hierarchy, as kings and nobles fall prey to "the weakest of the Saints" and the true church emerges victorious.

In the remaining portion of Cary's prophecy, her "Application," she examines in some detail the revelatory course of recent political events. Putting history into the past tense, she attempts to pin down the nature of the movement in which she is involved:

> But since the Bishops grew worse and worse, and became more prophane, and filthy, and wicked (as all that do usurp authority over the consciences do and the Bishops of Rome did), I say since Queen Elizabeths time, that they grew worse and worse, they have grown higher and higher in the persecution of the Saints; so that a reall godly minister could scarce be suffered to abide in the kingdome: but they were fain to fly to Holland and New England. . . . And this England did remain a horn of the beast, and a part of Babylon, because there was a power retained, that did exercise authority over the conscience. (*Res,* 86)

Like Lanyer and Davies before her, Cary traces the "Fall" of the church to the years succeeding the death of Queen Elizabeth. Its decline is, for her, coterminous with the Stuart ascendancy and the English clergy who have become increasingly visible in their ceremonial emphasis and in the Romish powers they assert over the private consciences of the church's membership. Much as Milton does, she argues that it is they and not women who "usurp authority," borrowing Paul's phrase to turn the tables upon them.

On the other hand, Cary notes, the "reall godly ministers" are appropriately called "Purintents," their names coinciding with their inner lives. As "the most precious saints of Jesus Christ" (*Res,* 88), they have become the new Foxeian martyrs. Their true faith has exposed them to the Romish persecution of the bishops who rage against Puritan purity: "For [the Bishops] cannot endure those torments, that the Prophets of Jesus doe inflict upon them, when they hold forth the truth of Christ, so as to overthrow their devilish doctrines, and turn their waters into blood; when they do so hold forth the truth, as to throw down the pomp and pride of their clergy . . . and admit to partake of sealing ordinances" (*Res,* 96–97). In "holding forth the truth"—very much as Una interprets Duessa's letter at the close of Book 1 of *The Faerie Queene*—true prophets such as Cary "throw down the pomp and pride" of the enemy by displaying their "sealing ordinances," their union with Christ. For a final time, then, Cary focuses on the prophets of the true church, but now Christ's "beloved wife" engages in a far darker and more violent image of communion; she turns "waters into blood."

Cary's habit of erasing gender distinctions and, like her male contemporaries, laboriously explicating the Apocalypse, actually reinforces her bid for spiritual and intellectual equality. If her concept of a revelatory and egalitarian community is taken seriously, it becomes clear, no identification or privileging of gendered voices would occur. The Spirit's encounter with the soul would be, to her way of thinking, neuter, entirely open and free to all.

Anna Trapnel, also a Fifth Monarchist, shares with Mary Cary a social and political vision involving the complete reformation of society. While she too offers a forceful prophetic critique of contemporary realities, she is less taken up with the recent demise of the monarchy and more with the corruption apparent in the New Model Army under Cromwell. In her *Legacy for Saints*, her most immediate source is not the Apocalypse but the recent experience of the prophetess Sara Wight, whose autobiography enables Trapnel to understand and represent herself for others. Beneath this rather personal autobiographical account however—in the temporal plot of Trapnel's physical illness and the various forms of her imprisonment—we hear intertextual echoes of the death of Christ and the repeated sufferings of Paul.

Appropriating and transforming these biographical narratives in the story of her own life, Trapnel traces a series of interconnections. Thus, what is "stampt on her Spirit" as she lies ill and incapable of eating is the phrase, "It is finished, be it according to thy faith." In this case, the prophecy she receives unites Christ's statement from the cross with his repeated healing of the sick. Initially overlooking the first part of this revelation, Trapnel repeatedly informs those attending her that she will be healed. But she quickly discovers at the "ninth hour" the torture of Christ's final moments. "An extreme pain" seizes her, causing her throat to become "very sore" (*Legacy*, 31), an experience that clearly replicates Christ's "I thirst" spoken prior to his moving "It is finished" (John 19:28, 30).

Just as she believes, however, Trapnel's throat is healed when she awakens in the morning, and it is at this point that her experience begins to coincide with the apostle Paul's. Now she realizes that her revelations must, like the apostle's, be attended by humbling afflictions to keep her from being "exalted above measure" (2 Cor. 12:7). Perhaps for this reason, Trapnel speaks to her attendants with the very words that Paul uses while on trial in Rome. Paul then tells Agrippa: "I would to God, that not only thou, but also all that hear me this day, were both almost, and altogether such as I am, except these bonds" (Acts 26:29). Paul's "bonds," recontextualized by Trapnel, are apparent in her recurring physical weakness as well as in her imprisonment under Cromwell. It is this "weakness" and these "bonds" that she would not wish upon her friends, though the visions are quite another matter: "I could wish you all as I am except my weakness, and if I could speak to you as it was spoken to me (I told them) it would appear far more glorious: but it comes from men at second hand, which is as water running through the channel, but it came to me as water out of a fountain" (*Legacy,* 32). Here distinguishing between what is spoken and therefore mediated and what is originary, Trapnel employs the simile of a fountain to highlight what no longer comes "from men at second hand" but from direct contact with the divine. While her experience is "far more glorious," it is not reducible to human speech, so she pauses, like Paul, on the threshold of incommunicable mysteries.

Throughout her autobiographical entries *Legacy for Saints* and the *Report and Plea,* Trapnel continues to trace the various details of her life as they are illuminated by Paul's visions, afflictions, incarcerations, miraculously broken fetters, storms at sea, and shipwrecks. In events at once intertextual and highly personal, she recapitulates the narrative of the persecuted church in Acts 16:27 as she experiences it under the oppressive "Lord Protector" Cromwell.

One of the most obvious intertextual parallels occurs when Trapnel refashions Acts 16:24 in her *Report and Plea.*[8] In the biblical account, Paul and Silas are thrown into the "inner prison," their "feet fast in the stocks." Even when an earthquake occurs and their chains are broken, Paul remains to convert the jailer. The two are legally freed the next morning, but Paul refuses to leave until the authorities who have placed him in prison apologize for violating his rights. Trapnel recapitulates the same series of events as she too is thrown into prison. Initially she tells us, "The Lord made that little storm, to work abundance of good to me many ways: and all things

---

8. Trapnel, *Anna Trapnel's Report and Plea.* I quote from the text printed in Charlotte Otten, ed., *English Women's Voices, 1540–1700,* 64–78; future references will be designated *Report* and cited parenthetically within the text.

that were afflictive, the Lord quickly broke such fetters" (*Report,* 71). The "fetters" broken in Trapnel's case are psychological; she experiences the joy of the divine presence despite the foul-smelling and rat-infested conditions of prison. When her friends tell her to petition for consideration, she takes the opportunity to comment briefly on Cromwell's lack of involvement: "The Protector said, he did not know that I was put in Bridewell, till I had been there above a week, that one went and informed him" (*Report,* 72). As far as she is concerned, Cromwell is implicated both in his ignorance and in his failure to reprove those who have incarcerated her. Consequently, when she is later offered freedom, her response is the same as the apostle Paul's: "I told him they should fetch me out that put me in; had they put me among thieves and whores, and now did they send for me out without acknowledging the reproach they had brought upon me?" (*Report,* 74). The stand she takes against Cromwell is personal, spiritual, and political as she demands an acknowledgment of the way she has been mistreated. Once in their presence, she asserts that Cromwell merely takes the place of the old, corrupt monarchy that the Fifth Monarchists had hoped to leave behind:

> And as for him you call your Protector, you do not give him that tithe in love to him more than to another, nor so much as to old King Charles and to his son, who is in your hearts, you love a King dearly. Oh that you did love King Jesus, he would never fail you, he would teach you to make your indictments truer, and not upon persons undeserving, he would teach you not to use his children as witches, and vagabonds when they come into your parts. (*Report,* 77)

Now putting her jurors on trial, Trapnel reads the divine bill against them, citing in her list of errors their false allegiance, corrupt legal system, and misguided spirituality. They have sold out to another king, she informs them, and in doing so have committed treachery against the only "protector" who matters.

Through these moments that are at once intertextual and experiential, a matter of record and a matter of what cannot be recorded, Trapnel's autobiographical prophecies attempt to trace in words written with her own hand a life shaped as much by silence as by ecstatic, irrational outpourings of the Spirit. In all of her texts Trapnel is fascinated by the nature of "sealing ordinances," and it is this metaphor of divine union that holds her autobiographical *Legacy* together. Thus, "sealing ordinances" link in one volume the "sealed" letter of Daniel, the "sealed" book of Revelation, and the "sealed" mark of the Holy Spirit upon his bride, the church. As Trapnel traces the movement of the Spirit within her, she moves back and forth between silence and speech, between law and liberty, between being struck dumb and being filled with lyrical, often uncontrollable music.

Consequently, the moment of Trapnel's sealing is as extraordinary as the ecstatic activities that succeed it:

> I had the representation of a seal set upon the wax, the spirit as fire made my stony spirits pliable for it to leave its mark or impression upon, as fire fits the wax for the seal; a glorious impression and stamp was set on my spirit, now I felt, saw and heard, that I never did before: O that Arras of glory, that now was my clothing! Now I was made like my Saviour, a crown given me, not made with pearls or rich diamonds, but far richer, not to be valued.[9]

Trapnel's representation fuses all three "sealing" metaphors as she highlights the literary, prophetic, and Christological implications of her empowerment. In the visionary clothing that she wears and in the likeness with Christ that she enjoys, she pauses on the very threshold of verbal expression: "Sure no tongue is able to speak it out, the pen of the readiest writer cannot write this, it may give some hints of the seal, but for depth, length, and breadth, who can give a full description or relation of it, it is a thing impossible to be published? O then you sealed ones, come admire with me, who can tell forth Sions glory? Could not Paul tell what he saw in the third heavens?" (*Legacy,* 11). Appropriating the divine speech of the Psalmist, "My tongue is the pen of a ready writer" (Ps. 45:1), Trapnel negates it to heighten the unspeakable nature of what she sees; her signifiers refer to the ultimate sign that resists even partial disclosure, that can be only hinted at, experienced as mystery.

What then can the *Legacy* offer? Trapnel suggests that she leaves as her final endowment the opportunity to "read, not my works, but the spirits works, and so admire him who is most worthy, when I am gone hence, and shall be no more seen" (*Legacy,* 12). As a record of the spirit, her text engages readers in that experience of awe that occurs at the end of language, propelling them into that space beyond the visible, material world, beyond the referential letter, beyond the "Law," beyond any sense of an ending.

Voyce for the King of Saints opens a window on this world as Trapnel escapes all of the limitations imposed by written form; in a state of trance and

---

9. Trapnel, *Legacy for Saints,* 11. Future references will be designated *Legacy* and cited parenthetically within the text.

unaware of what she is saying, singing, or doing, her songs are transcribed by her listeners as if from another world. Led by the Spirit and sealed with his impression, Trapnel begins to reveal, with all the authority found in otherworldly ecstasy, the place of women in the Gospel. Only from this vantage point does her voice at last take flight, enabling her to clarify in far more specific terms the writing of Revelation, the nature of the Antichrist in the temple, and the origins of feminist prophecy.

The prophetic text begins, as we might expect, with the song of the bride, who celebrates Christ's coming to the poor and the lowly:

> This is King Solomon, saith she
> That looks upon poor one,
> And cometh forth with love so free
> To daughter and to son.[10]

Christ as "Solomon" opens himself in love to both "daughters and sons," refusing to discriminate on the basis of gender. He overlooks educational distinctions as well, sharing his wisdom with all who approach him. Thus, like Aemilia Lanyer, Trapnel focuses on the presence of the Queen of Sheba whose wisdom brings her to Christ:

> O Shebas Queen thou cam'st from far
> Was't not a glorious sigh?
> What didst thou ever see like him
> That had such wisdom high
>
>   (*Voyce*, 3)

The Presbyterians who fly from Christ, on the other hand, reveal their fallen Babylonian ignorance as they attempt to consolidate their positions of power by rejecting free and "originall" grace for the bondage of the law:

> You call your wise men for to plead
> And speak for Sinai breath
> It comes not from originall
> But Babylon doth preach.
>
>   (*Voyce*, 11)

---

10. Trapnel, *Voyce for the King of Saints and Nations or A Testimony*, 3. Future references will be designated *Voyce* and cited parenthetically within the text.

Trapnel remains unaffected by "dark Sinai noyse," despite its continual ringing in her ears, and is soon carried away to "Mount Sion's joy" (*Voyce,* 16). Once here, the bride celebrates her arrival in a more visionary landscape by disclosing another intertext:

> O the sweet spouse did shew before
> A pattern to thy song,
> And brought her Epistle to be
> A pattern unto John.
>
> (*Voyce,* 16)

Using the love song of the bride as the model of his own, John unseals the letter he receives from her to unlock further mysteries; what he now discloses, through a prophetic indictment, is the corruption now occurring in the temple, perhaps most apparent in its "mixture" of divine and human intentions:

> King David, where is Gospel pure
> Do not mens fancy bring;
> Poor England hath a mixture that
> Doth not well please the king.
>
> (*Voyce,* 19)

Naturally, Trapnel expresses an answer to this dilemma in the annihilation of those ceremonial forms that the temple represents and in the new mode of worship that Christ inaugurates:

> Then shall there be no mixtures
> No Moses in that day
> But Jesus Christ shalt worship'd be
> In his own manner and way.
>
> (*Voyce,* 32)

She may be attacking as well the "mixture" of voices so apparent in the prophetic discourse of Andrewes, Donne, and Herbert who underscore the learning of the Fathers along with originary insight.

As Trapnel continues to unravel the mysteries revealed to John through her ecstatic music, she illuminates the importance of women in the Gospel narrative, in Christ's life, and in the Apocalypse itself:

O John he did speak of hand-maids
Whom Christ did love so dear,
And tells that Jesus Christ he did,
To hand-maids first draw near.
O John this record of the Son
Is very sweet indeed
He doth discover him to be
The glorious lovely seed.

(*Voyce*, 35)

What John "discovers," according to Trapnel, is the fact that Christ is the "lovely seed" of a woman. Moreover, John's willingness to trace Christ's responsiveness to women, in birth, life, and death gives him the same glimpse of the "Originall" that women enjoy:

John thou wilt not offended be
That hand-maids here should sing
That they should meddle to declare
The matters of the King.
John wilt not be displeased that
They sit about the throne
And go unto original
And nothing else will own.

(*Voyce*, 37)

In so easily dismissing "handmaids" as "poor silly ones" (*Voyce*, 38), Trapnel hints that her listeners miss the opportunity to come into contact with "Originall" grace. Yet it is this that she repeatedly offers:

Original is opened
O come that Book and view
That so it may raise up your souls
In pleasures that are new.

(*Voyce*, 43)

Inviting her listening audience into the ultimate mystery, Trapnel highlights the fact that the prophecy of Joel is now fulfilled in their hearing:

And thy handmaids were promised
Much of that spirit choice
And it is and it shall come forth
In a rare singing voice.

It shall be poured all along
While that the ages last
But Antichristian Rabbys do
Indeavor this to blast.

           (*Voyce*, 54)

The "rare singing voice" with which Trapnel identifies herself participates in the song "poured out" through the ages, despite the continual attempt of Antichrist to suppress it. Christ's song, then, is one with the song of the handmaids and one with Trapnel's own:

Though it comes from the mighty throne,
Virgin womb must it bring.
O what a glorious bodys this
That from eternity sprung
And did declare Virginity
To the rebellious sons.

           (*Voyce*, 58)

Christ reveals himself in his "Original" incarnation in the "Virgin womb" and thus in his difference from the "rebellious sons." Inverting the political hierarchy, the Spirit continues to take form in the weak and the powerless and thus to exalt Christ:

The Spirit loves for to make use of
The poor low foolish things,
That so he might thereby exalt
The Son as King of Kings.

           (*Voyce*, 79)

In conveying through "Scripture language" the social and political inversion that Christ's reign signifies, prophets such as Anna Trapnel continued to call into account the inequities and unrighteous actions of an unjust government. Like Mary Cary before her, Trapnel identifies herself with the persecuted martyrs to the faith, and, in the same way as Mary Cary had foreseen the end of the monarchy, she foresees the end of the Protectorate. In the ever changing contest between the true church and the Antichrist, the parliamentarian government is only the most recent group to make the country drunk with their fornication. They thus assume, along with the monarchy, the unwelcome title of the beast of the Apocalypse.

When the Quaker Margaret Fell defends women prophets in 1667, she chooses neither to obscure gender issues like Cary nor to disclose her feminist perceptions in an ecstatic, irrational mode of utterance like Trapnel. Rather, Fell, like several earlier prophets, confronts the Pauline mandate head-on.[11] And while many before her had attempted to escape the implications of the text by spiritualizing it, Fell argues in *Women's Speaking Justified* that Paul has been interpreted out of context and thus dehistoricized.[12] To correct this problem, Fell places Paul within the framework of all biblical utterance, choosing to "first lay down how God himself hath manifested his will and mind concerning women, and unto women" (*WSJ*, 363).

Beginning with Genesis, then, Fell argues that when God created "male and female," they together revealed his image and neither was subordinate: "Here God joins them together in his own image and makes no such distinctions and differences as men do; for though they be weak, he is strong; and as he said to the Apostle, his grace is sufficient, and his strength is made manifest in weakness (2 Cor. 12:9)" (*WSJ*, 363). Thus, Fell notes, all "distinctions and differences" are entirely man-made. Even the distinction of "weakness" (a privilege as well as a curse in the writings of Cary and Trapnel) is, for Fell, not gender specific. Male and female are both "weak," and God, out of grace, chooses to manifest himself in both.

When she turns to the Fall, Fell rejects the essentialist interpretation of Eve's behavior and thus the inherent female weakness that Aemilia Lanyer so easily attributes to the first woman. Even in sinning, Fell argues, Adam and Eve stood on level ground: "and so they were both tempted into the transgression and disobedience" (*WSJ*, 365). The two can be distinguished by their behavior afterward, however, especially by their utterance. Adam chooses to answer God's question by circuitously laying the blame on Eve and God, while Eve accepts responsibility with remarkable brevity: "The Serpent beguiled me, and I did eat" (*WSJ*, 365). Fell departs from biblical quotation to underline her point: "Here the Woman spoke the truth unto the Lord." Because God values this, Fell observes, he pronounces not a curse but the *protoevangelium*, and thereby "stops the mouths" of those who oppose "womens speaking": "Let this Word of the Lord, which was from the beginning, stop the mouths of all that oppose women's speaking

11. At the same time, Margaret Fell departs significantly from Cotton and Cole's attempt to spiritualize the Pauline mandate, arguing in effect that Paul aims at "weakness" in general rather than women in particular.

12. Margaret Fell, *Womens Speaking Justified*, in *English Women's Voices, 1540–1700*, ed. Otten. Future references will be designated *WSJ* and cited parenthetically within the text.

in the power of the Lord; for he hath put enmity between the woman and the serpent; and if the seed of the woman speak not, the seed of the serpent speaks" (*WSJ*, 365). By joining the introductory epithet that proceeds every revelation of the prophets, "the Word of the Lord," to the incarnational assessment of John, "which was from the beginning," Fell assigns the origin and continuance of all prophetic activity to the *protoevangelium*. These words spoken to a woman locate in the woman's seed the unfallen origins of a new humanity and establish, for Fell, the central opposition between divinely sanctioned female utterance and the satanic attempt to silence it.

This affirmation of women continues to appear in the language of the prophets as they repeatedly employ female metaphors. Rather than treating this utterance as symbolic (the most common strategy in ecclesiastical tradition), Fell literalizes the metaphors; the "woman forsaken," "King's Daughter," "Bride," and "woman clothed with the sun" are words and phrases that God himself chooses and approves: "the Lord is pleased, when he mentions his Church, to call her by the name of woman" (*WSJ*, 365). But Fell pushes the point further: "Thus much may prove that the church of Christ is a woman, and those that speak against the woman's speaking, speak against the church of Christ, and the Seed of the woman, which Seed is Christ" (*WSJ*, 366). Because "woman" is not merely a metaphor for the true church, but is indeed part of the true church, an attack on women is an attack on Christ.

Fell argues, furthermore, that in the initial stages of God's communication with humanity, he employs the *protoevangelium* and the language of the prophets to reflect God's "will and mind" toward women. Later, Christ's actual appearance in the flesh seals the intimacy of their relationship. Listing the biographical details in which Christ gives attention to women, Fell notes how he repeatedly goes out of his way for the woman of Samaria, Mary and Martha, the woman with ointment, Mary Magdalene, Mary his mother, and numerous others. In each case, he often says more to them, she argues, than "ever he said in plain words to man or woman (that we read of)" (*WSJ*, 366). Indeed, Christ spoke first to women following his resurrection because they were "so united and knit to him in love, that they could not depart as the men did" (*WSJ*, 368). They were accordingly the first to carry the news of the Resurrection, yet, Fell asserts, her contemporaries would doubtless have silenced them: "Mark this, you that despise and oppose the message of the Lord God that he sends by women, what had become of the redemption of the whole body of mankind, if they had not believed the message that the Lord Jesus sent by these women?" (*WSJ*, 368). Underscoring the bodily part women played in redeeming the "whole body of mankind," both in carrying Christ and in carrying his Word, Fell turns her prophetic edge against her male opposition.

Continuing her chronological overview of Scripture, Fell moves from the critical role women played in the Resurrection to the part women played in the early days of the church, focusing specifically on Priscilla's teaching of Apollos. Having at last arrived at the appropriate historical period for a consideration of Paul, she also takes up the Pauline mandate.[13] Advising those who interpret this passage first to "seriously read" (*WSJ*, 369) 1 Cor. 14 in its entirety, Fell proceeds to make her case. She notes first that the entire congregation was in a state of confusion in the Corinthian church, and that for this reason Paul had, in the course of his letter, advised not just the women but also the men to remain silent. Such silence was necessary, she asserts, because some of them (both men and women), were still under the "Law": "Here the Apostle clearly manifests his intent, for he speaks of women that were under the Law, and in that transgression as Eve was, and such as were to learn, and not to speak publickly" (*WSJ*, 369). Having not yet experienced the liberty that comes with the life of the Spirit, many of the women and men of the time were still in training. But this was not true, Fell argues, either of all of the women in the church Paul addressed or of all of the women in the present church: "And what is all this to women's speaking, that have the everlasting gospel to preach, and upon whom the promise of the Lord is fulfilled and his Spirit poured upon them according to his word, Acts 2:16–18" (*WSJ*, 370). Having experienced the anointing of the Spirit and a liberation from the "Law," women must move in response to God and not remain silent—nor, Fell argues, does Paul command them to.

But the passage in 1 Cor. is not the only one being employed against "women's speaking," and Fell quickly moves on to 1 Tim. 2. Stating that Paul advises women regarding their relationship to their husbands in this passage, Fell sidesteps Paul's problematic interpretation of Genesis. She calls attention instead to the fact that Paul does not advocate the silence of women in the church here, but rather requests them not to teach their husbands. Within the larger context of the passage, she notes, Paul is concerned about godly behavior, particularly about feminine dress and demeanor. The fact

13. In " 'vesells fitt for the masters use': A Transatlantic Community of Religious Women, the Quakers, 1675–1753," Bonnelyn Young Kunze examines the interconnections that Quakers found between the letter-writing communities of the Pauline churches and the letter-writing communities they themselves were forming (183–84).

that women in the past have occasionally behaved inappropriately in this matter is all the more reason for women in the present church to respond to the Spirit's calling: "Must not they speak the word of the Lord because of these undecent and unreverent women that the Apostle speaks of, and to, in these two scriptures? And how are the men of the generation blinded that bring these scriptures, and pervert the Apostle's words, and corrupt his intent in speaking of them?" (*WSJ*, 371). Underlining the fact that the "men of the generation" only reveal their blindness when they misread the Word and pervert Paul's intention, Fell ties this attitude to her overarching argument: these fallen interpreters are the "seed" of the serpent in Revelation who is determined to "bind up" all:

> But all this opposing and gainsaying of women's speaking hath risen out of the bottomless pit, and spirit of darkness that hath spoken for these many hundred years together in this night of apostasy, since the revelations have ceased and been bid, and so that spirit hath limited and bound all up within its bond and compass, and so would suffer none to speak but such as that spirit of darkness approved of, man or woman. (*WSJ*, 371)

To acknowledge this corrupt authority and thus to speak or grow silent in response to it is to be implicated in it and enslaved by it. Refusing to let this occur, Fell exposes the corruption apparent in all spiritually sanctioned sex discrimination: "Those that speak against the power of the Lord and the spirit of the Lord speaking in a woman, simply by reason of her sex, or because she is a woman, not regarding the Seed, and Spirit, and Power that speaks in her, such speak against Christ and his church, and are of the seed of the serpent, wherein lodgeth the enmity" (*WSJ*, 366). Margaret Fell could not be clearer.

By historicizing the Pauline mandate, interpreting it not only within the context of the biblical canon but also within the culture of the early church, Fell calls her male contemporaries and their interpretations into question. If her culture is to be liberated from the bondage caused by the misrepresentation of these words, she must herself articulate the nature of that freedom. Consequently, after establishing the divine intention registered in the conversations between God and women throughout history, Fell completes her polemical argument by allowing women to speak for themselves. She returns to the biblical text to retrieve and highlight the words that women have spoken across time, setting them in dialogue with the patriarchal and repressive voices of the seventeenth century. Here, the voices of women become increasingly dramatic and powerful, allowing Fell to articulate through the format of prophetic debate the profound place that women have always had in shaping divine revelation.[14]

The first three women in Fell's chorus of voices are Hulda, Miriam, and Hanna, women prophets "who were not forbidden during the time of the Law" and so prophesied freely. Thus, Hulda the prophetess in 2 Kings 22 pronounced judgment on all in the kingdom who had forsaken God; at the same time, she preserved the life of the king of Judah, both because he willingly sought her counsel and because he humbled himself before God. Upon quoting Hulda's words in full, Fell turns the point of Hulda's prophecy against her contemporary opponents: "Now let us see if any of you blind priests can speak after this manner, and see if it be not a better sermon than any you can make, who are against women's speaking?" (*WSJ*, 373). Highlighting male distance from divine speech and prophetic empowerment, Fell underscores their all too damning silence. In this case, the "blind priests" she addresses are the presbyters under Cromwell who are here called to account for their refusal to hear the women prophets in their midst.

Fell turns next to the "handmaids" who fulfill Joel's prophecy, both the women in Acts 2 and Mary and Elizabeth who prophesy at the conception of Christ. Again, after quoting Mary's Magnificat, Fell chastises her opposition in the most specific of prophetic indictments: "Are you not here beholding to the woman for her sermon, to use her words to put into your common prayer?" (*WSJ*, 374). In precisely this way, Fell argues, women's "sermons" in the Bible have been appropriated by men and colonized, stripped of the powerful feminist content they repeatedly disclose.

To highlight this sense of inversion, Fell goes on to quote one prophetic text after another, giving voice to the words of Hannah, the Queen of Sheba, Queen Esther, and Judith. In suppressing the gender of these women in contemporary sermons, she argues, male preachers have corrupted their messages to sanction their own economic, social, and spiritual advancement: "Yet you will make a trade of women's words to get money by, and take texts, and preach sermons upon women's words and still cry out, 'Women must not speak, women must be silent.' So you are far from the minds of the elders of Israel, who praised God for a woman's speaking" (*WSJ*, 375). By

14. Mack contends that women prophets "rarely presented themselves in public as the courageous Queen Esther, the heroic Jael, the praise-singer Miriam, or the militant judge Deborah; instead they spoke as virtual incarnations of angry male prophets" (*Visionary Women*, 174). I believe, however, that Fell associates her own voice directly with the voices of biblical women, as Aemilia Lanyer, Eleanor Davies, and Anna Trapnel do before her.

twisting the words that women speak in the Bible to serve their own "trade," Fell notes, contemporary Presbyterians turn the woman prophet into profit and violate her socially as well as spiritually. Such behavior suggests that they have nothing in common with the "Elders of Israel" and they, consequently, will have no part in the restoration of Israel either.

But Fell offers an even more compelling indictment of the present Presbyterian system, as, in concluding, she focuses on the bride and whore of the Apocalypse. Following in the apocalyptic tradition of Spenser, Brightman, Napier, and others, Fell's whore is affiliated with the pope. However, in a particularly significant addition to this interpretation, the whore's offspring are those who would silence women: "For the Pope is the head of the false church, and the false church is the Pope's wife, and so he and they that be of him, and come from him, are against women's speaking in the true church, when both he and the false church are called 'Woman,' in *Revelation* 17" (*WSJ*, 376). The corrupt whore who opposes the bride is a political and patriarchal power, linked for Fell, as for Cary and Trapnel before her, with the Presbyterian priesthood. Despite the Presbyterian attempt at suppressing women's utterance, however, Fell's "bride" has the last word: "Is not the bride compared to the whole church? and doth not the bride say, 'Come?' Doth not the woman speak then, the husband, Christ Jesus, the 'Amen,' and does not the false church go about to stop the bride's mouth? But it is not possible, for the bridegroom is with his bride, and he opens her mouth" (*WSJ*, 377). It is the bride who continues to speak in the interim between the present moment and the end of history, her words a continual invitation to him and to his body, the church. If Christ has opened woman's mouth and authorized her to speak, argues Fell, no man has any authority to shut her mouth or silence her. On this triumphant note, she brings her argument to an end, but not without adding a final "Postscript." It is almost as if Fell recognizes, beyond the last word that she writes, another opposing voice, a further argument that she must address.

And address that argument Fell does, her "P.S." opening as if in reaction to an immediate, accusatory voice: "And you dark priests, that are so mad against women's speaking and it's so grevious to you, did not God say to Abraham, let it not be grievous in thy sight because of the lad, and because of thy bondwoman? In all that Sarah hath said to thee, hearken to her voice (mark here) the husband must learn of the woman, and Abraham did so" (*WSJ*, 377). Fell now returns to the same argument that Cornelius Agrippa outlined a hundred years before and that Aemilia Lanyer embraces in the pages of *Salve*. In the event that her readership have failed to see that women in Scripture prophesy not only to nations but also to instruct their husbands, Fell cites the examples of Sarah and Samson's mother. Even in this most intimate of relationships, she argues, women are not silent partners. This time, when Fell does conclude her tract, her last words are poignant, even haunting: "And this was a woman that taught" (*WSJ*, 376). In Fell's case, the medium and the message are one.

9

Henry Vaughan's Concealed Temple

For the Church cannot dwell but in the State. Ye never read that she fled out of
the State into the wildernesse, but when some Dragon persecuted her. Revel. 12.
—William Laud, A Sermon before Parliament

I T SHOULD come as no surprise that the exiled members of the English
Church turned to apocalyptic rhetoric during the Interregnum since it
now reflected their marginalized positions.[1] They too were the woman in
flight from a corrupt state, hoping like their female counterparts to escape
the persecution of the parliamentarian "dragon." Beneath this unifying
metaphor was, of course, a very different ideology; their removal from
political and spiritual power was attended by a tremendous desire to see their
"temple," the English Church, restored to view, and by a prophetic vision that
was ardently royalist and hierarchical. In short, they were re-dressing Una,
the woman clothed with the sun, not in the egalitarian clothing of "original"
insight found in the women prophets, but in the patriarchal learning of
episcopacy. In their view, the temple's restoration would effectively eliminate
the "common wealth" who had come by their status through the basest
exchange of all: through murdering the head of the visible church.[2]

This marginalized, once orthodox position is given voice in Henry
Vaughan's 1650 and 1655 *Silex Scintillans*. After experiencing the upheaval
of the English Civil War, Vaughan had returned home, leaving behind his
city of residence, his career, and his poetry. He fled London for Wales,
renounced law for medicine, and abandoned his secular verse for a poetics
"baptized" in the lines of George Herbert. His subsequent religious poetry,

1. Hill elegantly traces this rapidly shifting paradigm in *Antichrist*.
2. Gordon J. Schochet analyzes as one of the factors of revolution the desire for the reform
of an outmoded economic and social structure and a redistribution of wealth and power
("The English Revolution in the History of Political Thought" 1–20). These issues are taken
up not only by the lady in *Comus* but also by the women prophets. They are, of course,
treated quite dismissively here.

published during the Interregnum, conveys its messages through a rhetoric of allusion derived from biblical parables, apocalyptic allegory, and contemporary writers.[3] Acknowledging his exclusion from the structure of power, Vaughan marks his discourse off from the incendiary prophecies of his contemporaries, both men and women, by calling attention to the pacifism of the true prophet of God. Thus, while he returns to the apocalyptic paradigm of Spenser to emphasize the ongoing contest between the whore and the bride, he weaves into this framework the pacifistic prophecies that have arisen in the intervening decades—the episcopalian harmonies of Andrewes, the all embracing true spouse of Donne, and the ancient temple of Herbert. Redressing the wrongs of his particular moment in history by re-dressing the woman of the Apocalypse a final time, he pieces together, out of the torn phrases and discarded fragments of his precursors, the unifying peace that once characterized the English Church.

Vaughan thus condenses into a single prophetic form both the marginalized and the orthodox perspectives we have been tracing throughout this book. The debates over authority, politics, and history reappear in his work, as does the class bias encoded in the prophetic exchange itself. Vaughan, however, invests his spiritual and material capital in an audience for the express purpose of producing a new social order by restoring an old one.

To achieve this, Vaughan directs his private, allusive poetics against contemporary institutions with a vengeance that his stated pacifism does little to diminish. He escapes like most prophets of the time by hiding behind both the allegorical character of the Apocalypse and a private, reflective intention. Unlike Andrewes, Donne, and Herbert, however, Vaughan does not turn his

---

3. Noel K. Thomas analyzes Vaughan's apocalypticism, and Cedric Brown considers the predictive sensibility that the Spirit offers to righteous men just before their deaths, discussing how Andrewes, Herbert, and Vaughan are recorded as possessing prophetic insight (Thomas, *Henry Vaughan: Poet of Revelation;* and Brown, "The Death of Righteous Men: Prophetic Gesture in Vaughan's 'Daphnis' and Milton's *Lycidas*"). James D. Simmonds discusses the importance of a number of genres, coming close to Vaughan's sensibility in his discussion of satire; he does not focus on prophecy specifically *(Masques of God: Form and Theme in the Poetry of Henry Vaughan)*. Jonathan F. S. Post notes that "Vaughan's Christ—the Christ he chooses to imitate—is decidedly unprophetic," but Post derives his understanding of prophecy from the apocalyptic strain traced by Wittreich (*Henry Vaughan: The Unfolding Vision,* 128). As we have seen, the men of the English Church consider Christ the ultimate prophet since he embodies the "sweetness" of redemptive sacrifice, humility, and wisdom. Claude J. Summers offers the most extensive treatment of Vaughan's prophetic vision to date, focusing on his political, ecclesiastical, and apocalyptic sensibility ("Herrick, Vaughan, and the Poetry of Anglican Survivalism").

focus inward to establish a public and inclusive harmony; he turns it inward to conceal a politically charged and subversive intention.

Consequently, when Vaughan re-covers the Babylonian whore, he gives her a parliamentarian dress. "The Proffer," in which she attempts to seduce him, carries little economic or sexual appeal. Perhaps, he suggests, she has the wrong man:

> No, No; I am not he,
> Go seek elsewhere.
> I skill not your fine tinsel, and false hair,
> Your Sorcery
> And smooth seducements: I'le not stuff my story
> With your Commonwealth and glory.[4]

Though Vaughan refuses to corrupt his "story" with the base exchange rate of her "commonwealth," he nevertheless introduces her into his poem to expose the "fine tinsel" of her glittering surfaces and the "false hair" of her artifice. She is guilty, however, of far more deadly transactions. Returning to the parable of the "tares" and the "wheat"—the terms for the ecclesiastical debates of his age—Vaughan assesses the corrupt economy she has repeatedly produced:

> There are, that will sow tares
> And scatter death
> Amongst the quick, selling their souls and breath
> For any wares;
> But when thy Master comes, they'l finde and see
> There's a reward for them and thee.
>
> (322.37–42)

The "tares"/tears in the visible church that she inflicts, Vaughan reveals, spring up because she has "scattered death" with the "breath" of her utterance, making her profit by trading in human souls. But, Vaughan affirms, this will not go on indefinitely. In the interim, his audience would do well to "keep the antient way" (322.43) traced out for them by the men of the English Church.

This "ancient way" is reflected in "The Constellation," where Vaughan observes the patterns in the starry heavens and remembers their relationship

---

4. Henry Vaughan, *The Poetry and Selected Prose of Henry Vaughan*, 321.31–36. Future references will be cited parenthetically within the text.

to the now lost bishops of the English Church. Again, he contrasts this ancient order with the commands of the parliamentarians who undermine the very authority upon which all order is based:

> But here Commission'd by a black self-wil
> The sons the father kil,
> The Children Chase the mother, and would heal
> The wounds they give, by crying, zeale.
>
> (302.37–40)

In following such "commissions," sons kill their father, the king, and children wound their mother, the church, not only breaking political, ecclesiastical, and domestic ties but destroying the family unit as well. Vaughan responds by recording the suffering of the woman in the wilderness, her "blood and tears" perfectly mirrored in the anguished passion of the Apocalypse:

> Then Cast her bloud, and tears upon thy book
> Where they for fashion look,
> And like that Lamb which had the Dragons voice
> Seem mild, but are known by their noise.
>
> (303.41–44)

Though the Puritans "fashion" themselves by this "book," Vaughan slyly suggests, they miss the ultimate irony: their loud voices are those of the persecuting "Dragon" rather than the "Lamb." Like the "wand'ring stars" (46) of Revelation, they are completely incapable of leadership since they have violated the very order by which heavenly, ecclesiastical, and political bodies move, and they will fall from their high positions. True order, on the other hand, can be found in following the stars of the English Church. Returning to the verbal harmonies of Lancelot Andrewes, Vaughan now highlights the position of the true subject:

> Settle, and fix our hearts, that we may move
> In order, peace, and love,
> And taught obedience by thy whole Creation
> Become an humble, holy nation.
>
> (304.53–56)

With the night sky illuminating his renewed vision of political and ecclesiastical order, Vaughan prays for a return of the "spouse" as well:

Give to thy spouse her perfect, and pure dress,
    Beauty and *holiness,*
And so repair these Rents, that men may see
And say, *Where God is, all agree.*
                                                        (304.57–60)

In desiring to recover the "pure dress" of the bride, Vaughan turns away from the purifying militancy of his contemporaries to the "beauty of holiness" found in the past, a vision of church order inscribed by Laud and celebrated by Andrewes, Herbert, and Donne. Once repaired, the church will regain its ancient and orderly rhythms, its liturgical harmonies themselves overcoming the dissonant, often contradictory voices of his contemporaries.

Vaughan continues to pursue this commitment to the "pure dress" of the English Church in a poem called "Dressing." Invoking the temple of the Apocalypse as Herbert does, he explores the losses that the English Church has incurred in the interim between Herbert's time and his own. Though he employs Laud's terminology, he escapes its rather subversive implications by remodeling the "temple" in his soul rather than the external church:

Open my desolate rooms; my gloomie Brest
With thy cleer fire refine, burning to dust
These dark Confusions, that within me nest,
And soyl thy Temple with a sinful rust.
                                                        (288.5–8)

Vaughan's wording, however, suggests a rather different program. By focusing on the "desolate" rooms that are closed to view, he calls attention to the locked doors of the present church. And the purification for which he hopes, the burning of "dark Confusions," extends beyond those that "nest" within him to include the disorder in the entire political body. Finally, the "rust" in the temple, a problem never encountered in Herbert's *Temple,* suggests the disuse and neglect occurring in the actual physical church structure.

In seeking the renewal and restoration of this temple, Vaughan establishes some clear differences between himself and Herbert; he now refuses to take the mediating tone toward ceremony found throughout *The Temple* and renounces as completely inappropriate not only the angels sitting "in order serviceable" at the end of Milton's "On the Morning" but also the "sitting" speaker at the close of "Love III":

> Some sit to thee, and eat
> Thy body as their Common meat,
> O let not me do so!
> Poor dust should ly still low,
> Then kneel my soul, and body; kneel, and bow;
> If *Saints*, and *Angels* fal down, much more thou.
>
> (288.37–42)

Applying the "Laudian" interpretation of Rev. 4:4 in which the angels fall down before Christ, Vaughan turns away from "sitting" as a possible option; one must kneel before Christ, kneel when one receives him. To do less is to make Christ's Body "common" rather than majestic and to eat in the manner of commoners. Clearly, the very reception of the sacrament is for Vaughan a political and social indicator: a sign of one's allegiance either to the commonwealth or the king.

This social and political distinction is apparent in "White Sunday" as well, a poem in which Vaughan characterizes his prophetic method by juxtaposing the false prophecies of the present against the genuine prophecy of the past. Vaughan turns back to Herbert's "Whitsunday" and Andrewes's "Whitsunday" sermons to renew what he considers the appropriate prophetic method and to apply that perspective. Consequently, in the opening stanza he makes a sharp distinction between God's "light" and man's:

> Wellcome white day! a thousand Suns,
> Though seen at once, were black to thee;
> For after their light, darkness comes,
> But thine shines to eternity.
>
> (319.1–4)

The "thousand Suns" that Vaughan identifies here extend the light beyond the "twelve suns" in Herbert's "Whitsunday" to that much larger group upon whom the Spirit fell in Acts. Receiving their "light" from the Holy Spirit, they were "crowned with prophetic fire." Once having been royally empowered, they established the visible lines of descent and succession evident in the Episcopalian priesthood and so become the standard against which the "new lights" of contemporary prophecy must be tested:

> Can these new lights be like to those,
> These lights of Serpents like the Dove?
> Thou hadst no *gall*, ev'n for thy foes,

And thy two wings were *Grief* and *Love.*
(319.9–12)

A kind of horror resonates in the phrasing and rephrasing of the question as Vaughan, like Andrewes before him, sets the "Dove" of the Holy Spirit off against the militant violence of the "Serpents" who, in the Apocalypse, war against God. Such spirits reveal their opposition to Christ whom they persecute. Even in dying, Vaughan makes clear, Christ forgave his enemies, founding his church on redemptive love rather than on animosity or violence.

Unfortunately, the inversion of spiritual value in which contemporary prophets engage—one in which peace gives way to war, humility to pride, divine transactions to human ones—does not stop with Christ's murder. Men continue to highlight their prophetic powers, hoping to cover the absence of the Spirit with the fire of zeal:

> Though then some boast that fire each day,
> And on Christs coat pin all their shreds;
> Not sparing openly to say,
> His candle shines upon their heads.
> (319.13–16)

These false prophets have "shredded" the coat of Christ and divided the church, not only removing his head but also dismembering his body. They have, in short, enacted the murder of Christ in seventeenth-century England:

> Again, if worst and worst implies
> A State, that no redress admits,
> Then from thy Cross unto these days
> The *rule* without *Exception* fits.
> (320.33–36)

"Redress" will be possible, Vaughan now suggests, only when subjects are purified by a divine economy in which royal grace descends and displaces the corrupt exchanges of the "commonwealth":

> As thou long since wert pleas'd to buy
> Our drown'd estate, taking the Curse
> Upon thy self, so to destroy
> The knots we tyed upon thy purse,

So let thy grace now make the way
Even for thy love; for by that means
We, who are nothing but foul clay,
Shal be fine gold, which thou didst cleanse.
(320.53–60)

In Vaughan's view, only that divine fire received from on high can turn "foul clay" into "gold" and put royal benefits, rather than "common wealth," back in circulation. Vaughan accordingly has one last request:

O come! refine us with thy fire!
Refine us! we are at a loss.
Let not thy stars for *Balaams* hire
Dissolve into the common dross!
(321.61–64)

Turning his focus outward, Vaughan prays for the cleansing of his readership and the purification of prophetic form. In equating the Puritans and radical sectarians of his time with Balaak who hired Balaam to prophesy falsely against God's people, Vaughan requests God to keep his "stars," the true prophets of seventeenth-century England, above the "common dross" who trade in God's Word out of profiteering self-interest. Balaam managed to withdraw from this evil in the nick of time, predicting instead the fall of God's enemies and the ultimate redemption of his people:

I shall see him, but not now:
I shall behold him, but not nigh:
there shall come a Star out of Jacob,
and a Sceptre shall rise out of Israel,
and shall smite the corners of Moab,
and shall destroy all the children of Seth.
(Num. 24:17)

Vaughan identifies himself as a "star" after this divine pattern, looking just as steadily and in the same visionary way for the redemption of England.

While the "redress" that Vaughan envisions here takes its apocalyptic focus from the marginalized spouse so compelling to the women prophets, Vaughan registers a difference between his own position and what Mary Cary calls the "pure intents" of the Fifth Monarchists: he chooses a woman with whom the women prophets seldom identify—Mary Magdalene. Rather like Donne's true "spouse" and Herbert's speaker in "Love III," she, as the elect church, is purified by her relationship to Christ, her past adultery remembered only to emphasize the nature of divine forgiveness and the love born out of redemptive grace. For Vaughan and many other English Churchmen, she is the ultimate ecclesiastical model of the Reformed Church of England—an Una who has erred and been forgiven. Because of her past, she determines to embrace those similarly "fallen," rather than choosing with the Puritans to exclude the impure. She is, in this sense, a fully redeemed New Testament version of Hosea's erring wife.

In examining her portrait, Vaughan exclaims, "Dear beauteous Saint! more white then day" (343.1). He thus contests the much celebrated "purity" of the saints, who, like Milton's lady in *Comus,* attempt to escape the corruption of episcopacy, asserting that it will somehow taint them. Highlighting the fact that it was Christ who "sainted" Mary Magdalene—a status she never attained on her own—Vaughan turns the Puritan quest for "purity" into an exercise in self-authorizing hypocrisy. Their actual disease, Vaughan suggests, goes far deeper, becoming much more horrific than the external measures they employ to cover it up: "He is still leprous, that still paints: / Who Saint themselves, they are no *Saints*" (344.71–72). Vaughan undercuts the feminist orientation of the Fifth Monarchist and Quaker prophets as well by revealing Mary Magdalene's relationship to divine authority as an "art of tears" rather than words:

> Learn, *Ladies,* here the faithful cure
> Makes beauty lasting, fresh and pure;
> Learn *Marys* art of tears, and then
> Say, *You have got the day from men.*
> (344.45–48)

Mary's willingness to sacrifice her costliest perfume at the feet of Christ discloses the appropriate role of woman to those in authority; she enacts her "art" as a passive, penitent subject, not as an authoritative messenger of divinity. Nevertheless, it is this willingness to be "subject," Vaughan suggests, that is the appropriate model both for England and for the English Church:

> Dear *Soul!* thou knew'st, flowers here on earth
> At their Lords foot-stool have their birth;
> Therefore thy wither'd self in haste
> Beneath his blest feet thou didst cast,

> That at the root of this green tree
> Thy great decays restor'd might be.
>
> (344.27–32)

Mary Magdalene's self-sacrifice at the foot of her Lord opens the way for her complete restoration, not only removing her "great decays" from view, but also making her a saint. In her redemptive history lingers the past adultery and present purity of the visible church, for she is recovered whore and true spouse both.

Through Mary Magdalene, Vaughan manages to contain the populist, increasingly open inspiration of the women prophets and Presbyterians by linking inspiration to episcopal lines of succession and by turning the fallen woman into a model of the reverent subject. But he recognizes in the conformist position certain errors as well, particularly the desire for inclusivity that Andrewes, Herbert, and Donne made so central to their vision of the temple. Consequently, in "Jacobs Pillow and Pillar," he warns, " 'Tis number makes a Schism: throngs are rude, / And God himself dyed by the multitude" (363.5–6). One must not, he now believes, seek to embrace everyone as Andrewes, Herbert, and Donne did, for a familiarity with the temple and the spouse only breeds contempt: "Man slights his Maker, when familiar grown, / And sets up laws, to pull his honor down" (364.19–20). Consequently, in a final twist on the controversy over the visible and invisible temple of the Apocalypse, Vaughan appropriates Thomas Brightman's model of the invisible temple, but he does so to place the visionaries of the English Church safely inside of it, locking the Presbyterians outside in the corrupt courts:

> Yea *Bethel* shall have Tithes (saith *Israels* stone)
> And vows and visions, though her foes crye, None.
> Thus is the solemn temple sunk agen
> Into a Pillar, and conceal'd from men.
>
> (364.33–36)

Appropriating the very terms of invisibility and concealment that Laud had once feared would destroy the English Church, Vaughan aims it at the visible Presbyterian Church with remarkable force. God, he hints, will restore the English Church to view. But in the interim, he

> . . . is contented, that this holy flame
> Shall lodge in such a narrow pit, till he

With his strong arm turns our captivity.
(364.38–40)

The captivity of the English Church and its prophets is even now, Vaughan hints, on the verge of liberation.

Henry Vaughan thus provides a stunning final instance of the way in which the Apocalypse, throughout the seventeenth century, encoded subversive and orthodox attitudes toward the church, sometimes simultaneously. As the lines shifted between "public" prophecy and "private" lyric, between the visible and the invisible temple, between the "spouse" as the "body of the Church" and the spouse as the gendered body of women, this text, perhaps more than any other, enabled numerous prophets to invest their poetic talent in the sociopolitical and spiritual transformation of their world.

Beneath the pens of Andrewes, Herbert, and Donne, the temple and the spouse are represented as open, inclusive, and engagingly accepting, offering a loving embrace to all who enter. Their bride's mediating language and pacifistic intentions differ markedly from Brightman's woman clothed with the sun who flees the corruption of royal and ecclesiastical power to sequester herself in a hidden Presbyterian temple. When she emerges from her wilderness journey, she has a voice and a vision for the future. Consequently, Milton's lady as true church not only speaks with a prophetic power that undoes the canon law of the English Church, but she rises from the chair of episcopacy as well. In similar fashion, Aemilia Lanyer, Eleanor Davies, Mary Cary, Anna Trapnel, and Margaret Fell break free of the Pauline strictures that have long bound women to silence, locating in the Queen of Sheba, the Virgin Mary, and the bride of the Apocalypse that egalitarian and divine empowerment that enables women, as a gender, to reproduce divine truth. Vaughan, of course, contains both the feminist and the Presbyterian movements by reverting to Andrewes's harmonies and Herbert's *Temple* in a visionary attack on the present political structure. And he gains access to this subversive power through the very invisible temple once employed by the Presbyterians to undermine the episcopal structure of the English Church. The circle has closed, perhaps, but the Apocalypse itself remains open, its allusive and contestatory poetics beckoning the next generation of prophets.

Bibliography

Agrippa, Henricus Cornelius. *Declamation on the Nobility and Preeminence of the Female Sex.* Ed. and trans. Albert Rabil Jr. Chicago: University of Chicago Press, 1996.

———. *Of the Nobilitie and Excellencie of Womankynde.* Trans. David Clapam. London, 1542.

Alpers, Paul. *The Poetry of the Faerie Queene.* Princeton: Princeton University Press, 1967.

Alter, Robert. *The Art of Biblical Poetry.* New York: Basic Books, 1985.

Andrewes, Lancelot. *Tortura Torti.* N.p., 1609.

———. *The Works of Lancelot Andrewes.* 11 vols. Oxford: John Henry Parker, 1967.

Anselment, Raymond. "'The Church Militant': George Herbert and the Metamorphoses of Christian History." *HLQ* 41:4 (1978): 299–316.

Ariosto, Ludovico. *Orlando Furioso in English Heroical Verse.* Trans. John Harington. 1591. Reprint, New York: Da Capo Press, 1970.

Articles of Religion: Agreed upon by both Houses, and the principall Divines thorough all England and Wales, for the avoiding of diversities of Opinions. Whereunto is added His Majesties Declaration in confirming the same. Printed for Theophilus Brown. London: His Majesties Speciall Command, 1642.

A True Testimony. London, 1654.

Audley, Ann. "The Trial and Condemnation of Mervin Lord Audley." In *English Women's Voices, 1540–1700,* ed. Charlotte F. Otten, 33–40. Miami: Florida International University Press, 1992.

A Variorum Commentary on the Poems of John Milton. Vol. 2, pt. 3. New York: Columbia University Press, 1972.

Bale, John. *The Image of Bothe Churches after the moste wonderfull and heavenly Revelacion of Sainct John the Evangelist, Contayning a very frutefull exposicion or Paraphrase upon the same. Wherin it is conferred with other scripturs, and most auctorised historyes.* 1548. Reprint, New York: Da Capo Press, 1973.

Bancroft, Richard. *A Survay of the Pretended Holy Discipline.* 1593. Reprint, New York: Da Capo Press, 1972.

Beilin, Elaine. *Redeeming Eve.* Princeton: Princeton University Press, 1987.

Berger, Harry. *Revisionary Play: Studies in Spenserian Dynamics.* Berkeley and Los Angeles: University of California Press, 1989.

Bergvall, Ake. "Between Eusebius and Augustine: Una and the Cult of Elizabeth." *ELR* 27:1 (1997): 3–30.

———. "The Theology of the Sign: St. Augustine and Spenser's Legend of Holiness." *SEL* 33 (1993): 21–42.

Bernard, Richard. *Plaine Evidences: The Church of England is apostolicall.* London, 1610.

Berry, Boyd M. *Process of Speech: Puritan Religious Writing and Paradise Lost.* Baltimore: Johns Hopkins University Press, 1976.

Bilson, Thomas. *The True Difference betweene Christian Subjection and Unchristian Rebellion.* 1585. Reprint, New York: Da Capo Press, 1972.

Bloom, Harold. *The Anxiety of Influence: Theory of Poetry.* Oxford: Oxford University Press, 1973.

The Book of Common Prayer. London, 1629.

Brightman, Thomas. *Against Bellarmine, the Confuting of that Counterfaite AntiChrist.* Amsterdam, 1615.

———. *The Revelation of St. John.* N.p., 1644.

———. *A Revelation of the Apocalyps that is, the Apocalyps of St. John.* Amsterdam, 1611.

———. *A Revelation of the Revelation that is . . . the Revelation of St. John.* Amsterdam, 1615.

Brown, Cedric. "The Death of Righteous Men: Prophetic Gesture in Vaughan's 'Daphnis' and Milton's *Lycidas.*" *GHJ* 7 (1983–1984): 1–24.

———. *Milton's Aristocratic Entertainments.* Cambridge: Cambridge University Press, 1985.

Browning, John. *Concerning public prayer and the fasts of the church.* London, 1636.

Buckeridge, John. *A Discourse concerning Kneeling at the Communion.* London, 1618.

Burton, Henry. *Israel's Fast.* London, 1628.

Cairo, Ann Baynes. "Writing in Service: Sexual Politics and Class Position in the Poetry of Aemilia Lanyer and Ben Jonson." *Criticism* 35:3 (1993): 357–76.

Campbell, W. Gardner. "The Figure of Pilate's Wife in Aemilia Lanyer's Salve Deus Rex Judaeorum." *Renaissance Papers* (1995): 1–13.

Carnes, Valerie. "The Unity of George Herbert's *The Temple:* A Reconsideration." *ELH* 35:4 (December 1968): 505–26.

Cartwright, Thomas. *A Christian Letter of Certaine English Protestants.* 1599. Reprint, New York: Da Capo Press, 1971.

Cary, Mary. *England's Fall from (the Mystical Babylon) Rome.* In *English Women's Voices, 1540–1700,* ed. Charlotte F. Otten, 100–103. Miami: Florida International University Press, 1992.

———. *The Little Horns Doom and Downfall.* N.p., 1651.

———. *The Resurrection of the Witnesses.* London, 1648.

———. *A word in Season to the People of England.* London, 1647.

Charles, Amy M. *A Life of George Herbert.* Ithaca: Cornell University Press, 1977.

Charles I, King. *His Maiesties Declaration to all his Loving Subjects.* Dublin, 1629.

Christianson, Paul. *Reformers and Babylon.* Toronto: University of Toronto Press, 1978.

Christopher, Georgia. *Milton and the Science of the Saints.* Princeton: Princeton University Press, 1982.

Cixous, Helene. "Castration or Decapitation." *Signs* 7 (1981): 41–55.

Cogswell, Thomas. "England and the Spanish Match." In *Conflict in Early Stuart England,* ed. Richard Cust and Ann Hughes, 107–33. New York: Longman, 1989.

Collinson, Patrick. "If Constantine, Then Also Theodosius: St. Ambrose and the Integrity of the Elizabethan *Ecclesia Anglicana.*" *Journal of Ecclesiastical History* 30:2 (April 1979): 205–29.

Coolidge, John S. *The Pauline Renaissance in England: Puritanism and the Bible.* Oxford: Clarendon Press, 1970.

Cooper, Thomas. *An answer in defense of the truth against the Apology of private mass.* 1562. Reprint, New York: Johnson, 1968.

Cope, Esther S. *Handmaid of the Holy Spirit.* Ann Arbor: University of Michigan Press, 1992.

Cosin, John. *The Works of the Right Reverend Father in God, John Cosin.* Ed. J. Sansom. 5 vols. Oxford: John Henry Parker, 1843–1855.

Cullen, Patrick. "Imitation and Metamorphosis: The Golden-Age Eclogue in Spenser, Milton, and Marvell." *PMLA* 84:6 (1969): 1559–70.

Cust, Richard, and Ann Hughes, eds. *Conflict in Early Stuart England.* New York: Longman, 1989.

Davies, Catherine. "'Poor Persecuted Little Flock' or 'Commonwealth of Christians': Edwardian Protestant Concepts of the Church." In *Protestantism and the National Church in Sixteenth-Century England,* ed. Peter Lake and Marial Dowling, 78–102. London: Crook Helm, 1987.

Davies, Eleanor. *Amend, Amend, God's kingdome is at hand.* N.p., 1643.

———. *The Prophetic Writings of Eleanor Davies.* Ed. Esther S. Cope. Oxford: Oxford University Press, 1995.

———. *The Restitution of Prophecy.* 1651. Reprint, University of Exeter: The Rota, 1978.

———. "Strange and Wonderfull Prophesies by the Lady Eleanor Audeley." In *Fugitive Poetical Tracts,* ed. W. C. Hazlitt, 1–4. London: Chiswick Press, 1875.

Davies, Julian. *The Caroline Captivity of the Church: Charles I and the Remoulding of Anglicanism, 1625–1641.* Oxford: Clarendon Press, 1992.

Dixon, John. *The First Commentary on "The Faerie Queene."* Ed. Graham Hough. Stansted: Privately published, 1964.

Dobin, Howard. "Milton's Nativity Ode: 'O What a Mask Was There.'" *Milton Quarterly* 17:3 (1983): 71–80.

Donne, John. *The Complete Poetry of John Donne.* Ed. John Shawcross. New York: Anchor Books, 1967.

———. *The Sermons of John Donne.* Ed. Evelyn M. Simpson and George R. Potter. 10 vols. Berkeley and Los Angeles: University of California Press, 1953–1962.

Downame, George. *A Sermon defending the honourable function of Bishops.* London, 1608.

Eusebius. *The Auncient Ecclesiasticall Histories.* Trans. Meredith Hanmer. London: Thomas Vautrollier, 1585.

———. *The Ecclesiastical History.* Trans. Kirsopp Lake. 2 vols. Ithaca: Cornell University Press, 1977.

Ezell, Margaret. *The Patriarch's Wife: Literary Evidence and the History of the Family.* Chapel Hill: University of North Carolina Press, 1987.

Facey, Jane. "John Foxe and the Defence of the English Church." In *Protestantism and the National Church in Sixteenth-Century England,* ed. Peter Lake and Maria Dowling, 162–92. London: Crook Helm, 1987.

Fell, Margaret. *Womens Speaking Justified.* London, 1667. Modern edition available in *English Women's Voices, 1540–1700,* ed. Charlotte F. Otten, 363–78. Miami: Florida International University Press, 1992.

Fincham, Kenneth, ed. *The Early Stuart Church, 1603–1642.* Stanford: Stanford University Press, 1993.

———. *Prelate as Pastor: The Episcopate of James I.* Oxford: Clarendon Press, 1990.

Fincham, Kenneth, and Peter Lake. "The Ecclesiastical Policy of King James I." *Journal of British Studies* 24 (April 1985): 169–209.

Firth, Katherine. *The Apocalyptic Tradition in Reformation Britain, 1530–1645.* Oxford: Oxford University Press, 1979.

Fish, Stanley. *The Living Temple: George Herbert and Catechizing.* Berkeley and Los Angeles: University of California Press, 1979.

Fisher, John [John Percy]. *A Treatise of Faith.* N.p., 1605.

Forbes, Patrick. *A Learned Commentary upon the Revelation of Saint John.* Middleburg: Richard Schilders, 1614.

Fowler, Alastair. *Spenser and the Numbers of Time.* New York: Barnes and Noble, 1964.

Foxe, John. *Actes and Monuments of these latter perillous dayes.* London: John Day, 1563.

———. *The Acts and Monuments of John Foxe.* 8 vols. New York: AMS Press, 1965.

Froom, Le Roy Edwin. *The Prophetic Faith of Our Fathers.* Washington, D.C.: Review and Herald, 1950.

Froula, Christine. "When Eve Reads Milton: Undoing the Canonical Economy." *Critical Inquiry* 10 (1983): 321–47.

Fuller, Thomas. *The Church History of Britain.* 3 vols. London: William Tegg, 1868.

Gardner, Samuel Rawson, ed. *The Constitutional Documents of the Puritan Revolution, 1625–1660.* Oxford: Clarendon Press, 1889.

The Geneva Bible: A Facsimile of the 1560 Edition. Madison: University of Wisconsin Press, 1969.

Gless, Darryl J. *Interpretation and Theology in Spenser.* Cambridge: Cambridge University Press, 1994.

Goekjian, Gregory F. "Deference and Silence: Milton's Nativity Ode." *Milton Studies* 21 (1985): 119–35.

Goldberg, Jonathan. *James I and the Politics of Literature.* Stanford: Stanford University Press, 1989.

Gottlieb, Sidney. "The Social and Political Backgrounds of George Herbert's Poetry." In *"The Muses Common-Weale": Poetry and Politics in the Seventeenth Century,* ed. Claude J. Summers and Ted-Larry Pebworth, 107–18. Columbia: University of Missouri Press, 1988.

Gray, Dave, and Jeanne Shami. "Political Advice in Donne's Devotions." *Modern Language Quarterly* 50:4 (December 1989): 337–56.

Greene, Thomas. *The Light in Troy: Imitation and Discovery in Renaissance Poetry.* New Haven: Yale University Press, 1982.

Gregerson, Linda. *The Reformation of the Subject.* Cambridge: Cambridge University Press, 1995.

Grose, Christopher. *Milton and the Sense of Tradition.* New Haven: Yale University Press, 1988.

Guibbory, Achsah. *The Map of Time.* Urbana: University of Illinois Press, 1986.

Gyffard, George. *Sermons upon the whole booke of the Revelation.* London, 1596.

Hall, Joseph. *The Old Religion.* Vol. 8 of *Works,* ed. Philip Wynter. New York: AMS Press, 1863.

Halpern, Richard. "Puritanism and Maenadism in 'A Mask.'" In *Rewriting the Renaissance,* ed. Margaret W. Ferguson, Maureen Quilligan, and Nancy J. Vickers, 88–105. Chicago: University of Chicago Press, 1986.

Hankins, John E. "Spenser and the Revelation of St. John." *PMLA* 60 (1945): 364–81.

Hannay, Margaret Patterson, ed. *Silent But for the Word: Tudor Women as Patrons, Translators, and Writers of Religious Works.* Kent: Kent State University Press, 1985.

Harvey, Elizabeth. *Ventriloquized Voices: Feminist Theory and English Renaissance Texts.* New York: Routledge, 1992.

Heale, William. *An Apologie for Women.* 1609. Reprint, Amsterdam: Theatrum Orbis Terrarum, 1974.

Henderson, Katherine Usher, and Barbara F. McManus, eds. *Half Humankind.* Urbana: University of Illinois Press, 1985.

Herbert, George. *The Works of George Herbert.* Ed. F. E. Hutchinson. Oxford: Oxford University Press, 1953.

Heylyn, Peter. *A Briefe Answer to Henry Burton.* 1637. Reprint, Amsterdam: Theatrum Orbis Terrarum, 1976.

Heywood, Thomas. *A True Discourse of the Two infamous upstart Prophets Richard Farnham Weaver of White-Chappell, and John Bull, Weaver of Saint Butolph's Algate, now Prisoners, as Also of Margaret Tennis, now Prisoner in Old Brideswell.* London, 1636.

Hill, Christopher. *Antichrist in Seventeenth-Century England.* London: Oxford University Press, 1971.

————. *The English Bible and the Seventeenth-Century Revolution.* London: Penguin Press, 1993.

————. *The Experience of Defeat: Milton and Some Contemporaries.* New York: Viking Penguin, 1984.

Hobby, Elaine. *Virtue of Necessity: English Women's Writing, 1649–1688.* Ann Arbor: University of Michigan Press, 1989.

Hodgkins, Christopher. *Authority, Church, and Society in George Herbert: Return to the Middle Way.* Columbia: University of Missouri Press, 1993.

Honeygosky, Stephen R. *Milton's House of God: The Invisible and Visible Church.* Columbia: University of Missouri Press, 1993.

Hooker, Richard. *Of the Laws of Ecclesiastical Polity.* 2 vols. 1907. Reprint, London: J. M. Dent and Sons, 1954.

————. *The Works of that Learned and Judicious Divine, Mr. Richard Hooker.* 2 vols. Oxford: University Press, 1850.

Hovey, Kenneth Alan. " 'Wheel'd about . . . into Amen': 'The Church Militant' on Its Own Terms." *GHJ* 10:1–2 (fall 1986–spring 1987): 71–84.

Hull, Suzanne W. *Chaste, Silent, and Obedient.* San Marino, Calif.: Huntington Library, 1982.

Hume, Anthea. *Edmund Spenser: Protestant Poet.* Cambridge: Cambridge University Press, 1984.

Hutcheon, Linda. Introduction to *Romantic Parodies, 1797–1831,* ed. David A. Kent and D. R. Ewen. Toronto: Farleigh Dickinson University Press, 1992.

Hutson, Lorna. "Why the Lady's eyes are nothing like the sun." In *New Feminist Discourses: Critical Essays on Theories and Texts,* ed. Isobel Armstrong, 154–75. London: Routledge, 1992.

Irigaray, Luce. *Speculum of the Other Woman.* Ithaca: Cornell University Press, 1985.

James I, King. *The Peace-Maker.* London, 1618.

————. *The Workes of the Most High and Mightie Prince, James.* London: R. Barber and I. Bill, 1616.

Jewel, John. *The Works of John Jewel.* Vol. 20. Cambridge: Cambridge University Press, 1845.

Jordan, Constance. *Renaissance Feminism.* Ithaca: Cornell University Press, 1990.

Kelly, Joan. "Early Feminist Theory and the *Querelle des Femmes,* 1400–1789." *Signs* 8 (1982): 4–28.

Kerrigan, William. *The Prophetic Milton.* Charlottesville: University Press of Virginia, 1981.

King, John. *Spenser's Poetry and the Reformation Tradition.* Princeton: Princeton University Press, 1990.

Kunze, Bonnelyn Young. " 'vessells fitt for the masters use': A Transatlantic Community of Religious Women, the Quakers, 1675–1753." In *Court, Country, and Culture: Essays in Early Modern British History in Honor of Perez Zagorin,* ed. Bonnelyn Young Kunze and Dwight D. Brautigam, 177–97. Rochester: University of Rochester Press, 1992.

Lake, Peter. *Anglicans and Puritans? Prebyterianism and English Conformist Thought from Whitgift to Hooker.* London: Unwin Hyman, 1988.

———. "Anti-popery: the Structure of a Prejudice." In *Conflict in Early Stuart England,* ed. Richard Cust and Ann Hughes, 72–106. New York: Longman, 1989.

———. "Constitutional Consensus and Puritan Opposition in the 1620s: Thomas Scott and the Spanish Match." *Historical Journal* 25:4 (1982): 805–25.

———. "Lancelot Andrewes, John Buckeridge, and Avant-Garde Conformity at the Court of James I." In *The Mental World of the Jacobean Court,* ed. Linda Levy Peck, 113–33. Cambridge: Cambridge University Press, 1991.

———. "The Laudians and the Argument from Authority." In *Court, Country, and Culture: Essays in Early Modern British History in Honor of Perez Zagorin,* ed. Bonnelyn Young Kunze and Dwight D. Brautigam, 149–76. Rochester: University of Rochester Press, 1992.

———. "The Laudian Style: Order, Uniformity, and the Pursuit of the Beauty of Holiness in the 1630s." In *The Early Stuart Church, 1603–1642,* ed. Kenneth Fincham, 161–85. Stanford: Stanford University Press, 1993.

———. *Moderate Puritans and the Elizabethan Church.* Cambridge: Cambridge University Press, 1982.

———. "Presbyterianism, the Idea of a National Church, and the Argument from Divine Right." In *Protestantism and the National Church in Sixteenth-Century England,* ed. Peter Lake and Maria Dowling, 193–224. London: Crook Helm, 1987.

———. "The Significance of the Elizabethan Identification of the Pope as Antichrist." *Journal of Ecclesiastical History* 31:2 (1980): 161–78.

Lake, Peter, and Maria Dowling, eds. *Protestantism and the National Church in Sixteenth-Century England.* London: Crook Helm, 1987.

Lambert, Sheila. "Richard Montagu, Arminianism, and Censorship." *Past and Present* 124 (August 1989): 36–68.

Lanyer, Aemilia. *The Poems of Aemilia Lanyer.* Ed. Susanne Woods. Oxford: Oxford University Press, 1993.

Laud, William. "A sermon before Parliament." London, February 6, 1625.

———. *A Speech Concerning Innovations in the Church.* 1637. Reprint, Amsterdam: Theatrum Orbis Terrarum, 1971.

———. *The Works of the Most Reverend Father in God, William Laud, D.D.* Ed. W. Scott and J. Bliss. 7 vols. 1848–1860. Reprint, New York: AMS Press, 1975.

Leishman, J. B. *The Monarch of Wit.* London: Hutchinson, 1951.

Lewalski, Barbara K. "Of God and Good Women: The Poems of Aemilia Lanyer." In *Silent but for the Word: Tudor Women as Patrons, Translators, and Writers of Religious Works,* ed. Margaret Patterson Hannay, 203–24. Kent: Kent State University Press, 1985.

———. *Protestant Poetics and the Seventeenth-Century Religious Lyric.* Princeton: Princeton University Press, 1979.

———. "Re-writing Patriarchy and Patronage: Margaret Clifford, Ann Clifford, and Aemilia Lanyer." *Yearbook of English Studies* 21 (1991): 87–106.

———. *Writing Women in Jacobean England.* Cambridge: Harvard University Press, 1993.

Lieb, Michael. "Milton's *Of Reformation* and the Dynamics of Controversy." In *Achievements of the Left Hand: Essays on the Prose of John Milton,* ed. Michael Lieb and John T. Shawcross, 55–82. Amherst: University of Massachusetts, 1974.

Lockyer, Roger. *The Early Stuarts.* New York: Longman, 1989.

Low, Anthony. "The Holy Ghost Is Amorous in His Metaphors." In *New Perspectives on the Seventeenth-Century English Religious Lyric,* ed. John R. Roberts, 201–21. Columbia: University of Missouri Press, 1994.

Lyle-Scoufos, Alice. "The Mysteries in Milton's Masque." *Milton Studies* 6 (1976): 113–42.

Lynch, Kathleen. "George Herbert's Holy 'Altar,' Name and Thing." *GHJ* 17:1 (fall 1993): 41–60.

———. "*The Temple:* 'Three Parts Vied and Multiplied.'" *SEL* 29:1 (winter 1989): 139–55.

Mack, Phyllis. *Visionary Women: Ecstatic Prophecy in Seventeenth-Century England.* Berkeley and Los Angeles: University of California Press, 1992.

———. "Women as Prophets during the English Civil War." *Feminist Studies* 8 (1982): 19–45.

MacLaren, I. S. "Milton's Nativity Ode: The Function of Poetry and Structures of Response in 1629." *Milton Studies* 15 (1981): 181–200.

Maltby, Judith. " 'By this Book': Parishioners, the Prayer Book, and the Established Church." In *The Early Stuart Church, 1603–1642,* ed. Kenneth Fincham, 115–38. Stanford: Stanford University Press, 1993.

Marcus, Leah S. *Childhood and Cultural Despair.* Pittsburgh: University of Pittsburgh Press, 1978.

———. *The Politics of Mirth: Jonson, Herrick, Milton, Marvell, and the Defense of Old Holiday Pastimes.* Chicago: University of Chicago Press, 1986.

Martz, Louis. *The Poetry of Meditation.* New Haven: Yale University Press, 1954.

Matchinske, Megan. "Holy Hatred: Formations of the Gendered Subject in English Apocalyptic Writing, 1625–1651." *ELH* 60:2 (1993): 349–77.

McGrath, Lynette. "Metaphoric Subversions: Feasts and Mirrors in Aemilia Lanier's *Salve Deus Rex Judaeorum.*" *LIT* 3 (1990): 101–13.

McGuire, Maryann Cale. *Milton's Puritan Masque.* Athens: University of Georgia Press, 1983.

Mede, Joseph. *The Name Altar.* London, 1637.

Milton, Anthony. *Catholic and Reformed: The Roman and Protestant Churches in English Protestant Thought, 1600–1640.* Cambridge: Cambridge University Press, 1995.

———. "The Church of England, Rome, and the True Church: The Demise of a Jacobean Consensus." In *The Early Stuart Church, 1603–1642,* ed. Kenneth Fincham, 187–210. Stanford: Stanford University Press, 1993.

Milton, John. *John Milton: Complete Poems and Major Prose.* Ed. Merritt Hughes. Indianapolis: Odyssey Press, 1957.

———. *The Prose of John Milton.* Ed. J. Max Patrick. Garden City, N.Y.: Anchor Books, 1967.

Milward, Peter. *Religious Controversies of the Jacobean Age.* Lincoln: University of Nebraska Press, 1978.

Montagu, Richard. *Appello Caesarem: A Just Appeale from two Unjust informers.* 1625. Reprint, Amsterdam: Theatrum Orbis Terrarum, 1972.

Morrill, John. "The Attack on the Church of England in the Long Parliament, 1640–1642." In *History, Society, and the Churches,* ed. Derek Beales and Geoffrey Best, 105–24. Cambridge: Cambridge University Press, 1985.

Mueller, William R. *John Donne, Preacher.* Princeton: Princeton University Press, 1962.

Napier, John. *A Plaine Discovery of the Whole Revelation of St. John.* Edinburgh, 1593.

Nardo, Anna K. "John Donne at Play in Between." In *The Eagle and the Dove: Reassessing John Donne,* ed. Claude J. Summers and Ted-Larry Pebworth, 157–65. Columbia: University of Missouri Press, 1986.

Nauert, Charles G., Jr. *Agrippa and the Crisis of Renaissance Thought.* Urbana: University of Illinois Press, 1965.

Nelson, Beth. "Lady Elinor Davies: The Prophet as Publisher." *Womens Studies International Forum* 8:5 (1985): 403–9.

Nohrnberg, James. *The Analogy of the Faerie Queene.* Princeton: Princeton University Press, 1976.

Norbrook, David. *Poetry and Politics in the English Renaissance.* London: Routledge, 1984.

———. "The Politics of Milton's Early Poetry." In *John Milton,* ed. Annabel Patterson, 46–64. London: Longman, 1992.

Northampton, Henry Howard. *A Defensative against the poyson of supposed prophesies.* 1583. Reprint, London, 1620.

Novarr, David. *The Disinterred Muse.* Ithaca: Cornell University Press, 1980.

O'Connell, Patrick F. "The Successive Arrangements of Donne's 'Holy Sonnets.'" *Philological Quarterly* 60 (1981): 323–42.

Otten, Charlotte, ed. *English Women's Voices, 1540–1700.* Miami: Florida International University Press, 1992.

Owen, Trevor. *Lancelot Andrewes.* Boston: Twayne Publishers, 1981.

Pagels, Elaine. *Adam, Eve, and the Serpent.* New York: Random House, 1988.

Parry, Graham. *The Golden Age Restored: The Culture of the Stuart Court, 1603–1642.* New York: St. Martin's Press, 1981.

Patrides, C. A., and J. A. Wittreich, eds. *The Apocalypse in English Renaissance Thought and Literature.* Ithaca: Cornell University Press, 1984.

Patterson, Annabel. "'Forc'd fingers': Milton's Early Poems and Ideological Constraint." In *"The Muses Common-Weale": Poetry and Politics in the Seventeenth Century,* ed. Claude J. Summers and Ted-Larry Pebworth, 9–22. Columbia: University of Missouri Press, 1988.

Patterson, Annabel Endicott. "The Structure of George Herbert's *Temple*: A Reconsideration." *UTQ* 34:3 (April 1965): 226–37.

Patterson, W. B. "King James I and the Protestant Cause in the Crisis of 1618–1622." *Studies in Church History* 18 (1982): 319–34.

Peck, Linda Levy. *Court Patronage and Corruption in Early Stuart England.* Boston: Unwin Hyman, 1990.

Post, Jonathan F. S. *Henry Vaughan: The Unfolding Vision.* Princeton: Princeton University Press, 1982.

Prynne, William. *A Quenche-Coale or a Briefe Disquisition and Inquirie.* N.p., 1637.

Ramsey, Paul. "Darkness Lightened: A. L. Rowse's Dark Lady Once More." *Upstart Crow* (fall 1984): 143–45.

The Reformation of Our Church. Middleburg, 1593.

Richey, Esther Gilman. "The Political Design of Herbert's *Temple.*" *SEL* 37:1 (1997): 73–96.

———. "To Undoe the Booke: Cornelius Agrippa, Aemilia Lanyer, and the Subversion of Pauline Authority." *ELR* 27:1 (1997): 106–28.

Riffaterre, Michael. "Compulsory Reader Response: The Intertextual Drive." In *Intertextuality: Theories and Practices,* ed. Michael Worton and Judith Still, 56–78. Manchester: Manchester University Press, 1990.

Roberts, John R., ed. *New Perspectives on the Seventeenth-Century English Religious Lyric.* Columbia: University of Missouri Press, 1994.

Rowse, A. L., ed. *The Poems of Shakespeare's Dark Lady.* London: Jonathan Cape, 1978.

Sanderson, Robert. *Ten Sermons.* London, 1628.

Sandler, Florence. "The Faerie Queene: An Elizabethan Apocalypse." In *The Apocalypse in English Renaissance Thought and Literature,* ed. C. A. Patrides and J. A. Wittreich, 148–74. Ithaca: Cornell University Press, 1984.

Schochet, Gordon J. "The English Revolution in the History of Political Thought." In *Court, Country, and Culture: Essays in Early Modern British History in Honor of Perez Zagorin,* ed. Bonnelyn Young Kunze and Dwight D. Brautigam, 1–20. Rochester: University of Rochester Press, 1992.

Schoenfeldt, Michael. *Prayer and Power.* Chicago: University of Chicago Press, 1991.

———. "'That Ancient Heat': Sexuality and Spirituality in *The Temple.*" In *Soliciting Interpretation,* ed. Elizabeth D. Harvey and Katherine Maus, 273–306. Chicago: University of Chicago Press, 1990.

Shami, Jeanne M. "Donne on Discretion." *ELH* 47 (1980): 48–66.

Sharpe, Kevin. *The Personal Rule of Charles I.* New Haven: Yale University Press, 1992.

Shuger, Debora K. *Habits of Thought in the English Renaissance.* Berkeley and Los Angeles: University of California Press, 1990.

Simmonds, James D. *Masques of God: Form and Theme in the Poetry of Henry Vaughan.* Pittsburgh: University of Pittsburgh Press, 1972.

Slack, Paul. "Religious Protest and Urban Authority: The Case of Henry Sherfield, Iconoclast, 1633." In *Schism, Heresy and Religious Protest,* ed. Dereck Baker, 295–302. Cambridge: Cambridge University Press, 1972.

Smart, Peter. *The Vanitie and Downe-fall of Superstitious Popish Ceremonies.* 1628. Reprint, Amsterdam: Theatrum Orbis Terrarum, 1977.

Smith, Nigel. *Perfection Proclaimed: Language and Literature in English Radical Religion, 1640–1660.* Oxford: Clarendon Press, 1989.

Spenser, Edmund. *The Faerie Queene.* Ed. Thomas P. Roche Jr. New York: Penguin Books, 1979.

Steadman, John. "Spenser's Icon of the Past: Fiction as History, a Reexamination." *Huntington Library Quarterly* 55:4 (1992): 535–58.

Stewart, Stanley. *George Herbert.* Boston: Twayne Publishers, 1986.

Strier, Richard. *Love Known: Theology and Experience in George Herbert's Poetry.* Chicago: University of Chicago Press, 1983.

———. "Radical Donne: Satire III." *ELH* 60:2 (1993): 283–322.

Stroup, Thomas B. " 'A Reasonable, Holy, and Living Sacrifice': Herbert's 'The Altar.' " *Essays in Literature* 2:2 (1975): 149–63.

Summers, Claude J. "The Bride of the Apocalypse and the Quest for True Religion: Donne, Herbert, and Spenser." In *"Bright Shootes of Everlastingnesse": The Seventeenth-Century Religious Lyric,* ed. Claude J. Summers and Ted-Larry Pebworth, 72–95. Columbia: University of Missouri Press, 1987.

———. "Herrick, Vaughan, and the Poetry of Anglican Survivalism." In *New Perspectives on the Seventeenth-Century English Religious Lyric,* ed. John R. Roberts, 46–74. Columbia: University of Missouri Press, 1994.

Summers, Claude J., and Ted-Larry Pebworth, eds. *"The Muses Commonweale": Poetry and Politics in the Seventeenth Century.* Columbia: University of Missouri Press, 1988.

Summers, Joseph. *George Herbert: His Religion and His Art.* Cambridge: Harvard University Press, 1954.

Sutcliffe, Matthew. *Ecclesiastical Discipline.* 1590. Reprint, New York: Da Capo Press, 1973

———. *Examination of Cartwright's Apology.* London, 1596.

Swanson, Donald, and John Mulryan. "Milton's *On the Morning of Christ's Nativity:* The Virgilian and Biblical Matrices." *Milton Quarterly* 23:2 (1989): 59–66.

Thomas, Keith. *Religion and the Decline of Magic.* London: Weidenfeld and Nicolson, 1971.

Thomas, Noel K. *Henry Vaughan: Poet of Revelation.* West Sussex: Churchman Publishing, 1986.

Trapnel, Anna. *Anna Trapnel's Report and Plea.* London, 1654. Modern edition available in *English Women's Voices, 1540–1700,* ed. Charlotte F. Otten, 64–78. Miami: Florida International University Press, 1992.

———. *Legacy for Saints.* 1654.

———. *Voyce for the King of Saints and Nations or A Testimony.* London, 1658.

Travitsky, Betty. "The Lady Doth Protest: Protest in the Popular Writings of Renaissance Englishwomen." *ELR* 14 (1984): 255–83.

———, ed. *The Paradise of Women.* London: Greenwood, 1981.

Trigge, Francis. *A Touchstone, whereby may easelie be discerned the true Catholike faith.* N.p., 1600.

Turner, James Grantham. *One Flesh: Paradisal Marriage and Sexual Relations in the Age of Milton.* Oxford: Clarendon Press, 1987.

Tyacke, Nicholas. "Archbishop Laud." In *The Early Stuart Church, 1603–1642,* ed. Kenneth Fincham, 51–70. Stanford: Stanford University Press, 1993.

Upton, John. *Notes on the Faerie Queene.* Ed. John G. Radcliffe. 2 vols. New York: Garland Publishing, 1987.

Ussher, James. *A Briefe Declaration of the Universalitie of the Church of Christ.* Preached June 20, 1624. London, 1687.

———. *The Whole Works of . . . James Ussher.* 17 vols. Dublin, 1847–1864.

Utley, Francis Lee. *The Crooked Rib.* New York: Octagon Books, 1970.

Vaughan, Henry. *The Poetry and Selected Prose of Henry Vaughan.* Ed. L. C. Martin. Oxford: Clarendon Press, 1957.

Veith, Gene Edward, Jr. *Reformation Spirituality: The Religion of George Herbert.* Lewisburg, Pa.: Bucknell University Press, 1985.

The Vindication of the Royall Commission of King Jesus against the Antichristian faction. Prefatory Letter, September 27, 1644. London, 1644.

Virgil. *The Pastoral Poems.* Trans. E. V. Rieu. Harmondworth, Middlesex, Eng.: Penguin Press, 1953.

Walker, John David. "The Architectonics of George Herbert's *The Temple.*" *ELH* 29:3 (1968): 289–305.

Wall, John N. *Transformations of the Word: Spenser, Herbert, Vaughan.* Athens: University of Georgia Press, 1988.

Walton, Izaak. *The Lives of John Donne, Sir Henry Wotton, Richard Hooker, George Herbert, and Robert Sanderson.* London: Oxford University Press, 1950.

Waters, D. Douglas. *Duessa as Theological Satire.* Columbia: University of Missouri Press, 1970.

White, John. *The Way to the True Church.* London, 1608.

Whitgift, John. *The Defence of the Answer to the Admonition.* Vols. 48–50 in *The Works,* ed. John Ayre. Cambridge: Cambridge University Press, 1851–1853.

Widdowes, Giles. *The Schismatical Puritan.* Oxford, 1631.

Williams, Griffith. *The True Church Shewed to all men that desire to be members of the Same.* London, 1629.

Wittreich, Joseph A. *Feminist Milton.* Ithaca: Cornell University Press, 1987.

Woodbridge, Linda. *Women and the English Renaissance.* Urbana: University of Illinois Press, 1984.

Yates, Francis. *Buildings, Faith, and Worship.* Oxford: Clarendon Press, 1991.

Young, R. V. "Donne's *Holy Sonnets* and the Theology of Grace." In *"Bright Shootes of Everlastingnesse": The Seventeenth-Century Religious Lyric,* ed. Claude J. Summers and Ted-Larry Pebworth, 20–39. Columbia: University of Missouri Press, 1987.

Index

Abbot, George, Archbishop: advice to King James, 3–4; *Treatise of the Perpetuall Visibilitie,* 111

Adam: command pronounced by God, 65; associated with Law, 65; representing limits of masculine knowledge and practice, 75; motivated by appearances, 76

Adam and Eve: as Una's parents, 28; subordination of Eve to Adam, as interpreted by Paul, 62–63; feminist reinterpretation of, 63, 75–78; and Milton's *Paradise Lost,* 165–72; as equally guilty, 212

Agrippa, Cornelius, 12; *Of the Nobilitie and Excellencie of Womankinde,* reinterpretation of Genesis and revision of Pauline mandate, 64–68; exposing gaps in biblical text, 65, 75, 83, 167, 170, 217

Alter, Robert, 180n12

Andrewes, Lancelot, 7, 10, 11, 12, 13, 111, 118, 119, 130, 133–34, 136, 144, 156, 209, 220, 222, 224; as defining pacifistic prophecy of visible church, 37, 39, 46–59; on Antichrist, 39; on containing violence, 47–48; on episcopal succession, 48–49; on softness, learning of prophetic speech, 49, 51–52; on Parliament and false profit, 50; on Pentecost as reversal of Babel, 52–53; on dreams/visions, 54–56; on women prophets, 55; on predictions, 56; on preaching, 57; on necessity of unanimity, uniformity, 57–58; on divine profit rather than economic change, 58–59; on feminine gospel, 60–61; on divine acceptance of Eve, 61; on Mary's

active participation in producing Christ, 61–62, 71

Antichrist. *See* Revelation

Apocalypse. *See* Revelation

Arminianism, 131

Audeley, Mervyn: as the biblical Joseph, 191–92

Augustine, 17

Augustus Caesar: return of golden age, 4, 133, 134, 174

Avant-garde conformists, 8, 10, 13, 36, 130, 132, 142, 144–45, 153

Bacon, Francis, 64

Bale, John: *Image of Both Churches,* 16, 17, 22, 73n24

Beilin, Elaine, 70

Belshazzar: as King Charles, 181–87

Bergvall, Ake, 17

Bloom, Harold, 163

Book of Common Prayer, 150, 177

Brightman, Thomas: on interpreting revelation, 2, 3, 10, 11, 36, 39, 87, 202; *Revelation of the Revelation,* 39–46; necessary zeal of prophets, 40–41; hidden temple of, 42–43, 108–9; egalitarian model of priesthood, 43; woman/Bride of, 43–46; on Constantine, 44, 108–9; *A Revelation of the Apocalypse,* woman as true church, 60–61; *Against Bellarmine, the Confuting of that counterfaite AntiChrist,* 109, 109n8, 116

Browning, John, 139

Buckeridge, John, 119n33

Buckingham, 111n17, 131

Burton, Henry, 147, 176

Caiaphas, 75
Calvin, John, 9
Calvinism suppressed in English Church, 8–9
Cartwright, Thomas, 19, 24; as cross-dresser, 23
Cary, Mary, 10, 13, 196, 197; absence of profit motive, 197; *The Resurrection of the Witnesses*, 197–204; concern with egalitarian communion and social justice, 200; prophets as Christ's beloved wife, 200–201; prophetic gifts open to all, 201–2; removal of gender coding in prophesying, 201–2; discussion of temple, 202; politics of "champion," 202–3; *Voyce for the King of Saints*, 207–11
Christ: as principal prophet, 2; as giving up position of royal authority, 24, 135, 161; as Arthur, 31; women as mirrors of, 66; choice of marginalized women to represent him, 66, 70, 73, 213; offers Queen of Sheba role as judge, 67, 81–82; silence of, 75; in temple, 140; Thrysis in *Comus*, 145–46; ignorance of end of world, 193; liberation of marginalized, powerless, 194; calling of friends, 199–200
Christopher, Georgia, 9, 141, 147
Chrysostom, 51
Church of England: attacks on, 5, 17, 40–41, 109; double government of, 18, 29; split over prophecy, 35, 36–59, 224–25; as inclusive, accepting, 89–90; as avoiding extreme positions, 89–90; as harboring Antichrist, 91, 109; as mother, 99–100; and newfangledness, 107; same foundation as Rome's, 111; history of, 112–13, 141–42, 158–60; bishops' plot against, 147; courtly origins of, 147; and "beauty of holiness," 153; reformation of, 175–76
Clifford, Margaret, 69, 79–80, 83
Conformists (in Church of England), 10, 11, 23, 37, 85, 106, 109, 110n11, 112n19, 123, 128
Constantine, 4, 11, 12, 17, 37–38, 108, 128, 135, 134, 162, 202; peace as corrupting, 11, 37–38, 42; temple of, 12, 35, 111, 127;

union of state and church, 17; Antichrist within temple, 109, 128–29
Controversies in Stuart church: over conformity, 8, 56–57, 92–93, 132, 139, 142–44, 150–52; over ceremonial order and worship, 8–13, 37, 56–57, 89, 93, 98, 109, 114–29, 130–40, 141–44, 146, 153, 162–63, 186–87, 193, 223–24; over clerical wealth, 8, 135n17, 136, 143, 147, 154, 162–63, 183; over attitudes toward church history, 8, 9, 11, 37, 42, 86–89, 106–7, 111–12, 149n34, 158–59, 162; over holiness and fear of spiritual corruption, 16, 17, 42, 109n9, 139–61; over Antichrist as international concern, 90–91; over meaning of the temple, 106. *See also* True Church.
Cooper, Thomas, 14n17
Cosin, John, 151
Cromwell, Oliver, 206, 216

Daniel, 180–87, 206
Davenant, John, 123–24
Davies, Eleanor, 10, 11; as feminist prophet, 13, 173–95; and redemption of English Church, 174; *The Appearance or Presence of the Son of Man*, 174–75; identification with Queen of the South [Sheba], 175; *Amend, Amend, God's kingdome is at hand*, 180–86; significance of numerology and hand writing, 181–82, 184, 194, 195; indictment of King Charles, 185–87; *The Restitution of Prophecy*, 187–95; and Pentecost, 188; identification with Mary, mother of Christ, and Bride of Lamb, 190; her talent buried by Laud, 193; containing infinite incarnations of the *Logos*, 194
Davies, Julian, 114n23
Debate. *See* Controversies in Stuart church
Dixon, John, 23
Donne, John, 7, 10, 13, 39, 117, 118, 130, 144, 152, 153, 157, 163, 193, 209, 220; "Holy Sonnet 18," 12, 86–89; controversy over true church, 87–89; Hosea as prophetic model, 91, 103–5; and support of James I, 93–96, 102; emphasis on peace, 94–95; admitting adultery in kingdom, 97–98; prophetic indictment of rich, powerful, 100; declines political critique

as prophet's role, 101; "A Litanie," 102–3; "Holy Sonnet 14," 103–5
Downame, George, 146n32

Ecriture feminine, 65, 65n10
Elizabeth Stuart: marriage to Frederik of Bohemia, 4, 91
Eusebius, 16, 17, 21, 108–9; *Auncient Ecclesiasticall Histories,* temple within, 112–29
Eve: God's acceptance of, 61; subjugation of, contested, 64–65; associated with grace, 65; not informed by God or Adam, 77; motivated by generosity, 77; seduced because of bad government, 84–85; pardoned, 188; second Eve, 192

Fell, Margaret, 10; and equality of genders, 212; *Women's Speaking Justified,* 212–18; on satanic attempt to silence women, 215; indicts sex/gender discrimination, 215; indicts male profit motives, 216; highlights words of women in scripture, 216–18; authorizes women to teach men, 217–18
Feminism: biblically sanctioned, 62; in Lanyer, 63, 68–83; women's speech as means of justifying, 74; validation of women by Christ, 81–82; and divine authority to prophesy, 174–76; and handwriting, 181–82, 194; and wisdom, illumination, 182
Fifth Monarchists, 10, 35
Fincham, Kenneth, 8, 9, 121n36
Fisher, John [John Percy], 84
Forbes, Peter, 3, 87, 134, 202
Foxe, John: *Acts and Monuments,* 4, 16, 17, 21, 29–30, 38, 107–8, 109, 110, 112, 140, 202

Genesis: reinterpreted by Agrippa, 64–68
Genevan church, 87–88
Goldberg, Jonathan, 10
Gottlieb, Sidney, 10
Green, Thomas, 112
Greenblatt, Stephen, 10
Grose, Christopher, 163n52

Guibbory, Achsah, 10
Gyffard, George, 134–35

Hall, Joseph: *The Old Religion,* 6; attacked by Laud and reformers both, 6n10
Harvey, Elizabeth: exploration of birth metaphors, 68n12
Heale, William, 167–68, 169
Herbert, George, 7, 9, 11, 39, 130, 144, 156, 157, 163, 220; *The Temple,* 14; "Sion," 106, 122–23; architecture based on Eusebius's model, 112–15; as response to ecclesiastical controversies, 114–29; "The Dedication," 115–16; "The Church Porch," 116–20; "The Altar," 120n35, 121–22; "The Windows," 123–25; "Love III," 125–26, 224; *A Priest to the Temple,* 126; "The Church Militant," 127–29
Heylyn, Peter, 176
Heywood, Thomas, 173
Hill, Christopher, 5n8, 6, 13, 22, 91
Hodgkins, Christopher, 9, 113n21, 122n37
Honeygoskey, Stephen, 9, 139–40, 163
Hooker, Richard, 1, 164–65
Hosea's wife, 91, 103–5, 227

Ibbotson, Robert, 186

Joel: and prophetic handmaids, 7, 66, 178, 184, 187, 189, 210
John the Baptist, 82–83
Jordan, Constance, 64

Kerrigan, William, 1
King Charles I: proposed marriage to Infanta Maria, 4, 91; marriage to Henrietta Maria, 5, 13, 190; influenced by churchmen, 8; difficulty with apocalyptic form, 12; peace negotiations of 1629, 131; taxes and reforms of, 131; "His Maiesties Declaration to all his Loving Subjects," 131–32; and Virgilian father and son, 132; and *Book of Sports,* 143; as Belshazzar, 181–87; contrasted with pure reign of Elizabeth, 190; rejection of Davies's prophecy, 192

King James I: *A Paraphrase upon the Revelation,* 3; pacifistic prophecy, 4–5, 12, 46; influenced by churchmen, 8, 12; and apocalyptic form, 12, 38, 39; as corrupting influence, 42, 46; foreign policy of, 91, 93; "Directions on Preaching," 94–95, appeal to antiquity, 96; and Abbot's treatise, 111n17; and Virgilian father and son, 132

King, John, 9, 19, 21, 22, 23

Kirchmayer, Thomas, 140

Lake, Peter, 8, 9, 18, 19n9, 24n25, 35, 36, 108n7, 119n31

Lambert, Shiela, 5n8

Lanyer, Aemilia, 10, 12, 85, 173, 175, 197, 208, 217; as dreamer, prophet, 68; *Salve Deus Rex Judaeorum,* 63, 65, 68, 69, 167, 169; exploration of gaps in New Testament narrative, 68; feminine reproduction of Christ, 68–72, 80; identifying with blackness of print, 70; noblewoman as Bride of Christ, 72; politics of incarnation, 72–73; on suppression of female voice, 73–75; reassessing politics of Adam and Eve, 75–78; feminine identification with Christ, 78; apocalyptic union of Christ and Bride, 79, 82; wisdom of Queen of Sheba, 80; liberation from patriarchy, 81–82

Laud, William, 99, 111, 163, 173, 191–93, 219; suppression of Calvinist sermons, 112

Laudian position, 12, 113n21, 116–29, 224

Lewalski, Barbara, 8

Luther, Martin, 9, 17

Lyle-Scoufos, Alice, 140

McGrath, Lynette, 70

Mack, Phyllis, 216n14

Marcus, Leah S., 143, 150, 156n45

Marlowe, Thomas, 65

Mary: active role in producing Christ, 61; as central to the Eucharist, 61–62; suffering of, 78, 188; reproduces *Logos,* Christ, 188–89, 211; annunciation of, 190

Mary Magdalene, 177, as appropriate model of English Church, 226–27

Matchinske, Megan, 174, 174n3

Metaphysical lyric: as public and political rather than private, 10; Miltonic parody of, 133; "somewhat" within, 156, 156n44; apocalyptic Temple turned into private lyric form, 157

Milton, Anthony, 5n8, 8

Milton, John, 8–11, 13, 109; and ecclesiastical controversy, 7; *Comus,* 7, 13, 130, 139, 140–62, 173, 176; "On the Morning of Christ's Nativity," 7, 13, 131–39; as indictment of pacifistic prophecy, 130–39, as critique of Charles I, 135; *Of Reformation,* 139, 162–65, 170; Lady representing Lady Ecclesia's encounter with Antichrist, 140; Lady's quest for brothers, 141; Comus's attempt to seduce true church, 143; Lady's resistance to conformity, 144; brothers as reformation protestants, 146; Comus: as "Star" and profiteering bishop of Church, 146–50; Lady and *Articles of Religion,* Canon 26, 151–53, 156; prophetic exchange exposing profit motives, 155; brothers and pacifism of temple, 157; Lady bound to corrupt ecclesiastical "chair," 157; *Paradise Lost* and tradition, 163, 163n52, 166; inspiration and feminist reassessments of the Pauline mandate, 165–72; liberty of illumination and diabolical coersion, 166–72

Montrose, Louis, 10

Napier, John, 3, 29, 87, 134, 202

Nashe, Thomas, 64

Norbrook, David, 5n8, 9, 154n42

Oecumenius, 51

Parable of wheat and tares representing true church. *See* True Church

Parliament, 13, 131, 177–78; of 1621 and of 1624, 6; and revision of Eleanor Davies' prophecy, *Amend, Amend,* 186–87; end of, 211

Pauline mandate: contested and revised by women prophets, 7, 12, 13, 62, 212; Andrewes' use of, 55; revised by

Agrippa, 64–68; revised by Lanyer, 75–78; reinforced by Milton in *Paradise Lost*, 165–72; interpreted out of context according to Fell, 212

Pebworth, Ted-Larry, 10

Pilate's wife, 66, 75–78

Post, Jonathan, F. S., 220n3

Presbyterian agenda, 10, 11, 13, 17, 18, 19, 21, 23, 35, 38, 43, 60, 88, 108–9, 208, 228; of Archimago, 22–23; and Red Cross's flight, 25; purification of temple site, 109n10; indicted, 217, 219–29

Prophecy: definition of, 1–2; openness, 1–2, 208; containment of radical dimension, 2–3, 193, 220; pacifistic alternative, 4, 8, 9, 13, 35, 46–59, 93–95, 135–36, 138–39, 175, 220–29; militant, apocalyptic focus, 8, 35, 38, 130, 132, 136, 138–39, 156–57, 174, 186, 229; debate over, 12; transcendent form as opposed to material "profit," 10, 14–15, 28, 100, 206–7; obscurity of, 12, 101–2; as Spenser's assessment of history, 20; division into two opposed forms, 35–36; as a letter, 39–42, 100–101; against Henrietta Maria, 97–98; as encoded indictments, 189–95; as beyond description, 207–8. *See also* Brightman, Thomas; Andrewes, Lancelot

Puritans: agenda of, 12, 38, 57, 90–92, 106, 113n21, 116–29, 176, 194; as "purintents," 203; indicted as false prophets, murderers, 222

Quakers, 35

Queen Anne, 71

Queen Elizabeth, 6, 64, 85, 108, 134, 135; as corrupting influence, 42, 46; her chaste rule and female power, 62, 190, 203

Queen of Sheba (of South): wisdom of, 80; identification with, 175, 208

Querelle des Femmes, 12, 63, 65, 68, 165

Revelation: interpretation of, 2–3, 9; politically charged readings of, 3, 5, 10, 45; whore within, 3–4, 8, 12, 91, 153, 217; imperial conquest within, 4, 91; suppression of commentaries on, 5, 5n8, 193; woman/Bride of, 6, 8, 12,

13, 14, 22, 60–61, 73, 79–80, 86, 89–91, 125–26, 134, 153, 162–63, 171, 175–80, 190, 208–9, 217; temple of, 8, 13, 14, 29–30, 42–43, 106–29, 153, 157; 200–202, 223–24; obscurity within, 12, 101–2; written during persecution of church, 16; meaning of 360 days/42 months, 29–30; as a letter, 39–41, 100–101; and Antichrist, 90–91, 93, 94, 98, 110, 128–29; as bittersweet, 185

Riffaterre, Michael, 116

Roman Catholic agenda, 11, 17, 18, 19, 21, 23, 86, 87, 92, 106–7, 181; of Archimago, 22–23; of Duessa, 26–27

Sarah, voice authorized in Old Testament account, 67; as interpreted by Hooker, 164–65; as interpreted by Milton, 165; as interpreted by Eleanor Davies, 180; as interpreted by Margaret Fell, 217

Sanderson, Robert, 5, 150

Schoenfeldt, Michael, 10

Sherfield, Henry, 123–24

Shuger, Debora K., 15, 91, 122n37

Sidney, Philip, 64

Smart, Peter, 106, 114–15, 130, 142–43, 151

Smith, Nigel, 197

Spanish Match, 4, 91, 93, 94, 132

Spenser, Edmund, 7, 8, 9, 11, 12, 14, 23n22, 24, 28, 85, 136; "Legende of the Knight of the Redcrosse, or Holinesse," 7, 11, 17–35, 141; Una, 6, 12, 19, 21, 23, 35, 85, 86, 134, 141–42, 204; false "Una," 11, 23; Duessa, 11, 12, 29, 86, 137; *The Faerie Queene*, and the popular voice, 19n9; history of false "Una," 19, 24–26; history of Duessa, 19, 26–27; Redcrosse, 11, 19, 21, 23, 24, 26, 29, 35; significance of Una and Redcrosse's protracted engagement, 18–19, 27, 35; Archimago, 21, 22, 23–24, 142; history of Redcrosse and Una's relationship, 24, 28–30, 28n34, 35, 141; "Letter to Raleigh," 24; history of Una, 24, 27–31, 28n33; Una's quest for Redcrosse, 26; Arthur, 27–28, 30–31; and the monarch's role, 28; apocalyptic numbers in, 29–30; Redcross's origin, name, and history, 31–34; Una and accurate church history, 33–34; Duessa's

letter, 33–34, 204; "Legende of Chastity,"
149, 160–61
Stewart, Stanley, 116
Strafford, 192
Strier, Richard, 9
Summers, Claude J., 10, 220n3
Sutcliffe, Matthew, 23, 24

Temple. *See* Herbert, George; Revelation;
True Church
Thirty Years' War, 3
Thomas, Noel K., 220n3
Trapnel, Anna, 13, 197; *Legacy for Saints,* as
Pauline and Christological autobiography,
204–6; sealing ordinances of, 206–7; *Voyce
for the King of Saints,* 207–11
Trigge, Francis: *A Touchstone, whereby may
easelie be discerned the true Catholike faith,*
85–86
True Church: debate over invisible or
visible status, 10, 11, 12, 18, 23, 31, 37,
38, 42–46, 97–99, 106–13, 140–42, 147,
219, 228–29; debate over presbyterian
or episcopal structure, 10, 11, 19, 38,
42–46, 106–13, 119–21, 149n34, 158–59,
162–63; debate over lay or episcopal status
of prophets, 11, 43, 49, 51–52, 201–2;
Spenser's "Legende of the Knight of the
Red Crosse" as history of, 11, 17, 19–20,
23–25; the return of, 14, 219; woman's
resistance to corruption, 16, 21, 42–46,
134, 139–61; as persecuted church in
Acts and Monuments, 17; represented in
parable of wheat and tares, 27, 31, 164,
221; as temple, 29, 42–46, 153, 106–29,
106n2, 223–24; before Luther, 34–35, 87,
107–8, 127; use of feminine metaphor
to describe, 61–62, 178; as spouse and
bride, 89, 98, 125–26, 153, 162–63,
206–7, 222–23; open admission of, 92, 99;
compared with Hosea's wanton wife, 97,

99, 103–5; chastity of, 105, 153–54. *See
also* Controversies in Stuart church
Turner, James Grantham, 167n56

Upton, John, 29, 29n37
Ussher, James, 110, 111, 127

Vaughan, Henry, 7, 14, 219–20; *Silex
Scintillans,* as re-dressing Bride, rebuilding
temple, 220; indictment of Presbyterians,
221–29; "The Proffer," 221; "The
Constellation," 221–23; "Dressing,"
223–24; "White Sunday," 224–26, "Mary
Magdalene," 226–28; "Jacob's Pillow and
Pillar," 228–29
Veith, Gene, 9
Virgilian Prophecy, 13, 132, 138; and golden
age restored, 133; as cyclical, 134
Virgil's Fourth Eclogue, 132, 135
Via Media, 4, 40

Wall, John N., 10
Waters, D. Douglass, 21
Whitaker, 90
White, John: *The Way to the True Church,*
37–38, 84–85, 86, 87, 178
Whitgift, John, 18–22, 90–91
Widdowes, Giles, 119
Williams, Griffith: *The True Church Shewed
to all Men,* definition of prophecy, 1–3;
difficulty of identifying pure church, 141;
"alluring" beauty of English Church, 144;
inclusion of masses in communion, 144;
need for charity in the church, 148
Wittreich, Joseph A., 167n56, 171
Women prophets, 7, 66, 68, 173–95,
196–219; use of Pauline theology, 196–97;
authorized to speak, 213–18; authorized
to teach, 217–18